CITY REGIONS AND DEVOLUTION IN THE UK

Also available in the Civil Society and Social Change series

Civil Society and the Family
By **Esther Muddiman**, **Sally Power** and **Chris Taylor**

HB £75.00 ISBN 9781447355526
208 pages October 2020

Putting Civil Society in Its Place
Governance, Metagovernance and
Subjectivity
By **Bob Jessop**

HB £75.00 ISBN 9781447354956
248 pages September 2020

The Foundational Economy and Citizenship
Comparative Perspectives on Civil Repair
Edited by **Filippo Barbera** and
Ian Rees Jones

HB £75.00 ISBN 9781447353355
200 pages September 2020

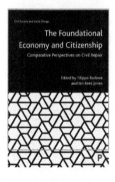

Published with the Wales Institute of Social and
Economic Research and Data

For more information about the series visit

bristoluniversitypress.co.uk/civil-society-and-social-change

CITY REGIONS AND DEVOLUTION IN THE UK

The Politics of Representation

David Beel, Martin Jones and Ian Rees Jones

First published in Great Britain in 2021 by

Policy Press, an imprint of
Bristol University Press
University of Bristol
1-9 Old Park Hill
Bristol
BS2 8BB
UK
t: +44 (0)117 954 5940
e: bup-info@bristol.ac.uk

Details of international sales and distribution partners are available at
policy.bristoluniversitypress.co.uk

British Library Cataloguing in Publication Data
A catalogue record for this book is available from the British Library

ISBN 978-1-4473-5501-4 hardcover
ISBN 978-1-4473-5505-2 ePub
ISBN 978-1-4473-5503-8 OA PDF

Cover design: Clifford Hayes
Front cover image: Black and white geometric pattern © Freepik.com
Bristol University Press uses environmentally responsible print partners.
Printed and bound in Great Britain by CPI Group (UK) Ltd,
Croydon, CR0 4YY

Contents

List of figures and tables   vi
List of abbreviations   vii
About the authors   viii
Acknowledgements   ix
Preface   xi

Introduction: Onward devolution and city regions   1

1   Northern powerhouses   23

2   Metro governance dynamics   41

3   Precarious city regions   63

4   Elite city deals   79

5   Beyond cities in regions   99

6   City-region limits   119

Conclusions: City-regional futures   139

Notes   155
References   157
Index   183

List of figures and tables

Figures

0.1	Deal-making and cities-first economic development in the UK	10
1.1	The geography of jobs across the Northern Powerhouse	26
1.2	Outline of Greater Manchester City Region and Sheffield City Region devolution and local authority membership	28
2.1	Sheffield City Region political geography	48
4.1	Cardiff Capital Region local authorities	87
4.2	Shifting governance of the Cardiff Capital Region	88
5.1	North Wales political geography	107
5.2	Gross value added per head, 2016	108
6.1	Swansea Bay City Region	122
6.2	Swansea travel-to-work flows	123
6.3	City region travel times	124
6.4	Swansea Bay City Deal project map	127
6.5	Swansea Bay City Deal revised project map	136

Tables

1.1	Participating Voluntary, Community and Social Enterprise groups	35
3.1	Actor strategies for opposing labour market policies	74
4.1	Business Council membership, 2018	88
4.2	City-deal cascading of representation	90
6.1	Swansea Bay City Region descriptive statistics	125

List of abbreviations

ABR	area based reviews
CA	combined authority
CCR	Cardiff Capital Region
CSP	City Strategy Pathfinder
DBIS	Department for Business, Innovation and Skills
DWP	Department for Work and Pensions
ESRC	Economic and Social Research Council
FE	foundational economy
GMCA	Greater Manchester Combined Authority
GMCR	Greater Manchester City Region
GVA	gross value added
LA	local authority
LEP	Local Enterprise Partnerships
MDA	Mersey Dee Alliance
NE	north east
NW	north west
NWEAB	North Wales Economic Ambition Board
NWGD	North Wales Growth Deal
RDA	Regional Development Agencies
SBCR	Swansea Bay City Region
SCR	Sheffield City Region
SME	small and medium-sized enterprises
UC	Universal Credit
VCSE	Voluntary, Community and Social Enterprise
WISERD	Wales Institute of Social and Economic Research and Data
WP	Work Programme
WSP	Wales Spatial Plan

About the authors

David Beel is Senior Lecturer in Political Economy at Manchester Metropolitan University where he is part of the Future Economies Research Cluster.

Martin Jones is Professor of Human Geography and Deputy Vice-Chancellor at Staffordshire University and a founding Co-Director of the Wales Institute of Social and Economic Research and Data.

Ian Rees Jones is Professor of Sociological Research at Cardiff University and Civil Society Centre Director, Wales Institute of Social and Economic Research and Data.

Acknowledgements

The chapters draw on aspects of previously published work, edited and updated to provide a narrative as *City Regions and Devolution in the UK: The Politics of Representation*. The authored and co-authored sources are listed below and we are extremely grateful to David Etherington, Warren Escadale, Alex Plows, the editors and reviewers of those journals and book chapters for helping us develop this work. We would like to thank Sam Jones (Wales Institute of Social and Economic Research and Data (WISERD), Cardiff University) for assisting with the production of figures. Laura Vickers-Rendall and Amelia Watts-Jones at Policy Press were helpful in bringing the book to completion and Abi Saffrey was a superlative copy editor. Thanks also go to Nicki Jones and Victoria Macfarlane for proof-checking assistance. Influence runs deep with the friendship and work of Bob Jessop. The responsibility for the text and all its faults is fully ours.

The Introduction derives in part from David Beel, Martin Jones and Ian Rees Jones (2016) 'Regulation, governance and agglomeration: making links in city-region research', *Regional Studies, Regional Science* 3: 510–31 (Open Access CC-BY-NC); Martin Jones (2019) 'The march of governance and the actualities of failure: the case of economic development twenty years on', *International Social Science Journal* 68: 25–41 (Open Access CC-BY-NC).

Chapter 1 derives in part from David Beel, Martin Jones, Ian Rees Jones and Warren Escadale (2017) 'Connected growth: developing a framework to drive inclusive growth across a city-region', *Local Economy* 32: 565–75 (Open Access CC-BY-NC); David Beel, Martin Jones and Ian Rees Jones (2018) 'Regionalisation and civil society in a time of austerity: the cases of Manchester and Sheffield', in Craig Berry and Arianna Giovannini (eds) *Developing England's North: The Northern Powerhouse, Devolution and the Political Economy of Place*, London: Palgrave, 241–60.

Chapter 2 derives in part from David Etherington and Martin Jones (2016) 'The city-region chimera: the political economy of metagovernance of failure in Britain', *Cambridge Journal of Regions, Economy and Society* 9: 371–389 (Open Access CC-BY-NC).

Chapter 3 derives in part from David Etherington and Martin Jones (2017) 'Devolution, austerity and inclusive growth in Greater Manchester: assessing impacts and developing alternatives' *Policy Brief*, Staffordshire Business School, Staffordshire University, Stoke-on-Trent; David Etherington, Martin Jones and David Beel (2019) 'The politics of austerity in city region: devolution and Greater Manchester's precarious economy', mimeograph, Staffordshire Business School, Staffordshire University, Stoke-on-Trent.

Chapter 4 derives in part from David Beel, Martin Jones and Ian Rees Jones (2018) 'Elite city-deals for economic growth? Problematizing the complexities of devolution, city-region building, and the (re)positioning of civil society' *Space and Polity* 22: 307–27 (Open Access CC-BY-NC).

Chapter 5 derives in part from David Beel, Martin Jones and Alex Plows (2019) 'Urban growth strategies in rural regions: building the North Wales growth deal' *Regional Studies* 54: 719–31 (Open Access CC-BY-NC).

The Conclusions derive in part from David Etherington and Martin Jones (2018) 'Re-stating the post-political: depoliticization, social inequalities, and city-region growth' *Environment Planning A* 50: 51–72 (Open Access CC-BY-NC).

City Regions and Devolution in the UK is dedicated to Martin Jones' father, Graham Jones (5 April 1937–2 March 2020), who died during the final stages of writing. Graham contributed much to civil society and economic life. He moved from (devolved) Wales to the Northern Powerhouse, then to the South East of England, to see what the new municipal agglomeration fuss was all about. Commenting on city-region devo-narratives, he once said, 'I had one of those, but the wheels fell off'.

Preface

City regions are riding high on the current political and policy agenda across the world. Their emergence is not accidental; they are being built in direct response to the deep ideological thinking exposed in key documents such as the World Bank's (2009) *World Development Report: Reshaping Economic Geography*. This set-in train 'new economic geography' influenced arguments closely following the work of policy advisors such as Krugman, Glaeser, and Katz on the 'new municipalism' and 'new localism', which collectively draw links between urbanism, city-region scales of state intervention, agglomeration economies, and more democratic socioeconomic development through business and civil society partnerships for prosperity.

In the UK, this motif is clearly evident in reports over the past decade, commencing with the 'Haywood Report' in Wales and the Royal Society of Arts' 'City Growth Commission' in England, which through the mantras of the Northern Powerhouse, Midlands Engine, and Western Powerhouse argued for the 'unleashing' of growth through a series of city regions or 'metros' – defined as the 'larger constellation of cities and towns that constitute a functional economy within build up areas' – as the main drivers of economic growth in an increasingly knowledge-driven, global economy. More recently, city regions are pivotal to the Conservative Party's post-Brexit governance-fix for 'spatially rebalancing' or 'levelling up' deep-seated geographical inequalities. In short, city regions are a conduit for redistributing prosperity, power and democracy from the South East to Northern 'left-behind' places, thereby reversing the long historical trend of uneven development and redevelopment. Or so the policy rhetoric goes ...

City Regions and Devolution in the UK: The Politics of Representation examines this and particularly tackles the missing social sphere of these competitive relationships, equilibrating tendencies, and the vacuum around the politics of city-region building on-the-ground. It reports evidenced-based research probing on questions of social and spatial agency in practice: why civil society stakeholders are involved; what the motives are for their engagement or a lack of engagement; reasons for mobilisation or marginalisation (by interest groups and by geographical location); and, in turn, whether city regions can sustain economic agglomeration, anchor socioeconomic development, and deliver virtuous or vicious growth. The book addresses this by offering a geographical political economy framework for understanding the dynamics of city-region building, highlighting the contradictions of state intervention, the experiences of civil society actors, and the ways in which policy problems are geographically played out.

Funded by the Economic and Social Research Council (ESRC) as part of WISERD Civil Society (Grant ES/L0090991/1), work package 'Spaces of New Localism', ESRC Impact Accelerator funding for 'Making City-Regions Work: Inclusive Governance, Skills, and Labour Market Disadvantage', and WISERD Civil Society (Grant ES/S012435/1) 'Changing Perspectives on Civic Stratification and Civil Repair', the book draws on case study research in Wales (Cardiff, Swansea and North Wales) and England (Sheffield and Manchester), to put city-region building in its place. The book does not cover developments in Scotland and Northern Ireland or make any claims about these territories. Phase one involved the analysis of economic development strategies, construed firstly in national level government documentation (Bills, Acts, White and Green Papers) and secondly how this is translated through the various sub-national structures and projects of the state. Phase two looked at experiences of economic development through state-making practices and civil society struggles.

Each of the case studies featured in this book were designed to explore how effectively the institutions and actors of economic governance have been able, or not, to meet the challenges of economic development within their various localities. Ninety-one semi-structured interviews were undertaken between 2014 and 2019 with a wide variety of actors working in, and connected to, the field of economic development, ranging from Director and Chief Executive levels, to civil society engaged in policy formulation and delivery on the ground. This sample size and actor cross-section was deemed appropriate for rigorous qualitative insight into city-region building processes within the five case study sites. The interviews were mostly city region *in situ* office-based, digitally recorded, and draw from the governance structures and various sub-groups of economic development. Stratified actor sampling was undertaken, complemented by snowballing sampling techniques to assess more vulnerable and impenetrable groups (see Atkinson and Flint, 2001; Hitchings and Latham, 2020). For reasons of confidentiality, the individuals are not named; anonymous quotations feature in some chapters and in others, the 'voices' feature in the analysis of policy. These interviews were supported and triangulated by the analysis of policy documents, and vice versa, including institutional minutes, policy briefings, strategy papers, and media analysis.

Introduction: Onward devolution and city regions

> The Government today outlines a new approach to local growth, shifting power away from central government to local communities, citizens and independent providers. This means recognising that where drivers of growth are local, decisions should be made locally. (HM Government, 2010: 5)

> The government has an ambitious programme of devolution. It has sought to decentralise power through structural and legislative changes. The introduction of directly elected mayors with specific powers and responsibilities has enhanced local control and accountability ... Just as the UK is bringing back power over its laws, money, borders, and trade from the European Union, *so local places are taking economic, social, and cultural policy away from Westminster and Whitehall.* (HM Government, 2018: 52, emphasis added)

> [T]he motivation behind much recent institution-building in city-regions is ultimately rooted in a powerful logic of subsidiarization that sits well with the mosaic-like geography of contemporary capitalist society. *Whether or not this trend enlarges the sphere of democracy and the right to the city remains a moot point depending precisely on the specific forms of political community that are put in place in any particular instance.* (Scott, 2019: 569, emphasis added)

It has now been ten years since the launch of the UK Government's 'Local Growth' White Paper (2010), which set in train a series of policy initiatives concerned with removing the barriers for 'civil society' actors to participate in economic and political life through empowered devolved structures and new institutions of governance. This in turn built on a previous decade of devolution and constitutional change, which had resulted in the Scottish Parliament, Elected Assemblies in Northern Ireland, Wales and London, plus (at that time) Regional Development Agencies (RDAs) and emerging city regions across England. This previous decade was the biggest shake-up to the UK state apparatus in recent times; in the words of Bogdanor, 'the most radical constitutional change this country has seen since the Great Reform Act of 1832' (1999: 1) – an Act that set in motion our modern democratic state.

Building on this, as the subtitle of 'Local Growth' reads, 'realising every place's potential' charted a further decade of 'participatory democracy', ending 'top down initiatives' that ignored the varying needs of different areas, instead creating active and real partnerships to bring together civil society, business, and civic leaders to 'set the strategy and take the decisions that will allow their area to prosper' (HM Government, 2010). Further, by extending the development of enterprise partnerships, city regions and leadership through directly-elected mayors, growth could be fostered and spatially agglomerated by giving more power to local areas. In short, making municipal decisions more accountable and responsive to local economic conditions was the driving force behind state intervention and public policy. Collectively, this was the dawn of a localism 'new era for cities' (Emmerich, 2017a: 101) – new in the sense of 'looking across the board' at how government could 'hand power back to people' through new forms of governance to modernise the United Kingdom (HM Government, 2010: 3).

The second quotation, taken from the UK Government's Civil Society Strategy, represents a confident stock-take of achievements made against this ambitious programme. It uses the phrase 'onward devolution' to capture city-region building to foster a sense of shared identity across the UK – improving integration among the people of a particular place and also among the people of the UK as a whole (HM Government, 2018: 52). As we discuss below, this involved legislation such as Cities and Local Government Devolution Act 2016, as well as increasing powers to Scotland, Wales, and Northern Ireland, to ramp up localist democracy. The foreword to this intervention boldly states that people have indeed been 'empowered to take responsibility for their neighbourhoods', as power has been 'decentralised so that local officials and professionals are properly accountable to local people, and trusted to do their job without bureaucratic interference'. Moreover, the provision of economic development and public services is seen as the 'business of the community', not solely the responsibility of government, as providers are invariably drawn from a broad range of suppliers from the public sector and beyond. All communities, then, 'regardless of levels of segregation and deprivation, are able to take advantage of these opportunities' (HM Government, 2018: 10), with the caveat being that 'places are not all starting from the same point' but state intervention has the 'potential to benefit all communities, regardless of circumstance' (HM Government, 2018: 52).

Sandwiched betwixt and between these landmark UK Government statements, critiques of these moments of localism over the past decade though have pointed to very different scenarios being played out in the 'evolution of devolution' (UK Parliament, 2016: 9). Four particular interventions are worth mentioning. First, the National Audit Office report on the 'Funding and Structures for Local Economic Growth' recognises that 'growth policy' has seen an accelerating sequence of initiatives over a number of decades, where structures and funding regimes are regularly replaced by devolved schemes, but 'local responsibilities and freedoms' on the ground are 'limited', tightly 'constrained', and 'poorly coordinated' (National Audit Office, 2013: 16). Second, the Institute of Government's *All Change: Why Britain is So Prone to Policy Reinvention, and What Can Be Done About It* also reveals limited devolution due to Whitehall's 'unwillingness to place trust in existing local institutions' (Norris and Adam, 2017: 14). This reports a 'policy-churn culture' of 'near constant upheaval', due to continuous centralisation through waves of 'decentralisation', with no evidence of strategic thinking, much policy confusion, costing annually £15 million for the continual reorganisation of a single government department alone (Norris and Adam, 2017: 3). In short, devolution discord is rife and awakened citizenry is somewhat limited.

Third, in a report called *Democracy: The Missing Link in the Devolution Debate* (Lyall et al, 2015), the New Economics Foundation analysed the arguments for devolution from a range of documents published between 2011 and 2015 by the central government, local governments, think-tanks, and civil society groups. The New Economics Foundation found that although economic growth was the most prominent outcome supporting devolution, it was poorly conceptualised and the distributional context was unknown. In particular, there was minimal reference to: austerity or structural problems affecting the UK economy; a more equitable distribution of growth benefits as reflected in living standards; improved working conditions, pay and job security besides the promised increase in levels of employment; and the way in which growth affects environmental sustainability (Lyall et al, 2015: 5).

Fourth, the UK2070 Commission – an independent inquiry into geographical inequalities, chaired by Kerslake, who ran the civil service from 2011 to 2014 – issued a final 'ultimatum' report (Pidd, 2020: 15): *Make No Little Plans – Acting at Scale for a Fairer and Stronger Justice* (UK2070, 2020a), which questions the localist 'benefits for all' philosophy and instead suggests 'nobody is winning' or being empowered. Official data (IFS, 2019) reveals that deep-rooted spatial inequalities persist in the UK, but the report notes limited debate about this, it suggests the 'economic potential of large parts of the UK is not being realised' and 'an imbalance of wealth and opportunity' exists in localist Britain, with 'increasing economic insecurity' (UK2070 Commission, 2020a: foreword). Understandably, government statements such as 'it is important that the public understand where power lies if the democratic process is to work effectively' (UK Parliament, 2016: 53) raise serious questions about devolution, governance, and civil society in the UK.

The third quotation, from Scott, puts these important geographical developments into a wider conceptual context, as they signal a deep intellectual concern with the academic fields of socioeconomic development, economic growth and spatial agglomeration, the politics of representation and dimensions of social polarisation, and, above all, critical concerns with democracy, governance and public policy in the context of political coordination and uneven development. Scott's evaluative review of city-region developments from around the world over the past 50 years highlights three global driving forces. These collectively claim that, firstly, urbanisation is a global phenomenon to be embraced at all costs and within this, city regions are the principal spatial scale at which this happens and people experience meaningful lived reality. Secondly, the economic basis of city regions rests on concentration and specialisation, which allows spatial agglomeration to take place and externalities to be maximised. The clearest state of this purpose is offered by Deas et al (2020: 6), where agglomeration 'envisages city-regions as dynamic nodes in the global economy, characterised by dense networks of firms and concentrations of skilled workers, underpinned by well-developed infrastructure, a business friendly fiscal and physical environment, and a host of cultural assets and residential amenities'.

Thirdly, cosmopolitan partnership policy management is required with a bold and confident voice, working with the grain of market logistics. This necessitates new 'spatial orderings' (such as governance frameworks) to lubricate agglomeration and provide efficiency by lowering transaction costs and promoting proximity, thereby liberating growth and allowing it to spread geographically for all to benefit. Last, as state spatial restructuring is 'materializing at a rapid pace' and new forms of regulation and governance such as 'city-regions are always at the same time conditioned by idiosyncrasies related to local material, social, and cultural circumstances', Scott notes the importance of these

(UK) policy developments for informing academic debates (Scott, 2019: 574). We certainly live in serendipitous times.

City Regions and Devolution in the UK: The Politics of Representation is situated in and contributes to these academic and policy concerns. It is concerned with the topics of devolution, localism, governance and the involvement of actors in city regions. The latter being under researched and silent in current debates. The book particularly questions social and spatial agency by analysing the representation and engagement of civil society to provide comparative windows on devolution and economic governance. Civil society is interpreted integrally as a 'shifting horizon of action rather than a fixed reality' (Jessop, 2020: xi) and where

> everything that goes on to link the world of government to the rest of society ... the sphere in which social movements are active, and where the popular challenges that sustain democracy's vibrancy are located; but it is also the space within which the political power of unequal wealth is wielded. (Crouch, 2020: 20–21; see also Heinrich, 2005)

We refer to 'encounters' (Jones, 2012) of city-region building through the endeavours of local government, trade unions, voluntary and third sector organisations, plus the plethora of social movements, based within and between places, thus situating civil society in the context of 'critical governance studies' (Jessop, 2020: xv).

Deploying case study research in exemplar Welsh localities (Cardiff Capital Region (CCR), Swansea Bay City Region (SBCR) and North Wales) and English localities (Sheffield City Region (SCR) and Greater Manchester City Region (GMCR)), the remaining chapters address key questions such as: what policy, strategy and institutional changes have taken place in the landscape of economic development since 2010 in England and Wales? How do these changes affect and involve civil society organisations? What are the narratives of devolution and community engagement and how are these being worked into policies and procedures for stakeholder engagement? Who is ultimately involved in the localism and how does this relate to forms of associational life and political engagement? How successful are city-region builders in realising the objectives of agglomeration, economic development, growth, and social empowerment? We answer these through empirical material and policy commentary undertaken between 2014 and 2020 – a six-year window on economic governance spanning the ascendency of the Conservative Party, starting first with the Tory-Liberal Coalition, and progressing to a Conservative dominated 'beyond Brexit Britain' (Bogdanor, 2019).

The remainder of this chapter provides a background to debates on city-region governance, economic development, and the politics of representation. It provides a 'geographical political economy framework' for grappling with city-region governance, which requires a consideration of the relationships between the state, economy and localism to understand historical specificities, trends, and counter-trends of state intervention. The chapter concludes by providing an overview of the arguments and chapters to follow.

City regions, devolution, the state and the politics of representation

City Regions and Devolution in the UK is about the big-picture academic concerns, anchored through small stories on the nature and scale of UK state intervention. It addresses Scott's (2019: 574) concerns to deploy city-region building to provide a window on 21st century capitalism and its distinctive social and economic features, as well as the contradictions of this model of production and growth. The book builds on previous 'governance geography' research, which argues that economic success within any given territory is not exclusively the result of a narrow set of economic factors, but instead is partially dependent on a whole range of social, cultural and institutional forms and supports, alongside concerns with social and spatial agency (Goodwin et al, 2012, 2017; Jones, 2019a, 2019b; MacKinnon, 2020). What is clear from the quotations above is that lots has been happening with regards to devolution, awakened citizenry, and city-region policymaking. What is less clear, as illustrated by concerns raised above, is whether this has enhanced or hindered the involvement of civil society actors and the capacity of the new institutions to deliver their economic strategies. The contemporary governance geography question, then, is why city regions and why now?

City-region solutions

As noted above, the notion of a 'city region' ushers into play areal units wherein socioeconomic and sociocultural relations can be effectively contained and developed – such as 'uniting a city and its surrounding suburbs and quasi-suburbs with rural areas beyond' (Redcliffe-Maud and Wood, 1974: 34). In this context, the planning tradition has held a longstanding interest in city regions as spaces for integrated development strategies, associated in turn with debates on the structure of local government, as well as forms of state intervention to address economic distributions of growth and opportunity for employment (Axinte et al, 2019). Debates have focused on stabilising city regions as 'functional realities' by aligning economic activity with administrative jurisdictions to create planning areas (compare Hall, 2009; Hall and Tewdwr-Jones, 2010; Harrison, 2007; Ward 1988). Healey though warns that the search for city regions that 'encompasses some *stable* "coherence" and "integration" relations may ... be misguided' (2009: 832, emphasis added). Historically, city regions are one of several territorial frameworks for anchoring economic development, with much geographical flux happening around the mechanisms, institutions and spaces of sub-national economic governance.

The UK, since industrialisation, has a long history of uneven development/redevelopment and spatial disparity, which broadly speaking has consistently focused the majority of economic growth and power within the Southeast of UK, specifically London (McCann, 2016). This relationship has been further exacerbated through processes of de-industrialisation, which has been coupled with an increased centralisation of governmental and financial power to London (Martin, 2015). The apparent regional disparity is often phrased in one of two ways, either as an overheating Southeast or that the other regions are underperforming and thus not reaching their full potential. Following Massey (1979), there is a need to move away from seeing 'regional problems' as related to merely spatial distribution and to think of such inequalities in holistic terms, namely how regions, and more specifically city regions, are being constructed and mobilised to capitalise on and gain competitive advantages in the global economy (While et al, 2013). The city region for urban elites developing policy in the UK, then, becomes an institutional agent and spatial scale on which capital investment (both internal and external) can be attracted to and acted on.

Since the identification of this disparity, there has been a significant number of attempts to address this imbalance and these have often shifted in their scalar focus (Jones, 2019a, 2019b). Under New Labour (from 1997 onwards) for example, the UK Government attempted to 'modernise' the UK state with a strong regional focus for both democratic delivery and economic development. This led to RDAs being created throughout the UK and for a number of reasons this modernisation process stalled under New Labour; there was the failure to 'sell' regional devolution to the English Regions, although Welsh and Scottish devolution were hailed as successes (compare, Rallings and Thrasher, 2006; Pike et al, 2015; Bogdanor, 2019). The Labour Party was also criticised for being overly centralist and not really wishing to cede power to the regions (HM Government, 2011), despite talking the language of decentralism. This was reflected in a strong emphasis on targets and measures for RDAs. There was also a belief that over time RDAs became bogged down in bureaucracy due to mission creep, as they were consistently being expected to do more with less. Finally, the global economic crisis and the removal of New Labour from office (2010) saw the end to the UK's experiment with a specifically regional growth model for development (Imrie and Raco, 2003).

With the supposed failure of RDAs and the 'regional approach' within England, as expressed by the Conservative-led coalition on coming to power, the focus then shifted towards a supposedly more flexible and localised city-regional scale for economic development (Pugalis and Townsend, 2012). This meant that in England, the RDAs were dismantled and replaced by Local Enterprise Partnerships (LEPs), which aim to be more locally strategic for doing economic development. They are also meant to give a more 'naturally' relevant scale on which economic activity takes place by bringing together different adjoining local authorities (LAs) whereby LAs negotiate which LEP they see themselves as being most appropriately based within. They were given an open remit to begin, with central government not wishing to dictate fully their terms of activity (HM Government, 2010), but LEPs have been expected to respond to the broader issues surrounding transport, planning, housing, local infrastructure, employment and enterprise, and the transition to a low carbon economy. This reflected a new form of institution building at the city-region level: boards largely made up of local business elites, alongside elected LA members – the vision being that such business elites can develop with elected members more appropriate locality-based, functional mechanisms for growth (BIS, 2010a). Critical here is the deep ideological belief in developing city-region based 'functional economic areas', which HM Treasury (2007) endorsed through the Sub-National Review.

Building on this 'local growth agenda', the Cities and Local Government Devolution Act 2016 formalised a move towards integrated governance with mayoral combined authorities (CAs) and also set in train a series of Devolution, City, and Growth Deals (reflecting the boundaries of some LEPs), done on a city-by-city basis and not uniform in their scope and reward (see National Audit Office, 2016). In England, during the first wave, the eight largest Core Cities outside London all received City Deals (HM Government, 2015a). The largest and most broad ranging of these has been the Greater Manchester Devolution Deal, set within the context of claims made for the Northern Powerhouse (Chapters 2 and 4) to direct power and resources into Northern Britain. There has subsequently been a Wave of City Deals with further deals for other city regions being progressed along weaker lines (Sandford, 2019, 2020).

Different processes of negotiation have been applied to the Celtic devolved territories, set within their different devolution settlements. Within Scotland, there have been six Deals, with Northern Ireland receiving Deals for Belfast and Mid Ulster. Following several amendments to devolution through Acts passed in 2006 and 2011, the Welsh Government Minister established a 'task and finish' group to consider the potential role of city regions in the future economic development of Wales. The task was to decide, on the basis of objective evidence, whether a spatially focused city-region approach to economic development, as opposed to the (national) Wales Spatial Plan (WSP), could deliver an increase in jobs and prosperity for Wales. The three reasons for adopting a city-region approach were: improving the planning system; improving connectivity; and driving investment through a stronger and more visible offering from an agglomerated wider region (see Welsh Government 2011; House of Commons Welsh Affairs Committee, 2019). A final report argued that: 'City-region boundaries must reflect economic reality and not political or administrative boundaries. Genuine engagement and meaningful collaboration across many local authorities will be needed. This will certainly involve ceding power, funding and decision making to a more regional level' (Welsh Government, 2012: 7).

Two city regions have been created: SBCR (Chapter 6) and CCR (Chapter 4), with both awarded City Deals in 2016. A North Wales Growth Deal (NWGD) followed in 2019 (Chapter 5), with a Mid-Wales Growth Deal currently under discussion. The structure of the deals in Wales is different as no such LEPs exist and responsibility for economic development is devolved to the Welsh Parliament (previously the National Assembly for Wales, 1999–2020). Given that the Welsh Parliament holds powers over LA powers and funding, there is 'therefore no devolution of financial levers and the deals so far agreed have been purely economic stimulus packages for the areas involved' (House of Commons Welsh Affairs Committee, 2019: 6).

The shift to the city region, then, represents a changing scalar relationship for both democracy and economic development in the UK, especially in English cities, with some Welsh and Scottish cities following, but devolution of powers is less of a factor for city deals in Wales, Scotland and Northern Ireland than it is in England. Figure 0.1

Figure 0.1: Deal-making and cities-first economic development in the UK

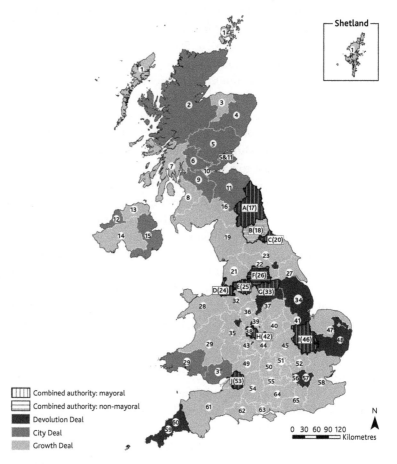

Source: Produced by Sam Jones, WISERD

Deal name	Deal type	Deal/ combined authority label
Islands Growth Deal	Growth Deal	1
Inverness and Highlands City Region Deal	City Deal	2
Moray Growth Deal	Growth Deal	3
Aberdeen City Region Deal	City Deal	4
Tay Cities Region Deal	City Deal	5
Edinburgh & South East Scotland City Region Deal/Tay Cities Region Deal	City Deal	5/11
Stirling and Clackmannanshire City Region Deal	City Deal	6
Argyll and Bute Growth Deal	Growth Deal	7
Ayrshire Growth Deal	Growth Deal	8
Glasgow City Region City Deal	City Deal	9
Falkirk Growth Deal	Growth Deal	10
Edinburgh & South East Scotland City Region Deal	City Deal	11
Derry and Strabane City Deal	City Deal	12
Causeway Coast and Glens Growth Deal	Growth Deal	13
Mid, South and West Region Growth Deal	Growth Deal	14

Belfast Region City Deal	City Deal	15
Borderlands Inclusive Growth Deal	Growth Deal	16
North of Tyne	Devolution Deal	17/A
North Eastern	Growth Deal	18/B
Cumbria	Growth Deal	19
Tees Valley	Devolution Deal	20/C
Lancashire	Growth Deal	21
Leeds City Region	Growth Deal	22
Business Inspired Growth: York, North Yorkshire and East Riding	Growth Deal	23
Liverpool City Region	Devolution Deal	24/D
Greater Manchester	Devolution Deal	25/E
West Yorkshire	Devolution Deal	26/F
Humber	Growth Deal	27
North Wales Growth Deal	Growth Deal	28
Mid-Wales Growth Deal	Growth Deal	29
Swansea Bay City Deal	City Deal	29
Cardiff Capital Region City Deal	City Deal	31
Cheshire and Warrington	Growth Deal	32
Sheffield City Region	Devolution Deal	33/G
Greater Lincolnshire	Devolution Deal	34
The Marches	Growth Deal	35
Stoke-on-Trent and Staffordshire	Growth Deal	36
Derby, Derbyshire, Nottingham and Nottinghamshire,	Growth Deal	37
Black Country	Growth Deal	38
Greater Birmingham and Solihull	GrowthDeal	39
Leicester and Leicestershire	Growth Deal	40
Greater Cambridge & Greater Peterborough	Growth Deal	41
West Midlands	Devolution Deal	42/H
Worcestershire	Growth Deal	43
Coventry and Warwickshire	Growth Deal	44
South East Midlands	Growth Deal	45
Cambridgeshire and Peterborough	Devolution Deal	46/I
New Anglia	Growth Deal	47
Norfolk and Suffolk	Devolution Deal	48
Gloucestershire	Growth Deal	49
Oxfordshire LEP	Growth Deal	50
Buckinghamshire Thames Valley	Growth Deal	51
Hertfordshire	Growth Deal	52
West of England	Devolution Deal	53/J
Swindon and Wiltshire	Growth Deal	54
Thames Valley Berkshire	Growth Deal	55
London	Growth Deal	56
Greater London	Devolution Deal	57
South East	Growth Deal	58
Cornwall	Devolution Deal	59
Cornwall and the Isles of Scilly	Growth Deal	60
Heart of the South West	Growth Deal	61
Dorset	Growth Deal	62
Solent	Growth Deal	63
Enterprise M3	Growth Deal	64
Coast to Capital	Growth Deal	65

captures this evolving piecemeal economic and political geography. The approach is not without its questions concerning an effective deployment as an equitable and spatial rebalancing strategy. The following section discusses these in considering why the city region has become the de facto model for urban and economic development and why this is deemed problematic for civil society actors.

City-region growth machines, neoliberalism and civil society

Work by Scott (2001, 2019) discussed above is a prime example in delineating the success city regions can have. The focus on scale is important as a key feature on their success has been for their urban centre's ability to dominate the region surrounding them. This allows for a suitable supply of labour, as well as the space to spread, as city agglomeration grows (Storper, 2013). This points towards the concept of agglomeration in urban theory whereby an urban centre enlarges by engulfing more land, labour and infrastructure into its region (Rigby and Brown, 2013). Agglomeration at the city-region scale, then, is the current ideological discourse that is dominant within the neoliberal growth model of urban development thinking (Haughton et al, 2013). Its various proponents (such as Fujita and Krugman, 1995; Harding, 2007; Nathan and Overman, 2013; Scott and Storper, 2003; Florida, 2014) all purport in different ways to a model, which celebrates the perpetually development of the urban, while running the risk of glossing over the structural inequality that it creates.

There has also been a strong influence on UK policymakers from North American accounts on urban development, where a focus on the 'Metro' areas and 'New Municipalism' approaches (see Glaeser, 2012; Barber, 2014; Katz and Bradley, 2014; Katz and Nowak, 2017; cf. Thompson, 2020) has had a strong influence on structuring UK urban policy (RSA, 2014). This is done by often focusing solely on 'successful' metro/regional case studies (Harrison, 2007), which are highly spatially selective, highlighting only a narrow narrative of economic success through agglomeration (Lovering, 2007). The proponents of this approach conceptualise the city region as the focus for generating growth (Harding, 2007) in which the city should be mobilised to pull in capital as best actors can. The city region is thus constructed as a 'growth machine' (Logan and Molotch, 1987; Jonas and Wilson, 1999), which aims to develop a critical mass of investment so that such growth can then lead to a trickle-down effect for the city region as a whole (Overman et al, 2007). At the centre of this is the belief that despite issues caused by uneven development, in overall economic performance terms, it is better to ignore economic and historical imbalances and to concentrate on continuing growth, rather than address distribution and inequality at the outset. In the words of an influential commentator on this perspective:

> Investing in more successful cities to either enhance the economy or reduce cost of living clearly exacerbates uneven spatial development. But I have tried to argue that this may make for good economic policy in a world where who you are matters more than where you are and the government can't do much to offset the market forces that make some places perform worse than others. Of course, adopting such a course, and prioritising growth over rebalancing makes for very difficult politics for constituency based politicians. (Overman, 2012: 1)

Pushing the mantra of neoliberalism, which is the ideological backdrop to this, 'success' creates success and the city region is thus seen as a tool for economic growth, which focuses on building an economic mass, the skills base and the transport links of the region (see Chapter 5). The political project of city regionalism is to, therefore, rescale the central city into a much larger territory and to bring surrounding territories under its purview. It pushes the dominant centre's identity and politics onto its hinterland (Deas et al, 2020; Vainikka, 2015) through an economic rationalism for growth and due to this, everything else becomes secondary concerns and social noise (see Peck and Tickell, 1994, 2012).

City-regional worlds, critiques and missing links

Critiques of this position have been varied and there have been a variety of heated debates in the academic literature, which have opened up discussions with regards to city-region development. This will be developed further below, but with regards city regions and agglomeration, Haughton et al (2014) neatly point out the failure of agglomeration to develop even growth, in spite of its boosterish potential. In discussion with Overman (2014), Haughton et al (2014) detail how a desire to relax planning constraints in urban areas for 'growth' suffers from 'short-term' thinking that focuses on the centres of successful agglomeration examples while ignoring the uneven growth this creates within the city and its surroundings (see Cochrane and Massey, 1989; Etherington and Jones, 2009; Massey, 2015). Such approaches fail to counter this evidence with empirical work from other less successful locations, therefore, not taking into account the way in which such processes, although potentially good for one city region, could be highly constraining for another (Henderson and Ho, 2014; Lovering, 1999). Harrison (2007) argues that this represents a shift in terms of the spatial scale on which economic competition takes place as 'New Regionalist' thinking (see Brenner, 2004; Keating et al, 2013) and is then rescaled to the city region. By moving from the region to the city region, the system of city-regional development only increases the competition between urban areas, rather than breaking it down, or it attempts to create uneasy growth coalitions such as the Northern Powerhouse (Chapters 2, 3 and 4), which is as fractious as it is cooperative.

Accordingly, critics of city-region deal-making policy have noted problems of governance complexity, which reproduces regional inequalities by focusing only on the most profitable and high-tech sectors of the local and regional economy (Etherington and Jones, 2016a). Moreover, there is little new money, 'more a "menu of specials", where: a number of items have been made available to most areas, but each deal also contains a few unique elements or "specials" (typically consisting of commitments to explore future policy options)' (Sandford, 2018: 9). Behind this, broader restructuring processes are at work. The principal historical function of LAs was the concern with public services in the context of addressing uneven development (Duncan and Goodwin, 1988). Merging LEPs with local government functions through the various CAs and mayoral CAs have shifted local state functions towards the ideological purpose of economic growth 'by negotiation' with central government (Hatcher, 2017; O'Brien and Pike, 2019). The need to compete in a relentless globalised economy and with the city region being seen as the appropriate scale to enact this (Scott, 2001) as Harrison (2007) suggests, then, forces city regions to compete for growth and territory (in some cases) in an attempt to secure their position of dominance. The deployment of depoliticising scalar processes are crucial here to limit opposition and resistance (Deas et al, 2020; Conclusions in this volume), alongside an ongoing process of joining up economic development with the welfare reform agenda (see Chapters 2 and 3), collectively seen as 'clearing the ground for a market solution' (Toynbee and Walker, 2017: 78). In the words of a Welsh councillor, giving evidence to a select committee on City Deals and Growth Deals, and in the process concurring with Darling (2016: 230) that when 'combined with a market-oriented transfer of responsibilities, depoliticization acts to constrain the possibilities of political debate and to predetermine the contours of those policy discussions that do take place':

> When I was told I would take part in negotiations on the growth deal, I expected there to be some kind of specific system or order, and I must admit that I am quite frustrated that the political meetings we have had with the Ministers have been a little – to use my son's word – 'random' and not particularly structured. There is no particular programme or agenda. I asked one Minister, 'Before we meet next time, what about having a programme of our meetings diarised so that we are clear when we are going to be discussing this with you? Let us have some action points from the previous meeting, if you like. We don't want detailed minutes, but what are the action points? You can report back on that, and we can then see where the problems are that we need to resolve'. But that really did not happen. (Dyfrig Siencyn, Gwynedd Council Leader, quoted in House of Commons Welsh Affairs Committee, 2019: 40)

There is also a need to think critically about the ways in which such an agglomerative approach impacts on areas outside of, or disconnected from, a metropolitan centre (Chapters 5 and 6). Due to the piecemeal process by which city regions are being delivered, whereby only certain cities are given a city deal, this raises a series of questions with regards to those places outside of the deal making process (Pemberton and Shaw, 2012). Figure 0.1 highlights a large number of cities and provincial towns, but also rural areas, that do not fall within the hinterland of a city-region deal. This is not to say economic development planning is absent, as every area in England is placed within a LEP, but it does again highlight the unevenness between metropolitan and non-metropolitan areas. The 'city-first' approach to sub-regional economic governance, whereby growth is delivered via agglomeration, not only has the potential to exacerbate uneven development in cities, but also to further entrench it in places external to the city region (Harrison and Heley, 2015). For them and Ward (2006), if not addressed, this will only perpetuate an existing rural development problem via the reproduction of place hierarchies that marginalises non-urban centres.

To date, then, there have been both theoretical and empirical literatures, operating at a variety of scales, arguing both for and against, the practices of city-regional development. What becomes apparent though is that there is a pressing need to contextualise, comprehend and place the current economic developments and growth orientated agendas of city regions (in the UK) within the broader processes of 'state spatial restructuring' (Brenner, 2004, 2019). This perspective has been offered by MacLeod (2001) and Jones (2001), who, contra Lovering (1999), remain sympathetic to the new regionalist project, but note a conceptual void around the *geographical political economy of city-region making*. As Ward and Jonas (2004: 2120) have previously highlighted, it 'appears to leave a lot out in terms of what actually drives regional economies in any given context' and similarly we would argue that city-region discourses appear to leave out far more than they actually contain. They call for the following to be addressed to take city-region debates forward:

> the economic and social conditions under which the city regional scale is politically constructed as a particular space (or scale of territoriality) for class and political alliance formation and struggle [and] the ways in which conflicts around production, social reproduction, and collective consumption with in and around city regions are managed and, consequently, the variety of struggles around state territorial structures in city regions. (Ward and Jonas, 2004: 2130)

This succinctly captures part of what is missing within the current deployment of the city-regional discourse – this form of state rescaling is fraught with tensions and conflicts that are often marginalised and this needs to be brought into the matrix of city-region building to expose the 'contestation of the political and economic consensus' (Deas et al, 2020: 2).

Tensions between economic, social and political governance and agency, labour control, service provision, welfare policies, democracy and citizenship, intra-metropolitanism, the politics of the urban environment, and sustainability are the unfinished aspects of this research agenda. *City Regions and Devolution in the UK* tackles these through the lens of civil society actors, in a sense providing a 'moral agency' (Normington and Hennessy, 2018: 14–15), or experiential and lived-integrity take on the regional world of agglomeration. This begins to dig down to the 'lived' experience of the city region and the ways in which policy begins to impact on daily lives and institutions.

We turn to this in the next section, suggesting the state as a sociospatial relation is a critical missing link in the city-regions debate.

Making links: the state, civil society and the politics of representation

The most general feature of the state (pre-modern as well as modern and pre-capitalist as well as capitalist) is that it comprises a set of institutions concerned with the territorialisation of political power. This involves the intersection of politically organised, coercive and symbolic power, a clearly demarcated core territory, and a fixable population on which political decisions may be made collectively binding. Thus, the key feature of the state is the historically variable ensemble of technologies and practices that produce, naturalise and manage territorial space as a relatively bounded container within which political power is exercised to achieve various, more or less well-integrated, and changing policy objectives. The state, then, is distinct and different from say a multinational corporation, by virtue of its territorial integrity and its political legitimacy. The state is also different in the various roles that it can play. States can respond to the contradictions, dilemmas and problems of capitalism by creating the general conditions for the production and social reproduction of the capital relation, that is, the environment for economic growth and development. The state does this in part by seeking to promote growth and development and/or by responding to the effects of this, that is, uneven growth, change and restructuring. The state though is omnipresent: due to its development and penetration into most spheres of life, it appears to be everywhere and nowhere at the same time (Jones, 2019a: 17–18).

Following Gramsci (1971), the state is a complex and broad set of institutions and networks that span both political society and civil society in their 'inclusive' sense, though these divisions between the state and the private or non-state sphere are purely conceptual and the two overlap in reality. Building on this insight, states can be viewed as strategic terrains, with emphasis being placed on strategic considerations and strategic actions. Offe (1984, 1985) discusses this arrangement by drawing attention to the state and its circuits of power and policy implementation, which provides a window on the patterning of state intervention and the everyday nature of policymaking and agency under capitalism.

Building on Offe and Gramsci, Jessop's approach to the state, has significantly moved forward these arguments. For Jessop (1990, 2002,

2008, 2016a), the state needs to be thought of as 'medium and outcome' of policy processes that constitute its many interventions. The state is both a social relation and a producer of strategy and, as such, it does not have any power of its own. State power in relation to the policy process relates to the forces that 'act in and through' its apparatus. According to this view, attempts to analyse the policy process need to uncover the strategic contexts, calculations, and practices of actors involved in strategically-selective, or privileged, sites. This draws attention to the intricate links between actors and forms of representation, institutions and their interventions and practices, and the range of policy outcomes available. The state, then, is both a strategic and relational concern, forged through the *ongoing* engagements between agents, institutions and concrete policy circumstances. This means the roles of civil society actors and their agency in city regions needs to be conceptualised in this strategic-relational political economy context.

Rhodes (2007: 1254, emphasis added) reminds us that 'patterns of rule arise as the contingent products of diverse actions and political struggles informed by the *beliefs of agents* as they confront dilemmas that are understood differently in contending traditions'. Heeding this call, Jessop and Sum (2013) deploy the notions of 'semiosis' and 'construal' in their cultural political economy framework of state-making. Semiosis refers to sense-making and meaning-making, whereby policymakers can give appreciation and meaning to their actions 'in the world', which is in turn predicted on 'construal' – how a particular policy problem is perceived and the solution constructed in response to this as a product of 'symptomology'. Put very simply: 'Policy makers are not faced with a given problem. Instead they have to identify and formulate their problem' (Lindbolm, 1968: 13) and deploy actors to resolve. The governance of economic development and the roles of agency are no exception here and the nature of the problem and the solutions to this have changed considerably over time and across space – perpetually in a state of flux and question, as noted above.

These concerns can be further rolled together through the idea of 'spatial fixes' (Harvey, 2011, 2016) and 'spatio-temporal fixes' (see Jessop, 2016a, 2016b), concepts deployed to comprehend the dynamics of state spatiality, state spatial restructuring and the geographies of state intervention specifically. The state performs the role of securing the relative stabilisation of society by endeavouring to manage the various economic and political contradictions within the state system. This is inherently spatial, as state intervention is articulated through the constructions of spaces (scales, levels, horizons, and so on) of intervention, the fixing of borders, the stabilisation of places, and attempts are being continually made to produce and reproduce a territorially coherent and functioning socioeconomic landscape. This has been referred to elsewhere as 'state spatial selectivity' – the processes of spatial and actor privileging and articulation in and through which state policies are differentiated across territorial space in order to target particular geographical zones, scales, and interest groups. In short, certain spatial actors and geographical locations have a greater space of engagement on the state arena than others (Jones, 1997, 1999).

The latter dimension forms an integral element of how legitimation and mobilisation occur within the state apparatus via the creation of territorial coalitions, or what Cox (1998) calls 'spaces of engagement', to mobilise strategically significant actors and exclude others where 'spaces of dependency' (interests and attachments) rule out their possibility for incorporation. The tension between engagement and dependency, of course, creates a politics of scale and a scaling of politics, where some city regions are either more or less engaged in networks of association beyond their immediate territories than are others (see Jonas and Wood, 2012). As we discuss in Chapters 2, 3 and 4 with regards to the Northern Powerhouse in Greater Manchester and Sheffield, this can be explored through Jessop's idea of 'spatial imaginaries': how semiosis, construal and symptomology are enacted through social and spatial agency as 'geographies of representation' (MacLeod and Jones, 1999). As Jessop (2012: 7) summarises, spatial imaginaries guide present and future (non-)decisions and (in-)actions and play a performative role, when intense expectations unfold to mobilise resources, produce incentives, and justify certain actions in preference to other ones (see also Granqvist et al, 2019; MacKinnon, 2020).

City-region building as process, not an event

Devolution is, as noted by the mantra in Wales, 'a process, not an event' (Torrance, 2020; see also Davies, 1999). It is important to highlight the contingent 'mechanisms' or 'processes' in and through which this city-region project is being politically made and contested with 'some forms of agency' to avoid 'over generalizations' (Le Gales, 2016: 168). Following Offe (1984: 37), a 'processual' approach is favoured in *City Regions and Devolution in the UK*, which seeks out the mechanisms ('cross-scalar relations' as Brenner et al, 2012: 60 put it) that generate events, highlight developmental tendencies, tease out important counteracting tendencies and create the opportunities for progressive civil society localisms. Despite the potential for progressive politics to develop, instances of governance failure across cities and regions are becoming ever more apparent. This is a symptomatic problem created by the near constant process of state policy(making) switching to maintain the neoliberal accumulation economy through periods of crisis. This means the state, as a perceived rational response, attempts to address such failure through economic governance policies. As noted above, state actors appear to be continually re-inventing policy initiatives, often in response to the problems and contradictions caused by previous rounds of state intervention, in a search to maintain state legitimation and power. As 'statecraft is inescapably, and profoundly, marked by compromise, calculation and contradiction' (Brenner et al, 2012: 45) this raises a series of questions: how are state and civil society actors dealing with these challenges? How is failure being presented, interpreted and addressed; can civil society effectively influence economic development arrangements within the context of devolved responsibility? *City Regions and Devolution in the UK* tackles this.

Outline of this book

Chapter 1 is the first of two chapters considering GMCR and SCR in the North of England. The chapter looks further at the spatial delineation of the city region, which has gained considerable renaissance as the de facto spatial political unit of governance driven by economic development. It suggests that this spatial realignment has been central to the construction of the Northern Powerhouse (since 2014) and has rested alongside other agendas such as devolution, localism and austerity. The chapter presents empirical findings from the two city regions, looking at the ways in which the city region is being constructed differently and the different ways in which civil society is attempting to negotiate its way through this changing governance landscape. Drawing on development in Greater Manchester, we illustrate how this has created a number of significant tensions and opportunities for civil society actors, as they have sought to contest a shifting governance framework. We, therefore, carefully consider how civil society groups are grappling with devolution; both contesting and responding to devolution, increasingly in the context of seeking a more socially inclusive city-regional mode of growth, but with limits.

Within the context of spatial rebalancing and the Northern Powerhouse, Chapter 2 explores the implementation of the devolution of employment and skills within the SCR. The chapter focuses on metro dynamics and suggests that notions of governance and metagovernance failure are important for analysing the development, tensions and contradictions of city-region economic governance within the context of the UK Government's devolution and localism agenda (in particular 'Devolution Agreements'). Governance failure arises because of the primacy of a neoliberal-dominated strategy orientation towards the market and its failure in the delivery of skills. Governance and metagovernance mechanisms are unable to sufficiently coordinate effective responses to address a legacy of de-industrialisation, characterised by deep-rooted labour market and sociospatial inequalities. This, in turn, raises serious questions about the role of civil society in skills, employment and welfare, and the inclusive claims made by the Northern Powerhouse and 'Devo Sheffield'.

The opportunities for and limits to civil society involvement in England's city regions are continued in Chapter 3. This chapter is about how social and institutional actors exercise agency within cities in terms of contestation and negotiation in relation to welfare reform and the politics of labour conditionality. Attention is drawn to the role of trade unions and LA unions, who as actors still have a voice within the 'growth' agendas and the increasingly precarious nature of the economy. This is undertaken by drawing on devolution developments in Greater Manchester and reading these through the lens of civil society within 'austerity urbanism'. We point to the need to have a better understanding of the processes of social and spatial agency, which shapes the way cities are becoming focal points not only in relation to austerity, but also in terms of assessing the distributional consequences and civil society consequences of retrenchment.

The book moves to Wales in Chapter 4. In the context of city regions being vaunted as the 'spatial imaginary' for engendering economic development, the chapter unpacks the role or influence civil society can have in shaping outcomes outside England. It follows the development of city-regionalism in Wales and specifically the unfolding of the 'elite-led' CCR City-Deal. We discuss the recasting of central–local social relations in Wales and the governance tensions between Whitehall and Wales. The chapter builds on notions of metagovernance and its failure discussed in Chapter 2 and brings inter-scalar governance relations to the fore. It reveals that the historical legacy of economic and governance failures has created new geographies of governance and these are playing out differently in Wales. Austerity and local government reorganisation have created different structures for City Deals, but civil society actors also remain entangled in complex elite power networks. Here, they are outside the CCR representational regime but still expected to play along in terms of engaging with the neoliberal growth model.

Chapter 5 discusses the NWGD. North Wales is primarily a rural region within the UK, without a core city or large metropolitan centre. This chapter examines how this urban dynamic, fostered around a pushing of the agglomerative growth model out of the city region, is being transferred largely across rural space and place in terms of where growth is envisioned and how policy is implemented. It raises the importance of the non-metropolitan city-regional alternatives in the context of the city-regional debate. Chapter 6 develops this argument further in the context of the SBCR City Deal. We consider the implications of the city region concept to a medium-sized city and question whether such an application of spatial policy is appropriate when the central city in question is not necessarily economically dominant or connected to its wider polycentric region. We argue that this leads to the further privileging of an urban metropolitan Swansea elite and the marginalisation of civil society actors.

Chapters 5 and 6 collectively develop the notion of 'interstitial spaces' – spatial formations that sit outside the dominant city region discourse and how they form their own approaches to delivering economic development. We suggest interstitial spaces, such as developing dispersed urban and peripheral rural regions, still sit within an economic policy focus that is too heavily skewed towards and driven by a mega-metro city region approach. In the context of Brexit and rural economic development, these chapters argue that the challenges of delivering on this in the context of North Wales and Swansea are pressing.

The conclusion seeks to address the challenges raised in previous chapters. We juxtapose the emergence of a post-political governance condition, where depoliticisation is framing and constraining the possibility of civil society discourses and spatial agency, with the more progressive community-building city-region infrastructural politics of the foundational economy (FE) school of economic development thought. The city-regional challenges and consequences of these two growth models are discussed and a post-script research agenda is offered for civil society spatial agency and civic repair in the context of the current crisis (advanced neoliberalism and the COVID-19 pandemic).

1

Northern powerhouses

Osborne never has an idea: he creates narratives, then everyone nods. (Kate Fall, former Deputy Chief of Staff to Prime Minister David Cameron, 2020: 47)

George Osborne had been thinking about his legacy for a while, embodied by his reading of Robert Caro and his books on Lyndon Johnson, the (Democrat) American President, and Robert Moses, the "powerbroker" who built New York. The outcome was a speech Osborne gave in July 2014 during which he announced the notion of the Northern Powerhouse – evocative of the nineteenth-century cities ... and invited cities to come forward with their proposals for devolution to help create it. (Emmerich, 2017a: 99)

Introduction

Since 2010, the UK Government has sought to reshape the ways in which economic development takes place and although this shift in governmental delivery began under New Labour, there has been a continuing emphasis on developing the city-region scale to unlock economic growth. As noted in the previous chapter, it was much vaunted by the Coalition Government elected in 2010 (Deas, 2013), whereby they replaced the RDAs with LEPs and latterly LEPs morphed into CAs. These policies were subsequently continued by the Conservative administrations (Conservative Party, 2015) through a variety of locality-specific 'devolution deals'. In this context, the rhetoric of the 'Northern Powerhouse' as a flagship policy for delivering economic growth for the North of England (Lee, 2017) has sat alongside a severe austerity programme that has seen LA budgets cut significantly. This, therefore, raises difficult questions with regards to the ability of CAs and LAs to address the current and future needs of their populations (Etherington and Jones, 2016a). Finally, although the context of 'Brexit' and the forever changing leadership and ministerial portfolios of the Conservative Party means the future of the Northern Powerhouse remains uncertain, the political territorialisation and regionalisation (Harrison, 2014) of the city region has problematised the position of civil society actors working in their respective city regions and those working outside or on the periphery of city regions.

Concurrently to this and historically within geography as well as more broadly the social sciences, as noted in the previous chapter, there have been a series of parallel debates simmering away for the past decade (see Jonas and Ward, 2007 for one such example). These debates have revolved around a well-developed series of discussions that consider the ways in which such spatio-temporal fixes either foster economic development through agglomeration (Harding, 2007) or continue to exacerbate uneven development and spatial disparities (Etherington and Jones, 2009). This chapter seeks to connect these themes with the *realpolitik* concerns of delivering devolution. To do this, we follow the development of city-regionalism through these different discourses and unfolding city deals to allow us to ask: within a language of localism, devolution and austerity, how have civil society actors in SCR and GMCR sought to deal with city-regional development approaches and the new governance structures that have been created? These are two key city regions in the North and were the first areas within the Northern Powerhouse to sign devolution deals with the government. Thus, focusing on their cases is central to comprehending what kind of Northern Powerhouse growth is being built, and whose interests are being represented, if this is to be more than an empty policy husk (see Lee, 2017; MacKinnon, 2020). In turn, the chapter is interested in mapping out the missing elements from the Northern Powerhouse recipe book for economic growth and social democracy. By looking at Manchester and Sheffield, if the Northern Powerhouse is a coordinating frame for city regions in the north of England in terms of their interaction with each other, the chapter is interested in understanding how these bodies are being shaped by, and also shaping, devolution.

Accordingly, the chapter sheds light on the ongoing processes of LA restructuring in Greater Manchester and Sheffield towards CA (city-region) approaches. Therefore, it highlights how 'policies are not, after all, merely being transferred over space; their form and their effects are transformed by these journeys' (Peck and Theodore, 2015: 29). We engage with the views of civil society actors on-the-ground, in terms of how they have responded to a shifting governance framework at the local state and city-region scale. The chapter, therefore, addresses the positioning of civil society within these processes by, firstly, giving greater context to the development of city regions as a process of regionalisation: the ways in which 'new regions', namely GMCR and SCR, are created territorially through changes in governance structures. In doing this, the chapter also considers how austerity has impacted on these processes. Second, the chapter assesses how, in this context, civil society is being repositioned due to the economic rationale of city regions, the changes in governance scale and the creation of new 'citizenship regimes' (Jenson and Saint-Martin, 2010). By focusing on the positioning of civil society actors, the chapter highlights how city-regionalism and the Northern Powerhouse, more broadly, offers insights into developing notions of an 'inclusive growth' approach (RSA, 2016, 2017; Chapter 3). The findings suggest that the main issue emerging from these complex processes concerns whether failure to deliver inclusive growth at the city-region scale will reflect a failure to deliver equitable growth within the Northern Powerhouse.

Building the city regions of the Northern Powerhouse

The government sought to reshape the map of governance in England through a series of reforms implemented from 2014 onwards. One part of the solution to this has been the creation of the 'Northern Powerhouse', seen as a policy-framing device, in which a series of ongoing projects have been placed (see Lee, 2017; Berry and Giovannini, 2018). As noted in Chapter 1, the powerhouse represents what Jessop (2016a: 38) would call a 'spatial imaginary' – a discursive phenomenon that distinguishes, by carving out distinctiveness, specific places and spaces 'from the inherently unstructured complexity of a spatialized world'. This is well represented rhetorically in Figure 1.1, whereby economic success and growth is emphasised by the role Northern Powerhouse cities have in providing employment in their metropolitan centres.

The Northern Powerhouse agenda has framed the more substantial restructuring of (some) LAs into CA city regions. This has been based on a city first approach whereby, to date, city-region devolution has focused around the existing metropolitan footprints of the core UK cities (Harrison and Heley, 2015; Jones et al, 2015). The momentum for this has been developed due to a number of factors, which the UK state has attempted to deal with. First, it was very much a post-financial crisis reaction in order to stimulate economic growth with the city region vaunted as the de facto scale for growth (Overman, 2012). This reflected both a dominant policy discourse in urban development (see Storper, 2013 for such an example) and a perceived failure of

Figure 1.1: The geography of jobs across the Northern Powerhouse

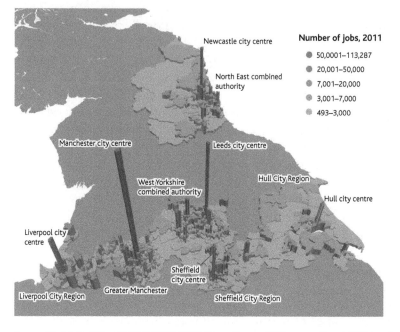

Source: Centre for Cities, 2015; NOMIS, 2015, Figure Census 2011, occupation, MSOA Level

RDAs (Pugalis and Townsend, 2012). Second, it has sought to address the longstanding issue of rebalancing the UK economy, whereby an overheating South is contrasted by an underperforming North (Gardiner et al, 2013; Clarke et al, 2016; Martin et al, 2016). Third, the UK state (with specific reference to England) is renowned for being the most centralised in Western Europe – in light of this, with the failure of regional devolution (beyond Wales, Scotland and London) under New Labour (Goodwin et al, 2005), devolution to a suitable scale within England has been sought (Pike et al, 2012). Fourth, via the deal-making approach, it has attempted to embed and deliver austerity into the reformulation of CAs through a process of block grant reduction and rationalisation.

Relatedly, as noted in the Introduction, the city-region scale has become the dominant discourse in urban development policy (see Storper, 2013). This is due to a number of reasons and analytical frames such as the rise of 'new regionalism' (Keating et al, 2013) and the influence of new economic geography in placing specific emphasis on the growing of regions for economic purposes (MacLeod, 2001). Within both these accounts of economic and regional geography, there is an implicit understanding given that the city region is both the 'natural' and 'functional' scale for economic development. It is suggested that where nation states have failed to deal with macroeconomic shifts in the global economy, city regions represent the suitable scale whereby they are 'small enough' but 'big enough' to deal with this challenge (Scott 2001, 2019; Hall, 2009).

Within this context, the Northern Powerhouse agenda – and the devolution deals that are associated with it – has a strong economic focus, which is also emphasised by the goal of soft-institutional organisations (Haughton et al, 2013) such as LEPs. Crucially, this led to a rescaling of the 'representational regime' of the city region (Jessop, 2016a; see also MacLeod and Goodwin, 1999; Cox, 1998), in spatially-specific and strategic ways. This, in turn, is linked to the creation of new 'citizenship regimes' for the governance of city regions. The concept of new citizenship regimes captures that: 'Who qualifies and is recognized as a model citizen is under challenge. The legitimacy of group action and the desire for social justice are losing ground to the notion that citizens and interests can compete equally in the political marketplace of ideas' (Jenson and Phillips, 1996: 112). In the context of the GMCR and SCR (see Figure 1.2 for a broad outline), the new business-orientated representational regime, by design, places civil society at the margins of the process. This means that what could broadly be termed as the 'social reproduction of the city' is given secondary status to its economic drivers (Jonas and Ward, 2007). This, in turn, positions civil society actors as no longer directly and centrally relevant within the context of chasing agglomerative growth.

Many scholars have been critical to this approach for a number of reasons, some of which were detailed in the previous chapter. First, there seem to be continuing patterns of uneven regional and city-regional development and redevelopment (Etherington and Jones, 2009, 2016a, 2016b, 2018), in terms of the failure for agglomerative approaches to trickle down to those that need it most. Second, this pitches city regions against each other in a competitive race to capture investment (Harrison, 2007), questioning the potential of the Northern Powerhouse as represented in Figure 1.1. Third, it is important to understand how such strategies empower and disempower within the city region. This last point is central to the aim of this chapter, as it highlights the implications that such an economically driven strategy has for those who sit outside of this rubric for growth.

The 'representational regime' (Jessop, 1990, 2016a; see also Rutherford, 2006) of the city region is central to this and to date, city-region devolution has only sought to strategically engage business communities in terms of dealing with government and market failure. This raises difficult questions for those that operate within what could

Figure 1.2: Outline of Greater Manchester City Region and Sheffield City Region devolution and local authority membership

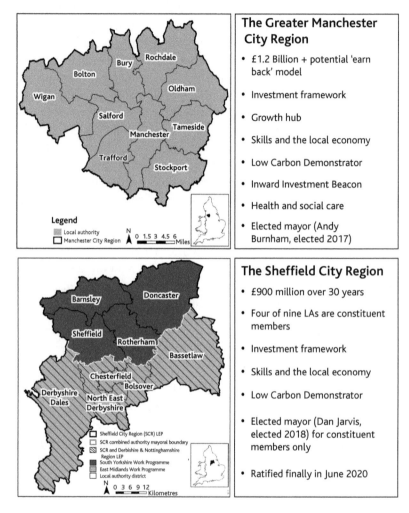

The Greater Manchester City Region

- £1.2 Billion + potential 'earn back' model

- Investment framework

- Growth hub

- Skills and the local economy

- Low Carbon Demonstrator

- Inward Investment Beacon

- Health and social care

- Elected mayor (Andy Burnham, elected 2017)

The Sheffield City Region

- £900 million over 30 years

- Four of nine LAs are constituent members

- Investment framework

- Skills and the local economy

- Low Carbon Demonstrator

- Elected mayor (Dan Jarvis, elected 2018) for constituent members only

- Ratified finally in June 2020

Source: Produced by Sam Jones, WISERD

be broadly termed 'civil society', who are often working with those who benefit least from agglomerative strategies. This reflects a failure to properly integrate a social or inclusive dimension into devolution, due to their stubborn and narrow focus on economic development. Despite many devolution deals having been put in place, the social and inclusive dimension of the reform is only starting to be discussed as a concern, in the continuing process of implementing devolution. An example of this can be seen in the Royal Society of Arts Inclusive

Growth Commission, which sought to identify practical ways to make local economies across the UK more economically inclusive and prosperous (RSA, 2016, 2017).

The aim of the next section is to build on these arguments and frame the role of civil society in processes of devolution in GMCR and SCR, and address the position of civil society more directly within this rescaling of governance.

Placing civil society in the city region

This section assesses the role and place of civil society within GMCR and SCR in the context of the unfolding devolution and the Northern Powerhouse agendas. Civil society is used as a catch-all term for a number of different types of organisation, which are separate from both the state and business. This includes organisations such as charities, those termed third sector, voluntary groups, community groups (of both place and identity), social enterprises, and housing associations. They all have very different relationships with both the local state and business in terms of how they operate. Some have contractual relationships, whereby they deliver specific services. Others act to give specific representation to minority groups, and different groups work on very different spatial scales – ranging from across the city region to very localised, neighbourhood development. What ties them together as a set of groups is their individual organisational remit to produce or engender some form of social benefit for their perceived communities. The interviews were not discussing the development of the Northern Powerhouse specifically, but more broadly the development of the city-region building agenda. However, as has been previously stated above, the development of city regions is central to development of the Northern Powerhouse as a 'spatial imaginary' and GMCR and SCR are two key cases in this respect. Hence the following analysis should be viewed in the context of what do such approaches to city regions mean for discourses surrounding the Northern Powerhouse.

In framing current developments in devolution from a UK state perspective and from within both SCR and GMCR, it is important to consider the ways in which civil society actors are dealing with this changing governance structure. Jones et al (2015) highlight how in Liverpool and Bristol, the changing governance landscape and the reduction in funding opportunities through austerity has made things more difficult for groups that sit within what is broadly termed civil society. This has been reflected in both GMCR and SCR, as austerity has impacted those hardest, in the most deprived areas of each city region (Beatty and Fothergill, 2016), where such groups are more active and needed. However, civil society members have also highlighted a number of opportunities to mitigate this (despite being problematic) within the context of devolution and in face of stringent austerity measures. Below we analyse how civil society actors have struggled with devolution, but also have attempted to find new positions and strategies on which to see their social agendas addressed against the economic framework.

Struggling with the economic rationale

A major observation that we wish to offer in this chapter is those questions around what sort of growth is being promoted by devolution from economic agglomeration approaches to creating and growing city regions. Evidence from our research suggests that inequality and social disadvantage actually hinders growth (see Etherington and Jones 2016a, 2016b; Jonas and Ward 2007; Lee 2019) or, at best, creates the wrong kind of growth due to it not being distributed evenly (see Bowman et al, 2014). The converse is that those policies that actively promote labour market inclusion will contribute to sustainable growth and also assist with maintaining productivity. The current model of growth though restricts access to employment and skills initiatives and hence the city region will accordingly struggle to meet targets. This is because it does not engage with the existing problems faced by a significant proportion of the population, who are under-skilled to access jobs in high growth sectors. We discuss the SCR case in depth in Chapter 2. This is identified in the below quote, as it spatially impacts on the development of the GMCR:

> 'I think of Greater Manchester as having a ring donut economy, it's a lot like a North American city. So, you have thriving city centre, which it didn't have twenty-five years ago. The suburbs actually doing ok and then the middle bit. If they do not do something about that, the powers that be will never achieve their economic goals of achieving a fiscal balance for this conurbation.' (Interview, Social Enterprise Leader, 2016)

The extract above highlights how from the outset there is a perception that the growth model proposed for GMCR fails to address the broader problems faced by the city region. This is caused by the ongoing geo-history of inequality, but it also shows how this is compounded by pursuit of an agglomerative growth strategy. Similar views emerged in SCR:

'Trickledown doesn't work for the most vulnerable and disadvantaged and you have to have strategies around social regeneration (for want of a better word) alongside economic regeneration. Those two things should come together and I don't think they do because the LEP is very purely focused on the economic policy … Feels like I'm in a rowing boat and my colleagues are in a rowing boat and we're trying to turn round this big tanker.' (Interview, Sheffield Community Development Group, 2015)

For both respondents, one a social enterprise, primarily focused on projects in Salford, and the other a community development organisation in a deprived area of Sheffield, the urban growth machine strategy (Logan and Molotch, 1987; Jonas and Wilson, 1999) is deeply problematic. They pick out how the 'trickle-down' approach, which implies a strategy of developing high level gross value added (GVA) uplift by bringing people to jobs within the city region (Etherington and Jones, 2016b), does little for the disadvantaged citizens they are attempting to support. This means that because they question the rhetoric of this growth model, they are left on the periphery of its strategic delivery. This is also reflected in the above quote, which highlights how such groups, operating at a local level, have little ability or remit in the context of devolution to act at the city-region level and there is an ongoing lack of accountability that marginalises local civil society through institutions such as the LEPs. As underlined by an interviewee in SCR:

'What opportunity will there be to genuinely involve civil society in the process? Because I think the LEP has been and I know it is an economic driver, fine and it's about inward investment, economic growth and the private sector is at the heart of that but there is very little in terms of any wider involvement. And maybe that's ok but when it comes to the combined authority, there needs to be more direct lines of accountability into localities and into local areas.' (Interview, Sheffield Community Development Group, 2015)

This suggests that the construction of a new 'representational regime' for the city region based on economic interests purposefully excludes civil society actors from the outset. This, in turn, allows for an uncontested agglomerative growth model to be developed. The following section addresses this by assessing how civil society is being positioned and marginalised differently at different scales.

Dealing with scale and representation

The struggles to have a voice within such processes, due to the failure for civil society groups to be integrated into the representational regime of the city region, has left some squeezed between the 'scale jump' of the city region (Cox, 1998) and austerity occurring at the same time. 'Scale jumping', in this context, is the redefining of territorial relations from the LA to the city-regional scale in such a way that it circumvents, where possible, certain locality 'politics of turf' (Cox, 1989). Scale jumping is, therefore, a process through which new networks of association can be built to prioritise practices of capital accumulation (Smith, 1990; Brenner, 2004, 2019). According to one interviewee:

> 'At one point they talk about localism but if you look at regionalisation, it's huge, it's huge and actually the local voluntary community sector can't even hope to engage with, let alone deliver against that agenda. Therefore, civil society is finding itself squeezed behind/between a rhetoric that emphasises its importance but a reality, which mitigates against its ability to capture the resources to deliver against that agenda.' (Interview, Bolsover Voluntary Organisation, 2016)

This quote highlights the difficulties for civil society organisations to deal with austerity and devolution at the same time. It also shows the way in which civil society groups are co-opted and recast into a neoliberal growth model. In short, civil society groups are both needed for the continuing function of the city region, but at the same time they are marginalised within rescaling processes too. There is also appreciation of how LAs are struggling to deal with this rescaling process too within the context of austerity:

> 'To be honest, they are holding what they can, both in Tameside and Oldham, they are holding everything that they can. We are predominantly funded through the local authorities, Tameside get us a fair bit from their CCG [Clinical Commissioning Group] but actually, we don't, as an organisation the make-up is a much greater split for local authorities. So they are doing all they can to protect us. I think the voluntary organisations with smaller grants are dwindling, the smaller amounts of funding for the sector are dwindling, which is in itself a risk and that's

something that we fight hard against. But strategically they do view us as important in terms of achieving their public service reform and in fact it has been said by the cabinet portfolio holders around in Oldham and others, that we are their answer to that, that's how they see the change in the relationships between citizens and the wider population and the public services.' (Interview, Oldham Voluntary Organisation, 2016)

The end of this quote touches on the important shifts within the positionality of civil society, as it acknowledges how the local state is a deeply contradictory 'agent and obstacle' (Duncan and Goodwin, 1988). On the one hand, civil society is drawn into the local state as a necessity of funding. On the other, it is also somewhat powerless in the context of restructuring and cuts, as civil society groups are further distanced from having a strategic voice. Here, the paradox of austerity in the context of scale suggests that at local level, civil society actors are needed more than ever, stepping into the austerity void (DeVerteuil, 2016) and increasingly being relied on to deliver public services. The work of Dear and Wolch (1987) represents an important framing point here, as they followed a similar trajectory of neoliberalisation of inner-city welfare provision in the US during the 1980s, charting the rise of what was then termed 'the shadow state'. This referred to the variety of civil society groups that stepped in to provide provision, as the state rolled-back and increasingly absolved itself of its social responsibility. This led though to a disintegration in the third sector's ability to deliver such services in US cities, as they could not cope with the demands being placed on them. This partially stemmed from a lack of engagement by the state with civil society and a similar sense of non-engagement, particularly with third sector groups, and is being conveyed within the GMCR. Hence for many respondents, successful devolution will ultimately rely on the sector being engaged. However, at a city-region level they are being afforded a marginal voice. This is especially true within the GMCR, due to the fact that the devolution deal for this area also includes health and social care. But similar issues have been noted also in SCR:

'I think it's probably changed enormously actually. I think – well there's a number of pros and cons, I think with the current government policy and the austerity measures everything that's going on in terms of shrinking the states, promoting using third sector organisations and growing civil society has brought some opportunities for the third sector. There's definitely, for example, funding streams that the third sector can access that statutory organisations can't access so having said that, they are highly competitive.' (Interview, Sheffield Youth Development Organisation, 2015)

As illustrated above, within the context of austerity, opportunities have arisen for civil society groups, even despite the highly competitive nature of funding. However, the 'jumping of scale' to the city region and realignment of governance alongside austerity has also created destabilising experiences. The following section looks at how civil society organisations have responded to these, drawing on developments in Greater Manchester.

Responding and repositioning within city regions

In this section, the responses of civil society groups to ongoing and overlapping processes of devolution, city-regionalism and austerity will be assessed primarily focusing on GMCR, as this is only area where, to date, a devolution deal has developed to a sufficient extent on-the-ground.

Indeed, within GMCR the problematic background highlighted in the previous section has generated a coordinated response from civil society groups via the Greater Manchester Voluntary, Community and Social Enterprise (VCSE) Devolution Reference Group (VCSE, 2016). The participating VCSE groups are detailed in Table 1.1. The Reference Group was formed in response to devolution due to the failure of Greater Manchester Combined Authority (GMCA) to engage such organisations in any meaningful way in the ongoing debate on the future of the city region. VCSE represents an attempt by the various actors to find a voice and influence the direction of devolution (and potentially, in turn, the Northern Powerhouse) by means of their collective knowledge and access to different parts of GMCA. According to one interviewee:

'The reference group was set up when we realised that all this was going on around us and nobody was going to come banging down our door ... So from that a little coalition of the willing emerged, completely undemocratically but again I think that's part of it. Stop waiting for permission; stop feeling like you have to get every detail right. Because actually things are moving so fast, we have to trust each to

advocate for what our sector wants to achieve collectively.'
(Interview, Manchester Voluntary Organisation, 2016)

This quote sheds light on a very important point. Although the VCSE group includes 'self-selected' groups and therefore does not give full democratic representation for civil society at large, its creation reflects a considerable attempt to 'jump scale' by organisations that for the most part do not exist on a city-regional scale. This potentially leaves smaller and more localised providers further away from decisions that may greatly impact on their organisation's future viability, which in turn creates a series of questions for GMCA in terms of how policy can be filtered and interpreted down to the local level. The VCSE sector already has a variety of different organisations working at and delivering across different geographical scales, whether this is at the community, LA or city-region scales. They have been consistently able to find ways to engage those individuals and groups, which are often hardest to reach or most in need, though this ability is becoming continually strained in the current era of austerity. For a more centralised form of 'local' city-regional governance not to appreciate the local could lead to a number of valuable services, with its nuanced delivery to beneficiaries, being lost in the short term, and possibly longer.

In this way, it could be argued that the VCSE epitomises a joint effort on the part of local civil society actors to exert agency at the city-regional level, and influence the process of devolution in Greater Manchester. However, the same extract also highlights how, to date, GMCA has failed to address the needs of civil society groups within the context of devolution, and the desire of these actors to be included

Table 1.1: Participating Voluntary, Community and Social Enterprise groups

Volunteer Action Oldham	LGBT Foundation
Macc	Unlimited Potential
Start in Salford	Stroke Association
GMCVO	Breakthrough UK
42nd Street	Big Life Group
Bolton CVS	Greater Manchester BME Network

Note: BME: black and minority ethic; CVS: Community and Voluntary Services; GMCVO: Greater Manchester Centre for Voluntary Organisation; LGBT: lesbian, gay, bisexual, and transgender.
Source: Authors' analysis

in the process. This shows the shortcomings of the representational regime emerging in GMCR. One interviewee develops this further:

'The pace of change of devolution has been about the public sector thinking about the public sector and their internal mechanism ways of working override that belief that we're important partners. I think we as a group, I'm going to use your term, 'civil society' but voluntary sector and social enterprises. By having that collective group that is able to in some part have representative round tables, to have the ability to talk to some of the key individuals, as a collective to be able to do that, that is important.' (Interview, Oldham Voluntary Organisation, 2016)

The VCSE Devolution Reference Groups, then, represents one model, which, within the context of devolution, can bring a broad coalition of diverse groups together alongside pre-existing organisations. The group aims to be representative of (rather than represent), and connect to, the broad spectrum of VCSE activity in GMCR. This takes in how such groups are positioned in different ways with very different approaches. The VCSE Devolution Reference group in its current form is not perfect and the group recognises that it will always need to evolve. Its ability to develop partnerships across a multifaceted range of organisations highlights a model that can be moved forward with devolution to create parallel forms of representation and governance. Such groups are at the hard end of delivering and enabling citizens to thrive in the very difficult circumstances of austerity. They have clear social purposes with regards to helping or enabling those in the most difficult circumstances to achieve, in order to 'eradicate' inequality in the GMCR. They also have a strong innovative spirit for delivery in a time of limited resources. This innovation could be harnessed more directly by including such organisations earlier in commissioning processes rather than just as respondents to funding opportunities. In doing this, there could be more attuned responses to inequality while giving the processes of commissioning more transparency. In the context of devolution, such activities should be folded into the processes of delivering devolution, rather than being a reaction to what is unfolding around VCSE members. This though raises questions of scale and representation and to the wider positioning of civil society as either an agent or obstacle to the development of city-region policy. As 'agent', they risk being complicit in policy that promotes agglomerative economic growth. Whereas an 'obstacle' positioning could see them marginalised further from the representational regime of the city region which could be precarious for organisations that can often rely on various forms of local state funding.

Moreover, while the voice of business leaders plays a prominent role in the devolution debate in GMCR, as the LEP works in conjunction with the GMCA, civil society groups have had to find alternative ways to reposition themselves within the CA. The VCSE is an attempt at generating 'critical mass' able to influence the process of devolution – but its impact is still marginal compared with that of the LEP. In this sense, the case of GMCR shows how the UK Government, with its emphasis on economic development in the context of 'devo deals', has sought to shape devolution from the top-down creating a distorted narrative of 'inclusive growth' which affects in turn the Northern Powerhouse agenda. By its very structure, it has defined who is and who is not involved in the debate that will shape the future of devolution deals to CAs and city regions – empowering certain groups (in particular business leaders), while marginalising and disempowering others (such as civil society groups). Although each city region will implement devolution deals differently, the 'rules of the game' have been shaped in one direction in terms of creating a new 'citizenship regime' under devolution. This raises serious questions around representation and recognition in the pursuit of economic growth and this is something that all respondents from civil society backgrounds have emphasised. By recognising this 'representational gap', civil society organisations have attempted to find new ways to place their agendas on inequality and the social production of the city region back into the processes of 'city-region building' and devolution. However, as these attempts at repositioning civil society are still unfolding, their potential impact and success will only become clear if and when devolution to city region CAs will be delivered in full, in the coming years.

Social innovation and economic growth

Devolution offers real opportunities to do things differently to the supposed model of growth offered by central government, but this opportunity has to be negotiated. The devolution of health and social care in Greater Manchester (unlike in other city regions) is one such opportunity, but this again needs radical rethinking if it is to fulfil its potential (see Etherington and Jones, 2017; Chapter 3). The sector has been one of the most dynamic in terms of thinking through how to deliver services to people and communities that are hardest to reach.

The opinion below, again from GMCR, highlights how the voluntary sector is already involved in taking a multifaceted thinking approach:

> 'We need to look at where are the skills and knowledge and solutions to fix any particular problem. Some of it may lie with the people who apparently have the problem, so if you want to solve homelessness, you've got to involve people who have experienced homelessness or who are currently homeless because it would be stupid not to take their ... so they would have knowledge that no-one else has. You've got to involve a whole range of other agencies who have touched with that problem in one way or another. And those who have got the overview. Collectively you might then start to come up with an answer to that.' (Interview, Voluntary Services Leader, 2016)

This desire to socially innovate by connecting up different agents to tackle problems, such as homelessness, exemplifies how new approaches can be found and are very much in tune with public sector partner thinking. VCSE groups can play a key strategic role due to their on-the-ground knowledge and their flexibility in delivering services. Indeed, understanding that the current inequality present in the GMCR is more than just an economic concern and that it is linked to a variety of other multifaceted problems is key to thinking about how groups within VCSE can have a very strong impact in terms of addressing these problems. The VCSE community represents one way in which complex activity and thinking (from small to large, from person to community and from place to identity) can allow for a stronger response to social inequality and to build a more inclusive economy.

Conclusions

This chapter has addressed the changes being created by the unfolding process of devolving power to two of the Northern Powerhouse's key city regions – GMCR and SCR. Within this, it has attempted to understand how civil society is being (re)positioned. It has emphasised that if and how the Northern Powerhouse is to be successful and be more than just a 'spatial imaginary' (Jessop and Sum, 2013) in which a 'rag bag' set of policies fall (Lee, 2017), there is a need to deal more seriously with issues surrounding inequality and uneven development within (and across) its city regions.

The Northern Powerhouse is presented as a project that will bring prosperity to the North of England. However, evidence suggests that its model of agglomerative economic growth, fostered on trickle-down economics, will only continue to exacerbate uneven development and undermine the project of spatial rebalancing, especially if this keeps perpetuating uneven dynamics of empowerment. By analysing the findings of interviews with civil society actors in GMCR and SCR, this chapter has highlighted how, in the context of city-region building, the current approach to city-regional economic development and governance is falling short of its promises. We have suggested that this is due, in part, to a clear divide between those who are enabled to have a voice and 'lead' with the devolution city-region agenda, and those who have been marginalised in this process. Further to this, findings in GMCR and SCR suggest that the new citizenship regimes implemented within city regions place civil society outside the decision-making processes that underpin devolution deals, while simultaneously – and somewhat paradoxically – expecting civil society to deal with the fallout from continuing uneven development, sociospatial inequalities and austerity. Importantly, in areas such as GMCR, where devolution deals are unfolding at a fast pace, civil society groups are trying to reverse these processes of representational marginalisation, as emphasised by the creation of VCSE. However, it remains to be seen whether these attempts at repositioning civil society will be successful.

The chapter has argued that the VCSE Devolution Reference Group is very much a response to the conditions of devolution in Greater Manchester but in that response, there is a model alluded to that, with further development, could address many of the gaps that have developed in the economic led thinking of city regions. If business interests and state restructuring are left to deliver devolution alone, without more holistically integrating the VCSE community, for instance, growth is likely to continue to be exclusive and devolution will not filter down to places, communities and people who have been left outside economic development. Therefore, in the context of inclusive growth, there needs to be stronger acknowledgement of the expertise this sector can bring and it should be a voice, alongside business and the public sector in terms of future devolution processes.

The Northern Powerhouse faces an uncertain future since the vote to leave the EU, and also due to the switch towards an Industrial Strategy for the UK and the largely repacking of existing committed expenditure with little new to create regional distinctiveness (compare Berry, 2016; HM Treasury, 2016). The pendulum of UK economic development may have turned away from the spatial imaginaries of the Northern Powerhouse and the city region to focus on the national level again, but the spatial dimensions and sub-national dynamics of this remain unclear. Moreover, as we have argued here, there remains a need to rebalance relationships between the economy, state and civil society, so that a more representational form of devolution can be delivered. We would suggest that this requires a much stronger attempt to integrate 'the social' alongside the economic within devolution if a more inclusive growth strategy is to be achieved.

2

Metro governance dynamics

Chimera: a thing which is hoped for but is illusory or impossible to achieve. Synonyms: illusion, fantasy, delusion, dream, fancy. (Oxford English Dictionary)

Introduction

Welcome to 'Devo Sheffield' – a city region that comprises the South Yorkshire council areas of Barnsley, Rotherham, Doncaster and Sheffield, alongside the East Midlands authorities of Bassetlaw, Bolsover, Chesterfield, Derbyshire Dales and North East Derbyshire. As discussed in the Introduction, with the ongoing processes of constitutional change and devolution in the UK, city regions in England are being brought to the centre stage of policy and politics to address, firstly, paraphrasing Lindblom (1968), the 'problem' of economic growth and a rebalancing of this geographically to iron-out issues of spatial combined and uneven development (see Martin, 2015), and secondly, the 'problem' of securing effective and accountable governance arrangements, whereby effective economic growth and development is contingent on open and transparent engagements with civil society. This model is being heavily influenced by the US 'Metropolitics' agglomeration thinking of Katz and others, transferred at speed into the UK through discourses such as the 'Northern Powerhouse', 'Metro-Mayors', and promises of additional functions to civil society actors to create the conditions for 'real control' (Wharton, 2016: 9).

'Devo Sheffield' was accordingly coined on 12 December 2014 (HM Government, 2014) and builds on a City Deal and Growth Deal to roadmap a 'journey that sees the people of Sheffield put in charge of their own economic destiny' (Otten, 2014: 1). Launched by Nick Clegg MP, as Deputy Prime Minister, and following 'Devo Manc' developments in Greater Manchester, subject to a directly-elected Mayor being in place, 'Devo Sheffield' promises to shift power from Whitehall to the SCR, anchored through a £900 million 'big pot of money' agreement (£30m of funding for 30 years, 'immune from any spending review'), and giving greater control over skills, transport, housing and business support. By combining skills with employment opportunities 'for all', the SCR is becoming responsible for the 'building a new skills system'. In short, 'Devo Sheffield' is a 'historic moment for the great city', giving responsibilities to local leaders to push forward plans that will seek to strengthen the economy and 'without waiting for Whitehall to do something to the regions of England', again (Beardmore, 2015: 8). As we argued in the Introduction, the promise of a new city-regional era has been made, providing the infrastructure for a 'second industrial revolution' to transform Sheffield's blighted post-industrial city region from 'slagheap to innovation district' (Burnett, 2016: 22).

These timely policy developments in England are not anecdotal or insignificant; they have deep ramifications for academic debates in economic and political geography and for how we think about contemporary urban and regional political economy. Firstly, building on the arguments in the Introduction, they hit head-on the new neoclassical urban economics city-region building agendas and critiques of authors such Storper, Overman, Glaeser and others. *Keys to the City*, the leading account on how economics, institutions, social action, and politics shape development, for instance, makes the bold claim that '[c]ity-regions are the principal scale at which people experience lived reality' hence understanding city-region development is 'more important than ever' and 'managing it will pose one of the most critical challenges to humanity' (Storper, 2013: 4). Focusing on the micro-foundations of individuals, households, firms and groups interacting to make city regions in successful North American cities, Storper's concern is with the notions of 'winning' and 'super-star' regions and cities (Hadjimichalis and Hudson, 2014: 213); the 'big game to be hunted' (Storper, 2013: 4) appears to be charting growth and change to find success. We hear much less in these literatures about 'ordinary' and left-behind regions that have experienced extensive de-industrialisation and continual challenges faced by civil society.

Secondly, building on the Introduction, 'Devo Sheffield' talks loudly to the decade of debates on the spatial restructuring of the state (Brenner, 2004, 2019) and changes to the landscape of economic governance more broadly (Keating et al, 2013). This restructuring has often involved a tendency towards devolving employment and labour market policies and functions to city regions. There is a now considerable body of literature that highlights the inherent tensions, conflicts and contradictions embodied in these governance changes – for example, the tensions and conflicts between central and local objectives, competition and cooperation, and entrepreneurial versus social inclusion objectives and also issues of power and representation (compare Danson et al, 2012; Goodwin et al, 2012; Pike et al, 2015). This chapter argues that, and demonstrates how, all this is being intensified, and not resolved, through the processes and practices of devolution.

This chapter accordingly also flags the need to seriously consider issues of regulatory capacity, regulatory failure and 'regulatory deficits' (see Painter and Goodwin, 2000). The next section bridges these concerns and analyses the nature and limits to devolved city-region building and particularly the involvement of civil society actors within devolved labour market governances, given these feature strongly in the 'Devo Sheffield' devolution settlement. We suggest that with limited regulatory powers and little direct control over additional financial capacity, 'Devo Sheffield' is deeply bound-up with the contradictions facing UK capitalism and the various government priorities in responding to them through devolution and city regions. This is a 'chimera' – an apt phrase that is only occasionally used in geographical analysis (see Zuege, 1999; Bailey and Turok, 2001) to describe state projects that are imaginative, even dazzling at times, though deeply implausible when unpacked in reality.

To push our conceptual and theoretical understandings further, we suggest that notions of governance and metagovernance failure are important in terms of understanding both the limitations to and contradictions of devolution and city-region building, and the role of civil society actors therein. Metagovernance – the 'government of governance' through 'overseeing, steering, and coordinating governance arrangements' (Bell and Hindmoor, 2009: 11) – has received minimal detailed attention in urban and regional studies (except by Fawcett et al, 2017; Whitehead, 2003), it is timely to engage with these agendas, show how civil society actors are involved, and we would go as far as to suggest that devolution through city regions in England is producing spatially-articulated metagovernance failures. Governance failure arises because of the primacy of a neoliberal dominated strategy, orientated towards the market and its failure in the delivery of skills. Governance and metagovernance mechanisms are unable to sufficiently coordinate effective responses to address a deep legacy of de-industrialisation, deep-rooted labour market and social inequalities. Depoliticised metagovernance coordination conflicts signal an ongoing democratic deficit in terms of accountabilities and transparency, which in itself leads to legitimation problems between the partnerships and in relation to wider civil society.

'Slagheap to innovation district'? Economic governance and skills in Sheffield

Sheffield is the fourth largest city in England and located in the South Yorkshire coalfield. Its economic base comprises steel making and engineering, and its politics also was formed from a strong labour and trade union movement tradition with the LA controlled for many years by the Labour Party and with an active Communist Party, which influenced workplace and city politics. Sheffield was the centre point of the 1984–85 miners' strike and prior to that the steel workers strike, which attempted to resist large scale restructuring and closures impacting on civil society. In the early 1980s, the city became a focal point of resistance to the Thatcher Government with the LA and civil society institutions taking a proactive role in developing local economic initiatives, particularly in terms of employment and training. It promoted a progressive redistributive strategy against the dominant neoliberal politics of Thatcherism (Goodwin et el, 1993).

From the mid-1980s though, both the economy and political governance landscape was to change markedly. Between 1979 and 1982, 45,000 jobs were shed in the core engineering and steel industries. Its employment and occupational structure have been transformed over the past 20 years, from a high-paid employment economy with a plentiful supply of skilled jobs, to an economy where many of the new jobs created in the service sector tend to be contingent and low-paid. Also, of importance is the existence of significant proportions of the working age population categorised as economically inactive and in receipt of sickness benefits and where labour market exclusion and poverty occurs at a significant scale. Skills polarisation and segmentation thus became integral features of the labour market. Sheffield faces some distinctive skills challenges on both the supply and demand side of the labour market equation. On the demand-side, the proportion of employers lacking any sort of strategic approach to the skills of their workforce is higher than the national average in Sheffield. On the supply-side, a smaller proportion of the northern workforce has a degree and a larger proportion has no qualifications. In some areas this results in a vicious circle of low skills and low productivity: or what has been terms the 'low-skills equilibrium' (Finegold and Soskice, 1988; Henderson et al, 2013).

During the 1980s, the Thatcher government's neoliberalism had two major impacts – first that the politics of redistribution was replaced by the politics of the market where private interests were accorded prominence in terms of access to and as beneficiaries of urban policy.

The second impact, and related, was the shift in representational structures that increasingly marginalised the role of local government and the electoral democratic process challenging traditional models of accountability in public services. A raft of private sector-led initiatives was developed including Training and Enterprise Councils, as devolved bodies to cities and sub-regions charged with making the skills and training market. Despite there being serious, historical evidence-based, limits to creating an employer-led training market, New Labour continued with supply-side and market-driven skills policies. The devolution of employment and skills was a key element of New Labour's skills strategy through 'centrally controlled' Local Skills Councils, along with RDAs and Sector Skills Councils charged with coordinating skills strategies across the regions. The City Strategy Pathfinder (CSP) pilot was accordingly established in 2006 with the primary aims of devolving welfare-to-work programmes for tackling worklessness and integrating employment and skills strategies. The CSP was seen as a vehicle to promote an element of devolved responsibility to local partnerships in delivering Pathways and was thus seen as a bottom-up process – partnerships and consortia were formed by local employment services along with LAs, the private, voluntary and community sectors where there was some discretion given to develop their own priorities and innovate with project development (Etherington and Jones, 2009).

The UK Government's skills policy, 2010–2015, was focused on further deregulation and on freeing colleges and training organisations from central and other external control in order to create a purchaser provider market for skills at the city level (see BIS, 2010b). Furthermore, the coordination of skills has been put in the hands of employer-led LEP, established at the city-region spatial scale with a remit to regenerate local economies through investment in business and infrastructure. The Sheffield LEP was established in 2011 bringing together local partnerships within the city-region partners envisaged some link up with both the employment (i.e. the Government's flagship welfare-to-work programme for long-term unemployed the Work Programme (WP)) and skills agenda (i.e. apprenticeships and work based vocational training) (McNeil, 2010). Within this new governance and policy regime, the Sheffield City Council initiated its employment and skills strategy in 2012, which is coordinated by the Sheffield First Partnership established under the previous New Labour administration.

The Government subsequently established 'City Deals' as a means of first seeking to resolve the coordination problems and political conflicts that accompany the new (and old) governance arrangements (see UKCES and Centre for Cities, 2015). Through skills and employment policies, City Deals are second seen as integral features of devolving funding to create the conditions for 'open innovation' – a perspective on innovation districts where economy shaping, place making and social networking come together, 'mingle' and are claimed to move places like Sheffield 'up the value chain of global competitiveness by growing firms, networks and traded sectors that drive broad-based prosperity' (Katz and Wagner 2014: 1). Sheffield LEP, in conjunction with the SCR's Skills and Employment Partnership, obtained the ability to control part of the skills budget so that it can respond more effectively to local business needs. The brokerage model, deemed necessary to 'stimulate businesses to invest in skills', outlined in the document 'Made in Sheffield – a deal for growth' (SCR Local Enterprise Partnership, 2013, 2014), sought to match local contributions (public and private) with national funding (on which, see Payne and Keep, 2011).

In turn, this has led to the 'Sheffield City Region Agreement on Devolution' (HM Government, 2014) and the later 'Sheffield City Region Combined Authority Devolution Deal' (HM Government, 2015b), which considered different options for improving local governance and accountability. The CA was to 'exercise management functions' in support of the LEP in implementing SCR's skills and employment strategies, 'represent' the democratic mandate of local leaders and 'provide accountability in terms of performance, finance and statutory obligations'. Moreover, SCR was to work with Government to deliver 'integrated skills and training systems across the local area, driven by the needs of the economy and led by the private sector, giving local businesses the skilled labour they need to grow'. A £17 million Skills Bank, governed not by local partners but by PricewaterhouseCoopers, operated alongside this to improve the skills base of the workforce, changing the way skills system operates, by placing the purchasing power of skills in the hands of employers.

The SCR would in turn receive devolved responsibilities in relation to adult skills funding and provision, with the LEP and CA forming a joint venture partnership with the Skills Funding Agency, responsible for ensuring a forward-looking system was in place by 2017. This arrangement covered: the Adult Skills Budget (other than participation funding for apprenticeships and traineeships); the Apprenticeship Grant for Employers; and through an enhanced version of its existing Skills Bank, SCR played a central role in enabling businesses, especially small and medium-sized enterprises (SMEs), to take up and invest in apprenticeships. Working within Government's reform agenda for apprenticeships, in which funding was to be routed directly to employers, the Deal looked set to empower businesses to liaise with the SCR Skills Bank or directly with Government.

Last, joint working between the Department for Work and Pensions (DWP) was seen as the way forward, with the possibility of joint commissioning for the next phase of the WP, which involves a 'provider led' approach in which welfare-to-work services for longer term unemployed will be delivered by the private sector – usually large scale organisations ('prime' contractors) where other support services are sub-contracted usually to the voluntary sector. A 'black box' approach to the tendering has been adopted, essentially leaving the 'prime' contractors to put together a package of employment support, which meets the specific needs of the local area. Contracting processes – steered from the centre by the DWP and a pricing structure with a payment-by-results performance framework – are central to the governance of this. As part of this model of delivery, the long-term unemployed can be sign-posted to training as part of their personalised support. The programme for the South Yorkshire contract area (covering the north of the SCR – see Figure 2.1) is delivered by two multinational companies –People Plus (formerly A4e) and Serco. Under the Devolution Agreements, the SCR was to be involved in 'local commissioning'. Whereby funding is combined through a single block allocation and implemented according to 'local informed choices'.

The central elements of the two strategies are quite similar – promoting employability skills for people of school leaving age, raising attainment levels and developing apprenticeships. For the LEP, a key element of its focus is on business growth and that strategies are linked to 'flagship' projects such as building on the 'knowledge sectors' and promoting the 'knowledge economy' (Sheffield City Region Local Enterprise Partnership, 2014). The changing governance landscape described above involved changes in party control of Sheffield City Council where the Liberal Democrats were replaced in 2010 by a majority Labour party. In essence, the 2000s were characterised by changing control of the LA between the two parties. The current administration has had to manage a rapidly changing governance landscape and negotiate new relationships such as the LEP and WP providers. Alongside this, the Sheffield Labour Party produced the Fairness Commission in 2012 in order to develop a more socially inclusive approach to employment, welfare and the environment (see Sheffield Fairness Commission, 2012). At least in terms of political and policy city-regional rhetoric, the SCR Devolution Agreements provide the basis for taking this forward. For policymakers promoting

Figure 2.1: Sheffield City Region political geography

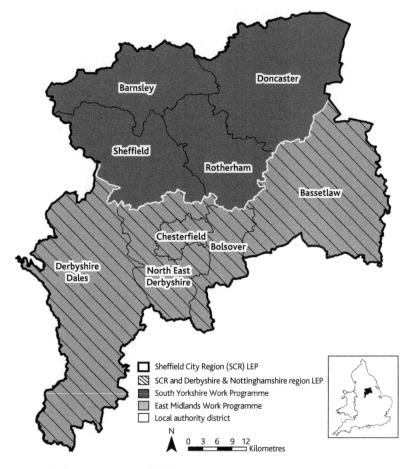

Source: Produced by Sam Jones, WISERD

Sheffield's Manufacturing Innovation District, which stands on the 'Orgreave site where Arthur Scargill led his members from the National Union of Mineworkers as police clashed with them' (Burnett 2016: 22), this is the 'dawn of a new era', providing the basis for a 21st Century export book beyond the volatile EU market with a high skilled, modern manufacturing economy, combining digital innovation; world class experience, academic research, and a strong global brand' (HM Government 2014, 2015b). We now turn to consider some of the emerging on-the-ground tensions of these shifts in the governance and regulatory environments of the labour market and the economy more broadly, particularly how these are being played out in and through civil society.

Restructuring of representational structures, new accountabilities and ongoing democratic deficits

The Government's 'localism' agenda has involved a shift in responsibilities for labour market and skills policy to city-region actors through the creation of the LEPs with a central role for the private sector in shaping strategic economic development policy (Pike et al, 2015). The emphasis on employer engagement and taking control of the skills agenda and market is a central plank of the LEP skills strategy (the SCR LEP Board is made up of ten 'business leaders' from the private sector and nine LA leaders). The shift towards the market in terms of purchaser provider relationship has created tensions within the LEP in terms of provider involvement in policy formation. The college networks have voiced concerns over their role on the LEP where their access to actually influencing or shaping skills policy rather than being seen as a 'provider' of skills (Davies, 2011). The LEPs role evolved over time, but its actual link with the existing raft of city partnerships remained unclear.

This is also exemplified in the way welfare-to-work programmes (i.e. the WP) are delivered in the city region. The WP has been devolved to regional/sub-regional contract areas (see Figure 2.1). The two providers, Serco and People Plus (formerly A4E), which cover the Sheffield area, involve a proliferation of sub-contractors mainly from the voluntary and private sectors. The influence of the LA on the way welfare-to-work policy is being implemented is minimal and its engagement highly constrained (strategically and spatially), limited to providing 'wrap around' services (social, health and basic skills training) for more disadvantaged groups who are unable to access employment.

The LA raised critical questions at the early stage of the implementation of the WP concerning the relationships between local partnerships and other services that support people into employment (Sheffield City Council, 2011). The privatisation model of delivery has been identified by some voluntary sector stakeholders as limiting the possibility of disadvantaged groups and communities in civil society in engaging and influencing policy. According to one source: "The competitive nature of the whole employment programme reduces it to a cattle market, where contracts are given based on criteria where unemployed and disadvantaged groups have no say" (Voluntary Sector Submission, Sheffield Fairness Commission, 2012). This view, concerning a lack of voice, seems to be common within the Sheffield community and voluntary sector. According to another source: "In recent times, involvement in voice, influence and participation in services has been reduced significantly. This is counter intuitive in the context of the localism agenda" (Interview, Sheffield Third Sector Assembly, 2014). The scepticism about the contracting model seemed to be prevalent among stakeholders. For example, health service professionals considered their views regarding the needs of people with long-term health conditions were not incorporated into the welfare-to-work programmes. The WP offers opportunities for the larger voluntary sector organisations to deliver welfare-to-work interventions, but there are no guarantees that the more experienced voluntary sector organisations in the welfare-to-work market, which have acquired the expertise in terms of delivery, will sustain themselves in light of their radically reduced grant allocations.

As the civil society community and voluntary sectors are incorporated into the welfare market so their influence on policy has been reduced. This occurred also under the previous CSP in Sheffield implemented under New Labour, which promoted local commissioning and contracting in welfare services. According to an interview with one stakeholder:

> 'the history of the role of the Sheffield partnerships seems to have given business interests a greater priority than an inclusive agenda. The aspirations of disadvantaged groups and communities has been neglected and there seems to be no indication that the new regime will be any different (the Labour Party took back control of the local authority from the Liberal Democrats in 2010)'. (Interview, Trade Union Official, 2014)

The increasing emphasis on private providers via the WPs seems to have led to greater disillusionment from the voluntary sector in terms of the ability to shape policies and decisions that affect disadvantaged groups. There is evidence that these tensions are prevalent within local government and NHS organisations. The impact of austerity and cuts in funding to social programmes seems to have further destabilised local partnerships.

Austerity, uneven development and the employment crisis

A crucial element of the politics of uneven development is the way funding cuts and austerity measures are impacting on employment and skills provision. The City Council has been facing a significant financial crisis – the revenue budget shortfall was estimated to be between £53 and £57 million in 2012/13 and £154 million and £170 million in 2015/16. Budget cuts initially took place within the local educational providers such as Sheffield College – a major public sector training provider that involved job losses and redundancies. In relation to skills, as Keep observes, the reductions in the government's Employment and Training spending announced in 2013 represent the point at which the entire edifice of traditional skills policy started to look unstable and probably unsustainable, particularly for provision beyond the compulsory phase of initial schooling. Between 2010/11 and 2014/15, cuts totalling 24.3 per cent have been made in the overall Department for Business, Innovation and Skills (DBIS) budget. Within this overall settlement, the DBIS and Further Education budget was reduced by approximately 25 per cent. On current projections, the overall reduction in the DBIS budget between 2010 and 2018 is estimated to be 42.5 per cent (Keep, 2014: 5).

Although there is no exact estimate of the skills funding gap in the SCR, skills surveys provide some insights into employer demand for skill funding. Businesses have reported, for instance, that they would be able to commit more financial resources to training if trading conditions were more stable or there was more certainty over the economy, and they would be more likely to use external training providers if there was greater public subsidy (42 per cent) or lower course fees (34 per cent), or if training was more tailored to their business needs (38 per cent). Providers in SCR were less likely to report being unable to meet demand, and over two-thirds of the providers in the SCR would have liked to be able to offer new or different provision, but feel they are unable to do so, mainly because of uncertainties over funding and/or the need for capital investment (Ekosgen, 2012). The 2014 SCR LEP Strategic Economic Plan sets out an ambitious funding and project plan in order to close the skills and employment gap within the city region which also entails considerable devolution of control of the way funding is managed and spent (Sheffield LEP, 2014). There is inevitably a question over whether the funding that will contribute to the creation of new jobs will be forthcoming from the Government in the context of current austerity plans.

The continued 'underperformance' of the city-region economy is a cause for concern among local politicians and stakeholders. An important example is the persistent jobs gap and shortfall, which characterises the labour market. The jobs gap is calculated by comparing the employment rates, i.e. the share of adults of working age who have jobs between different areas. The worst districts had an average employment rate of 68 per cent compared with best group of districts comprising 79 per cent. The number of jobs required in the worst districts to reach the national average and the 'best' districts is then calculated, and this involves a significant need for new jobs that need to be created (Sheffield First Partnership, 2010: 25; Beatty and Fothergill, 2014). Furthermore a 'prosperity gap' of over £1.1 billion due to a combination of economic inactivity, unemployment and low productivity sectors characterises the local economy. It is estimated that an additional 70,000 jobs will need to be created within the SCR to 'narrow the gap' with other parts of the country. However, it is important to view this challenge in the context that other comparator areas will also grow. Based on the forecast growth in other parts of the country, the SCR would need to create around 120,000 jobs to have closed the gap with the national average in 2024. This would require GDP growth of almost 5 per cent and 'nowhere in the UK grows at this rate for such a sustained period of time' (Sheffield LEP, 2014: 22).

Sheffield experiences skills polarisation and has a larger proportion of higher skilled people and University graduates than the national average. With weak labour market conditions, and limited job opportunities, graduates are often taking low-paid, lower-skilled jobs and there are significant numbers of people who possess no or low level qualifications (see Henderson et al, 2013). The number of pupils gaining 5+ GCSEs at grade A*-C including English and maths is low (49 per cent) compared to a national average (58 per cent). As such, Sheffield has moved from being the 3rd best Core City on this indicator in 2006/7 to the 7th best (of 8) in 2010/11. At a time when the skills levels required for many occupations continues to rise, this could preclude many young people from well-paid work (Sheffield City Council, 2013: 73). This contributes to a more competitive labour market and displaces other people further down the skills ladder (creating further unemployment), but it also under utilises the skills of graduates. Currently, SMEs are not considered as the 'normal' route for graduate jobs (despite the fact they represent 95 per cent of the business base in Sheffield) and graduates do not know how to access SME jobs. Furthermore, SMEs can be reluctant to take on graduates, often because they feel they cannot offer the time or structured training programmes graduates need to make the transition from university into the workplace (see Sheffield First Partnership, 2012, 2013, 2014, 2016a).

The economic downturn, the lack of good quality jobs and 'sustainable' jobs is a key issue for civil society in the SCR. In Sheffield, Job Seeker Allowance claimants have increased from around 8,000 pre-2009 recession, to over 17,000 (2013), with young people aged 16–24 being particularly affected and in total there are 48,000 people claiming out of work benefits (Sheffield City Council, 2013: 75). The ratio of job vacancies to unemployed people has declined dramatically which, when combined with a dramatic increase in long-term unemployment, is an important indicator of how the economic downturn is impacting on Sheffield. With a mean average weekly wage of around £410, low-paid jobs compound these labour market dynamics (see Sheffield First Partnership, 2014: 17; Sheffield City Council, 2011). Discussions have accordingly been taking place in recent years on the 'fragility' of the economy, with an increasingly unstable labour market and increasing poverty being witnessed (Sheffield First Partnership, 2013, 2016a, 2016b).

Vulnerable civil society groups in the labour market are experiencing the damaging effects of the emerging employment and skills crisis. For example, differences in occupations undertaken by women showed an underrepresentation of female managers in 2012 compared to the average in England, and the concentration of women employed in services – a sector notorious for its unstable employment and training opportunities. For example, 32 per cent of women were employed in caring and customer service occupations compared with 7 per cent of men (Sheffield First Partnership, 2013, 2016a). Disabled people claiming incapacity benefit make up the largest cohort of people outside the labour market and experience severe barriers in terms of accessing employment and skills (Sheffield First Partnership, 2012: 20).

Lone parents have also been targeted for welfare-to-work interventions through stricter benefit conditionality. This harsher work first regime is not seen to be effective in progressing lone parents into sustainable employment. As one Lone Parent Advisor commented:

> 'The new rules for lone parents make assumptions that people with children of school age are "ready" for the labour market and are able to engage with work related activity. The assumption is that the person has sorted problems such as debt and relationship breakdown and often this is not the case. Furthermore, one of the biggest barriers is accessing skills and this is currently a challenge due to the current funding arrangements.' (Interview, 2014)

The WP performance for 'signposting' disadvantaged groups into employment has generally been poor: employment outcomes compared with targets shows underperformance by Providers in South Yorkshire

(CESI, 2014). In theory, the WP should also be giving priority to sustaining employment (in employment for at least 26 weeks), which would mean that providers will give some priority to clients accessing skills. There is a lack of data held at the SCR level to assess this, although national evaluations show that the WP is not providing sufficient opportunities for unemployed people to access training (Devin et al, 2011: iii). The National Institute of Adult Continuing Education (NIACE, 2012) in its own survey of providers found that 11 of 18 prime providers are committed to providing some element of skills training although this seems to be at a very basic level (for example, online employability testing and basic IT skills). This suggests that: "those who are disadvantaged will be provided limited opportunities to break from the low pay 'no pay-low pay' cycle. This is why we see the skills strategy as important as welfare-to-work as a route into viable employment" (Interview with Sheffield City Council Officer, 2014). Because of the fear that contractors will override employment strategies produced by local partnerships, as occurred in certain instances under the previous CSP, the implementation of the WP is creating further challenges for the strategic partnerships. As one stakeholder commented "there is little incentive for the contractors to engage with the partnerships". Another interviewee observed: "contractors are advised to link with local partnerships and it is not mandatory. Nor is there likely to be any sanctions if they don't" (Interview, 2014). The lack of public transparency in terms of the delivery model of Serco and People Plus was seen as a problem. People Plus would not publicly consult on their delivery plan because of confidential reasons (Interview, 2014).

A central element in enhancing skills of unemployed people and workers in Britain over the past 25 years has been promoting the role of employer-sponsored training. Overall the track record for the UK is low compared with international comparator countries and Sheffield reinforces this pattern (see Lindsay et al, 2013). In 2010, for instance, less than half of all employers surveyed in the SCR (49 per cent) had a skills budget and had trained at least one member of staff. Furthermore, only 25 per cent of employers surveyed had invested, or were likely to invest in, apprenticeships. This pattern shows no signs of altering in the current (devolving) context: evaluation data highlights a 'reticence of employers to use cash to fund activity [which] suggests work is still required to sell the benefits of training' (BIS, 2015: 12). The result is persistent weak innovation, poor receptiveness to new technologies and, as a consequence, low productivity and weak competitive advantage (Sheffield First Partnership, 2013, 2016a, 2016b).

The political economy of governance and metagovernance

Despite the rhetoric of 'localism' and 'milestones' being claimed on a 'devolution journey' (HM Government, 2015b: 2), the different actors and coalitions of interests in the SCR are involved in a constant struggle to access, distribute and state a claim in resources and influence. Sheffield's Fairness Commission represents a turn towards a more socially inclusive agenda, although this is in the context of outsourcing, deep cuts to the local state and implementation of austerity policies by the Council. There is no indication that the Labour controlled Council is taking an oppositional position against austerity policies: the cuts are being implemented, managed and internalised within the Labour Party and the various partnerships. There is growing civil society unrest within the city and protests appear to be intensifying. This is the context to which local policies are now being implemented – increasing tensions and disaffectedness are now apparent within the Town Hall and the partnerships (see Sheffield First Partnership, 2016b).

Given that under 'Devo Sheffield' policymakers within the city and city region have given priority to upskilling and wider access to training, the gap between intentions and outcomes can never be greater, as the economy becomes more unstable and the continuing deregulated labour market gives rise to more pronounced social and spatial segmentation. The continued almost 'path dependent' nature of policy discourses around engaging employers and greater coordination of different stakeholders, policy regimes, budgets and partnerships represents a re-working of the governance arrangements to provide a 'best fit' model to address the employment and skills crisis. So far, despite the Fairness Commission's good intentions to recognise at least the social divisions that are endemic features of contemporary restructuring, policy actors, politicians and business leaders are locked into the market model of delivery, modes of representation, and subsequent failures in economic regulation. Sheffield clearly has a 'deficit in local regulatory capacity' and some state forms and functions are clearly 'counter-regulatory' (Painter and Goodwin, 2000). How can we interpret what is happening here and put civil society representation and positionality in its (city-region) place?

Governance failure – the 'failure to redefine objectives in the face of continuing disagreement about whether they are still valid for the various partners' (Jessop, 2000: 18) – is occurring. There are a number of dimensions to governance failure, which are embedded in local economic and social development. First, and as we have demonstrated, is the apparent tension between devolving responsibilities in relation to policy formation and implementation, and the tendency towards centralisation in decision making whereby local actors are charged with implementing nationally determined targets and programmes. The challenge here is the adaptation of national programmes to local conditions. Second is the increasing tendency towards institutional and policy fragmentation at the sub-regional level, with issues of accountability being raised. Governance becomes a new site for conflicts and political mobilisation as the nature and complexity of partnerships means that more and more 'actors' and 'stakeholders' are involved in design and delivery of labour market programmes. Outcomes at one scale may be dependent on performance at another scale of governance so therefore coordination dilemmas can occur. Furthermore, these coordination mechanisms may have different 'temporal horizons' and there may be continuous tensions between short-term and long-term planning goals in policy planning. Third, and related, is the failure of current policies to address deep-rooted problems of labour market inequalities that are integral to market failure. This is exemplified in Sheffield by the employment gap and lack of sufficient sustainable employment growth to 'revitalise' the city-region economy. Finally, governance in the form of economic partnerships, dominated by private-sector interests, is continuing to replace elected and representative government in terms of local economic development, which in itself poses a number of problems between government and its elected representation model of democracy and partnerships. These partnerships tend to be elite forming with blurred lines of accountability, often far removed from those who are disadvantaged and disenfranchised. Depoliticisation is occurring, as opaque representational structure and lines of accountability close down and restrict possibilities of negotiation and contestation (see Conclusions).

As noted by Bakker (2010), these processes have been neither 'tidy in practice' nor 'linear in fashion': market failures, state failures and governance failures coexist, 'exhibit a range of failures', and are used to justify the 'problem' requiring ongoing state intervention. Moreover, as forms of governance become more widespread, as we have demonstrated, 'the question of governance failure becomes more acute' (Bakker, 2010: 45). Given the timely nature of city-region building occurring across the globe, the answer to governance failure is where debates could fruitfully focus next. 'Metagovernance' offers one avenue for exploring this.

Metagovernance involves attempts to manage the ongoing complexity, plurality and tangled hierarchies, characteristic of prevailing modes of coordination (see Jessop, 2000, 2008, 2016a). It involves, then, continually defining and redefining and drawing boundary-spanning roles and functions, creating and recreating networking and linkage devices, sponsoring and redesigning new institutions, identifying appropriate lead strategic institutions to coordinate other partners (in this case, the SCR CA), and continually generating discourses and narratives on the economy (the 'shaping of context', according to Jessop, 2011) to facilitate relative geographical coherence through repetition of the 'problems' to be addressed and the solutions to this. Government plays an increasing role in metagovernance: providing the ground rules for governance and regulatory order in and through which governance partners can pursue their aims and seek to ensure the compatibility or coherence of different governance mechanisms and regimes. It seeks to balance and rebalance power differentials by strengthening weaker forces or systems in the interest of social cohesion or integration, and takes political responsibility in the event of governance failure (Whitehead, 2003). These emerging roles mean that networking, negotiation, noise reduction, and negative as well as positive coordination occur 'in the shadow of hierarchy'. It also means that, as Jessop reminds us, there is 'the need for almost permanent institutional and organizational innovation to maintain the very possibility (however remote) of sustained economic growth' (Jessop, 2000: 24). This is certainly the case in the SCR, which is being produced through a combination of political fiat, central government diktat, and local state opportunism. The research agenda put down by Jessop for doing metagovernance, which we have sought to answer head-on with 'Devo Sheffield', is the 'extent to which the multiplying levels, arenas, and regimes of politics, policy-making, and policy implementation can be endowed with a certain apparatus and operational unity horizontally and vertically; and how this affects the overall operation of politics and legitimacy of the new political arrangements' (Jessop, 2008: 222). Effective governance and metagovernance, in turn, depends on displacing certain governance problems elsewhere and/ or on deferring them into a more or less remote future. Whereas the positively-charged devolution city-region policy discourses framing the Sheffield problem point to a can-do 'steering optimism', where there is deemed to be a capacity to engage fruitfully and with purpose to produce temporary spatio-temporal fixes, our analysis in this chapter points to 'steering pessimism' and a crisis of crisis management. The chapter has highlighted the underlying long-term structural economic obstacles to effective governance and metagovernance, and that, 'by virtue of the simplification of the conditions of action, so often lead to the "revenge" of problems that get ignored, marginalized, displaced, or deferred' (Jessop, 2011: 117). This sort of simplification found in 'Devo Sheffield' is evident in attempts to define problems as societal in scope and as requiring consensual governance, rather than as conflictual effects of exploitation, oppression or discrimination that can be only resolved by addressing fundamental structural and strategic patterns of domination. A website, with postings since the launch of 'Devo Sheffield', offers some insights into this:[1]

> What is 'Sheffield City Region'? Is it an organisation, some sort of quango, a government department? And how is it to be held accountable? Where's the role for residents to steer changes and set the agenda?
>
> Sounds like a glorified talking shop. There has been virtually no discussion of these City Deals ... for me this is a backward step not a forward one.
>
> The problem is ... this handout to city-regions will be instead of a comprehensive devolution agenda, but is simply yet another last minute sticking plaster to hide the fact that nothing of substance has been achieved by yet another government.

Conclusions

Within the context of the Northern Powerhouse, this chapter has explored the implementation of the devolution of employment and skills frameworks within the SCR. The UK Conservative government has taken a 'localist' approach to urban regeneration, which positions sub-regional economic development and city-region building as the primary policy tools for growth, democracy, and also tackling spatial inequalities. There is certainly a gap in our knowledge in terms of how city-region growth strategies, welfare-to-work programmes, and employment and skills initiatives contribute to economic and employment growth. The chapter has highlighted the complex issues around facilitating access to employment and skills by disadvantaged civil society groups.

On this, we have highlighted three main tensions in the devolution settlement, as applied to the SCR through the Devolution Agreements. First, devolution is doing very little to address economic and social disadvantage in the SCR, which is stubbornly embedded on several levels: there is a relative low level of economic performance, with its GVA ranked 38 out of 39 city regions; the lack of employment demand and poor jobs growth compounds this with, as noted above, an additional 70,000 jobs needed to narrow the gap with other parts of the country; low pay, skills and in-work poverty mean that work is not an automatic route out of poverty; disability health and labour market disadvantage is a significant policy challenge; women and young people are particularly disadvantaged in terms of employment and pay, with a higher proportion of women paid below the living wage compared to men in the SCR, and some 22 per cent of those aged 16–24 years old unemployed (see Etherington and Jones, 2017).

Second, employment and skills provision are compounding this through policy fragmentation, limited transparency and accountabilities. According to some stakeholders, the city region as an economic entity faces challenges primarily due to overlapping boundaries – three LAs are in two city regions, and the Derbyshire LAs are also involved with employment and skills initiatives developed by Derbyshire Employment and Skills Board. The cross-border involvement of Chesterfield and Bassetlaw (in Derbyshire) LAs in a South Yorkshire deal subsequently led Derbyshire County Council to seek a (successful) judicial review (on the breadth of the consultation, on its fairness, on the means used to consult, and on the complexity of the information surrounding transfer of powers) of this devolution process, effectively putting back the mayoral election timetable to run the city region's development corporation. These 'custody battles' and 'regional rows' (Perraudin, 2016), illustrating how 'the power of the state is the power of the forces acting in and through the state' (Jessop, 1990: 270), increased during 2017 through the ambitions of Barnsley and Doncaster's LAs to be part of a wider Yorkshire Devolution Deal, culminating on 18 September with their withdrawal from, and 'derailing' of, the SCR devolution process (Burn, 2017). This triggered central government to withhold the £900 million financial offer, with a possible mayor de facto powerless, while austerity romps on. This situation was not resolved until Dan Jarvis MP was appointed Mayor in 2018 and in 2020 when Barnsley and Doncaster LAs finally ratified the deal (see Hoole and Hincks, 2020). All the time, welfare cuts had continued to bite deep, and austerity impacting further on Sheffield City Council's budget equated to 50 per cent of funding (£475 million) over the period 2010 to 2020 (Dore, 2020: 1).

The lack of boundary alignment also underlines an inherent problem with coordinating city-region and LA employment initiatives with

WP providers. The growth model in itself will contribute to increased numbers of jobs but there is a view that these will not be accessed by disadvantaged groups. There is a concern that this model is weak in terms of social inclusion policies and that it restricts the voice of disadvantaged groups being heard within the city-region policy process. Moreover, there have been weak links between welfare-to-work programmes and city-region initiatives and partnerships. The WP seems to have been 'parachuted' into the regions with relatively little consideration in terms of how provision is coordinated with local services.

Third, in the context of austerity, funding cuts are adversely impacting on the employment and skills system and the devo 'big pot of money' (see above) is not plugging this gap. The National Audit Office (2013) reports that over the 5-year period 2010/11 to 2014/15 the government will have spent £6.2 billion on local growth programmes, including that spent via RDAs and their legacy and spending on new funds and structures. By comparison, the RDAs spent £11.2 billion over the preceding 5-year period 2005/06 to 2009/10. Adult Skills budget cuts have been ongoing for a number of years and, we would argue, are unsustainable. The Government is prioritising apprenticeships in terms of skills policies and funding and an issue raised is how disadvantaged groups are to access Apprenticeships, given the importance of Further Education colleges (which are experiencing funding cuts) in providing training for disadvantaged groups. A significant funding gap is emerging within local government as a result of this and we have underlined how LA cuts are undermining and hindering the effectiveness of skills and employment programmes. Those services that are crucial to assisting civil society disadvantaged groups into employment are delivered or coordinated by LAs and are being cut back. We would argue that these cuts are hindering city-region growth objectives.

City-region building frameworks clearly have a long way to go to address these dilemmas, and the current obsession with deal-making public policy, which is 'founded upon territorial competition and negotiation between central and local actors unequally endowed with information and resources, leading to highly imbalanced and inequitable outcomes across the UK' (O'Brien and Pike, 2015: 14), will only compound the deeply historical problem of uneven growth that is occupying much media attention in the UK (see Pike et al, 2016). Devolution deals are concerned with arrangements for individual city regions and beyond the aspiration for a larger collective contribution to national economic output; there is no focus on the relationships with and between city regions and hence the overall functioning of the economy is bereft of strategic planning (Goodwin et al, 2017). In effect, there is an asymmetric distribution of powers: the devolution deals encourage competition over collaboration between city regions, which exacerbates existing inequalities, whereas the fantasy of 'neoliberalism promises that everyone will win' (Dean, 2009: 72) prevails in policy and political discourses. This is heightened by the welfare and LA cuts, as many of the policies that previously distributed the proceeds of the UK's finance-centric economic model have been ended by the broader austerity agenda. We maintain that public sector and public investment should play key roles in supporting and leading growth, but this stance 'is being directly hampered by a big withdrawal of state funding for this purpose' (RSA, 2016: 6).

Building on the innovative thinking of colleagues seeking to effectively spatial rebalance the economy in advanced capitalism (Martin, 2015), we would favour approaches that: offer growth based on social inclusion for civil society (adopt options which ensure that economic activities are more jobs rich, the poorest benefit the most); exercise redistribution and fairness (central government needs to acknowledge that the poorest areas, after decades of de-industrialisation and underinvestment, need a 'hand up'); and promote excellent public services to attract economic success (we need a new central–local relationship, founded on trust and a genuine localism, which appreciates the wider value of local government activity and strengthens local capacity to act in the interest of local people, communities and places). This in turn suggests the need for inclusive and accountable models of governance and commissioning; a needs-based approach to employment and skills; a targeted job creation programme; refocusing the outcomes of employment support on earnings and not performance indicators based on benefit off-flows; and targeting funds around integrated employment and skills to provide in-work support and progression.

Last, in terms of its analytical contribution, the key arguments put forward are that concepts of governance failure and metagovernance are important for analysing the development, tensions and contradictions of city-region economic governance within the context of the UK Government's devolution and localism agenda (in particular 'Devolution Agreements'). Using the tools of geographical political economy, it is time to grasp the contradictions of space and start thinking about 'devolved' city-region building as spatially-articulated metagovernance failure, where different and multiple spatial frameworks appear to be operating at the same time and evoking a crisis of crisis management (Jessop, 2016a, 2016b).

On this, and building on Rancière (2007), there is an urgent need to consider the links between, in this case, the ongoing depoliticisation of economic development and its governance in and through the existence of what have been termed 'post-democratic' and 'post-political' frameworks of performative and situated (apparent) consensus building (see Allmendinger and Haughton, 2012), and the ongoing 'march of neoliberalism' (Hall, 2011: 6) as a market-making machine continually depoliticising civil society through its economisation. Behind the chimera of the SCR is an ongoing brutal logic of labour market segmentation, flexibilisation and shifts in power relations between capital and labour through the weakening of collective bargaining and employment rights, creating the conditions for control over work arrangements and the casualisation of employment (part-time, temporary and zero-hour jobs). We must, as Rancière (2007: 106) points out, 'repoliticize [these] conflicts so that they can be addressed, restore names to the people and give politics back its former visibility in the handling of problems and resources'. The next chapter tackles this agenda through the lens of 'austerity urbanism' and city regions.

3

Precarious city regions

Introduction

The impact of austerity in cities has been framed around 'austerity urbanism'. This is a concept initially developed by Peck (2012, 2014) and extended more recently by Davidson and Ward (2018) to describe a strategy of fiscal policies and cuts focused on cities. This is in part a neoliberal response to previous policy failures to generate sustainable economic growth, which would influence the local tax base (Kennett et al, 2015). This 'austerity urbanism' approach has received criticism for being primarily overly 'US centric' and that it underestimates the role of global as well as national economic processes, shaping the way cities are becoming focal points, for 'managing' the distributional consequences of fiscal crises and retrenchment (see Hastings et al, 2017; Pike et al, 2018).

This critical engagement is extended further, to include how social and institutional actors exercise agency within cities in terms of contestation and negotiation (Meegan et al, 2014; Newman, 2014). Much of the work to date precludes agency and the ways urban actors can either resist or at least mitigate the impact of austerity. This point has been extended by Blanco and colleagues (Blanco et al, 2014; Davies and Blanco, 2017) and similarly by Bristow (Bristow and Healy, 2015; Webber et al, 2018), where attention is drawn to the importance played by agency in relation to LAs as 'regulatory intermediaries' adapting, responding and reacting to austerity crisis. LAs devise various strategies to protect the poor and disadvantaged groups who tend to depend on LA services (see Donald et al, 2014; Fuller, 2017, 2018).

Building on Chapter 2, this chapter is interested in how civil society social actors exercise agency within city regions in terms of the contestation and negotiation of austerity-fuelled welfare reform and the emerging 'politics of labour conditionality and discipline'. Attention is drawn to the role of trade unions and LA unions, who as actors still have a voice within the 'growth' agendas and in particular in terms of the growing precarious nature of the economy. This is undertaken by drawing on devolution developments in the GMCR, as noted in Chapter 1, considered to be one of the flagship devolution initiatives in England. This comprises, through city-region devolution, the LAs of Manchester, Bolton, Bury, Salford, Trafford, Stockport, Wigan, Oldham, Rochdale and Tameside to one (political) level. The inception of a mayoral CA, following waves of deal-making, has seen GM's 'Devo Manc' in the vanguard of recent devolution debates. This has been central to England's state spatial reconfiguration, with agglomerative city-region building and various rounds of 'spatial imaginaries' facilitating the decentralisation of budgets pertaining to economic and social development (Deas et al, 2020; Hincks et al, 2017).

The next section builds on the Introduction and charts the political economy of austerity in city regions. This is followed by an analysis of the implementation of welfare reform in the context of devolution in Greater Manchester and how these impact on civil society by reinforcing social inequalities. One of the key contradictions of austerity is how it undermines neoliberal objectives for a free market supply of labour. Building on Chapter 2, a subsequent section illustrates the increasingly unstable nature of the labour market because of the rise in precarious work. The chapter then focuses on the civil society institutional actors and explores the way they negotiate and contest austerity politics.

The political economy of austerity in city regions

Austerity is generally used to mean public expenditure cuts: reducing government budget deficits through a combination of public spending cuts and regressive tax hikes. There is a view that austerity involves an 'economic model' integral to neoliberalism with the aim of underpinning and reinforcing the power of ruling classes – that is, financial interests (Callinicos, 2012: 67). This restoration of 'class power' entails reducing wages and labour protections to make the workforce more 'flexible'. The 'disciplining of labour' is a key element of the austerity 'growth project' in terms of restricting its agency and capacities of mobilisation and resistance and this is facilitated by curtailing the bargaining power of labour via industrial relations and employment regulation. In addition, as we noted in Chapter 2, welfare and labour market policies involve the increasing use of conditionality in terms of reducing access to benefits and restricting the capacities of labour to negotiate and challenge the welfare system (see Etherington, 2020; Umney, 2018).

Austerity has generally led to widescale inequalities and markedly uneven growth which has particularly impacted on the northern and midlands former industrial regions (Beatty and Fothergill, 2016). Devolution and localisation share a joint purpose – to 'download' austerity to the regions, while at the same time seeking to manage its contradictions. Precarious economies, therefore, need to be understood in relation to the wider political economy of state restructuring and geographical uneven development. City governance, which operates at different spatial scales, now involves an array of actors, stakeholders and organisations; it is neoliberal in character in terms of the changing relations between state and market economy involving the increasing influence of corporate interests and privatisation of public services (Jones, 2019a, 2019b). Austerity plays a key role in the restructuring of modes of representation and democratic accountability, which are integral to devolution strategies. Interventions in managing civil society over the past few years have become more punitive and revanchist. Universal Credit (UC) now involves the amalgamation of six different benefits into one with a tapering system linked to in-work benefits and wages designed to 'make work pay'. This requires a more disciplinary and conditional welfare system through a tougher claimant regime in which sanctions are an integral feature. In turn, 'in-work conditionality' is a central feature of UC, with the requirement for claimants to attain 'earning thresholds' set at the level of effort reasonable for an individual to undertake. In short, the localisation of welfare performs societal depoliticisation by transferring aspects of social policy from the (collective) public to the (individualised) private sphere, articulated locally through the changing internal structures of the state. The Conservative Government's welfare reform agenda has, therefore, been established around moral and ideological messages in terms of rights, responsibilities and benefit 'dependency' drawing distinctions between 'strivers' (people who work) and 'skivers' (those who claim benefits) (Shildrick, 2018). As Wiggan (2012: 391) states: 'a hostile environment is slowly being constructed for all those who find they need to rely on social security, whilst the principle of solidarity that underpins support for more expansive public expenditure is eroded in favour of a market orientated system of punitive welfare'.

The onset of the 2008 financial crisis stimulated employer strategies towards labour flexibilisation and a key aspect of this is pay determination and the prevalence of low paid work, which is evidenced by this becoming a more prevalent feature of the UK labour market (D'Arcy et al, 2019). As such, working life in low-paying sectors has become more insecure and there is evidence that the movement between work and welfare becomes more common (see Peck and Theodore, 2000; Rubery et al, 2018). In turn, businesses shift the risks of the market on to workers, as the 'exit of qualified/skilled benefit claimants into low paying, precarious jobs, is uniformly considered a sub-optimal result of activation' (Raffas, 2017: 356). Indeed, the role of activation/welfare-to-work becomes clearly defined as a policy tool to ensure that precarious jobs are filled by claimants as a way of sustaining the new financialised business model of outsourcing and fragmentation. The removal and downgrading of employment rights and processes, which facilitate employee representation in negotiating workplace employment conditions, are key to facilitating this process (Rubery et al, 2018).

Our understanding of austerity in the context of devolution and civil society requires analysis of the role of social and spatial agency within the wider geography of insecurity. Both the attacks on civil society and the contradictions of neoliberalism and austerity are clearly expressed – and *visible* – on the local scale (Gough, 2014). Cumbers et al (2010: 53) make an important point when they state that 'our approach is to bridge the separation of production and reproduction (by) locating individuals within both their local labour market contexts and the broader webs of social relations through which they negotiate everyday life in the city'. We propose a deeper sense of agency through 'unpacking' resistance in the context of social struggles. As noted in Chapters 1 and 2, city regions are important sites of resistance to the downloading of or devolving austerity particularly in relation to local government and other state institutions. The labour market impacts of economic and state restructuring places demand and pressures on local institutions, trade unions and social movements in terms of resisting and negotiating the local impacts of austerity. However, devolved governance also opens a new space for civil society actors to mobilise their power resources and capacities, to engage in partnerships, and to try to shape local agreements (Gough, 2014).

The role of actors and collective action can, therefore, be extended to include the analysis of representational structures such as local government as 'anchor institutions' in the delivery of vital social investment and reproduction services and in terms of engagement with unemployed and disadvantaged groups (see Hastings et al, 2017). Referring to the role of local government, Newman coins the term 'landscapes of antagonism', contextualised within a 'contradictory field of political forces' (Newman, 2014: 3298). As Johnson et al (2017: 13) emphasise, as 'wider systems of welfare have retreated over the past 30 years or so, paradoxically local government has assumed a greater burden of responsibility for regulating the market in various ways'. In this way, the local state is a site where trade union densities and organisation are still relatively strong and often act as a focal point for negotiating and in some cases challenging the impact of welfare reform.

The GM 'city deal': austerity and uneven development

Chapter 1 outlined that the Northern Powerhouse was established to mobilise partnerships and local government to collaborate 'strategically' on key economic issues. This includes increased powers over transport and economic planning; electing their own mayors; some powers to manage health; new employment and skills power via apprenticeships; and in 2017, the co-commissioning of welfare-to-work. The GMCR Devolution Settlement now includes major infrastructure, planning, housing, health and social care, welfare and employment investment initiatives. In the area of employment and social inclusion, GMCA has piloted a health and employment programme 'Working Well', which was subsequently rolled out as a Work and Health Programme within the devolved welfare-to-work programme in 2017. The Work and Health Programme is commissioned nationally by the DWP by regional contract package areas, as was the case with the WP. However, as part of the Devolution Agreement, Greater Manchester is a distinct contract package area and the programme has been jointly designed based on the learning from the Working Well programmes. The GMCA and individual LAs have established internal and external partnerships in order to manage the implementation of UC and the 'managed migration' from 'legacy benefits' on to UC (Manchester City Council, 2019a).

The devolution settlement though has essentially involved the devolution of austerity, which impacts on civil society in a variety of ways, some of which have been highlighted above. The following further features need to be exposed:

- The Health and Work Programme, as described above, which is aimed at assisting those who are 'furthest away' from the labour market, will be smaller and more focused than the WP and Work Choice, formerly the major welfare-to-work programmes that were wound up in 2019. Both programmes comprised a combined expenditure of £540.8 million in 2015/16 (£416.4 million WP, £124.4 million Work Choice). This compares with the £130 million allocated for specialist employment support. Spending on specialist support under the new Work and Health Programme has a projected budget of £130 million representing a cut of more than 80 per cent from the WP and Work Choice alone.

- NHS devolution has major implications for welfare-to-work policies for claimants with long-term health conditions. Because of devolution, Greater Manchester was already a long way ahead of other areas in producing plans about transforming services, new models of care, improving outcomes, radical upgrades in population health, and prevention. But underlying it all is the 'financial challenge'. With a devolved health and social care budget for GM of just over £6 billion, the ten councils and NHS commissioners must find 'massive savings'. Nationally, Sustainability Transformation Partnerships are largely about making those massive savings, as well as exposing the NHS to even more private sector involvement (Bedale, 2016).
- Keep has observed that the nature and intensity of cuts to the Adult Skills Budget (post-2013) have been such that the system reached unsustainable levels (Keep, 2016). Keep's analysis is corroborated by the Institute for Public Policy Research, which states that 'by 2020/21 adult skills funding will have been nearly cut in half in real terms from 2010/11' (Dromey and McNeil, 2017: 3).
- Similarly, the area based reviews (ABRs) relating to the Further Education Sector, which devolved authorities must manage, involve a rationalisation based on major cuts in Further Education funding. Government guidance on the review process, included in a parliamentary briefing on post-16 ABRs, states that the ABRs need to be undertaken 'in a way which also addresses the significant financial pressures on institutions including a declining 16–19 population and the need to maintain very tight fiscal discipline in order to tackle the deficit'(HoC Library, 2018: 14).
- City region and LAs, which are subject to significant funding cuts, will have to absorb the impacts of the cuts in welfare within city-region and local areas (see Gray and Barford 2018; and below).

From welfare to increasing low pay and labour market insecurity

Greater Manchester had a large manufacturing base and in 1959, the manufacturing industry employed over half of the Greater Manchester workforce; today, it accounts for less than 1 in 5 jobs. The de-industrialisation of the latter 20th century hit the regional economy hard, as it did much of the UK's industrial north. Some parts of the city were particularly affected – East Manchester, a former centre for heavy engineering and chemicals, experienced 24,000 job losses between 1974 and 1984 alone. In contrast growth has been driven by the service sector. Financial and professional services account for one-sixth of all jobs, one-fifth of GVA and almost half of GVA growth in the decade leading up to the onset of the recession. The manufacturing sector contracted by 37.6 per cent over the period 1998 to 2008, reflecting the wider structural shift in the economy from manufacturing centre to service economy (Hunt, 2015).

Pike et al (2016) provide some empirical analysis of some of the embedded precarious and unstable nature of the regional economies described above. Their study addresses the question of how many more and better jobs need to be created to address the demand deficiency in the major industrial cities. They categorise the labour market in terms of the 'more jobs gap' and 'better jobs gap'. The more jobs gap comprises those people who are unemployed, inactive people who want to work, and underemployed workers who would like more hours such as people working part time. The better jobs gap incorporates those on low paid work, with those jobs classed as insecure such as temporary contracts, while workers prefer a permanent employment contract. In short, economic disadvantage within civil society is stark.

In this context, the number of people in GM who earned less than the low pay threshold (defined as two-thirds of national median income, or £7.74 an hour in 2014) increased to 233,500 in 2014 (New Economy Manchester, 2015). Furthermore, the chances of progressing out of low pay are limited. According to one key source:

> Most people who were low paid at the start of our period of study were low paid at the end. Our findings are in line with others that suggest that in many low wage labour markets, there is very limited scope for progression to better paid work. There appear to be substantial numbers cycling in and out of low paid work as they change jobs. Yet a relatively small minority show a clear sense of moving up out of low pay. (New Economy Manchester, 2015: 68)

Insecure and low-paid work is linked to the 'de-unionisation' and that people within the welfare system become vulnerable to exploitation. Trade union density (proportion of workers who are members of a trade union) is 26 per cent in Greater Manchester, slightly higher than the England average (23 per cent) and collective bargaining coverage is 30 per cent, also higher than the England average (27.9 per cent) (EWERC, 2017: 12). These figures show that most workers in Greater Manchester do not have access to, or are members of, trade unions. Furthermore, these are workplaces where trade unions have difficulties in accessing terms of recognition. According to the European Work and Employment Research Centre:

> For trade unions and civil society organisations, the proliferation of insecure jobs has caused a diminishing in the social and economic status of individuals. The more that employers depend on insecure employment forms and contractual forms of work that reduce entitlement to employment rights and social protection the greater the risk that segments of the more vulnerable workforce (whether due to age, disability, or limited education for example) are rendered 'invisible' and both the worker and their work become marginalised in the city ... For their part, unions are playing a clear role in promoting core rights to which all workers should be entitled to such as sick pay, holiday pay and the chance to contribute to a pension scheme. (EWERC, 2017: 8)

Yates's study of the labour market in respect to young people in Greater Manchester provides an interesting and insightful lens into these dynamics of low pay and welfare policies in terms of the way they tend to reinforce low pay and insecure work (Yates, 2017; Peck and Theodore, 2000). This argues that young people are a source of cheap labour and various policy instruments, such as training and welfare, reinforce their exclusion and marginalisation (see also Finn, 1987). With respect to training, there has been a trend towards a shift from training without jobs towards education without jobs as an increasing number of graduates compete for low paid jobs (see Allen and Ainley, 2013; Roberts, 2017). Apprenticeship programmes, where the majority offered in Greater Manchester tend to be run by low paying employers who offer below minimum wage rates, tend to be poor quality and undercut wages. The other factor that shapes the labour market transitions of young people is the discriminatory practices of the welfare system, where young people are denied access to benefits transferring the costs of social reproduction from the state on to young people and households. Yates adds:

> But since 2010 the dominant form which labour market interventions towards young people have taken are coercive and disciplinary. Young people have experienced removal of state welfare such as housing benefit and have been targeted by punitive active labour market policies such as the

'Work Programme' and 'Youth Obligation'; these schemes force young people to engage in compulsory training or work placements or have their already diminished welfare payments completely removed entirely. (Yates, 2017: 475)

Yates acknowledges that this trend has been shaped by the absence of trade unions and enforcement of employment rights (only a small percentage of young people are members of trade unions) in workplaces into which the majority of young people move (whether from the welfare system or outside it). In Greater Manchester, the lack of resources to support people of all age groups to retain their jobs with continued in work support is seen as a factor as to why many disadvantaged groups return to the benefit system. The impact of cuts to benefits and social support, including vocational training, underpins and shapes this trend towards poverty and exclusion. We discuss this impact in more detail below.

Implementing welfare reform and the reduction in social protection

The migration to UC from legacy benefits has been observed by the authorities to have major negative implications for people's incomes and wellbeing (see SSAC, 2018). This has had a major impact on disabled people claiming disability related benefits. A relatively high proportion of claimants were being found 'fit to work' even though many of these decisions have been challenged as being incorrect. One of the consequences of incorrect assessments is the relatively high proportion of sickness benefit claimants vulnerable to benefit sanctions and benefit cuts (GMLC, 2017). According to the GMCA (2018: 10), the migration numbers are significant in terms of the roll out in GM – involving 198,500 from out of work benefits (Employment and Support Allowance, Job Seeker Allowance), 211,000 from tax credits and 207,600 housing benefit claimants. The GMCA has emphasised the complex nature of the migration process and challenges in estimating the impacts. Furthermore, the GMCA has not been able to quantify the impacts except that there is a proportionally greater increase in the use of Trussell Trust foodbanks in the city region (19 per cent) compared with 13 per cent for the North West Region. In addition, the GMCA has through reference to national assessments identified the various 'threats' from UC in terms of reduction in incomes and vulnerability to financial hardship (GMCA, 2018: 5).

To sum up, benefit cuts hit the Greater Manchester area disproportionately as there are large numbers of out of work benefit claimants and those who are in low paid work claiming tax credits (Beatty and Fothergill, 2017: 8). Benefit freeze has significant financial consequences for families and individuals in the GMCR. Manchester City Council has summarised these impacts when it states:

> The combined and cumulative impact of these welfare reforms alongside the introduction of UC is difficult to monitor due to its complexity and the fact that individuals will have very different experiences based on their circumstances. However, evidence suggests that vulnerable residents in particular, who have barriers to employment could be at risk of greater poverty and housing instability. (Manchester City Council, 2017: 7)

As the new system involves cuts in social support this is leading to the undermining of benefits or social security as a safety net. Data collated by Beatty and Fothergill (2016) on the financial implications of welfare changes across civil society focuses on estimated changes to key benefit including Employment and Support Allowance, UC, Benefit Cap Extension and Benefit Freeze, which together amount to significant cuts in income for claimants. Accumulated loss in income from the post 2015–20 reforms and the implications of financial changes for working-age adults equates to nearly £1,000 per person across the GMCR. Accordingly, Whitham's study of local welfare support illustrates how austerity has impacted on the capacity to respond to increasing impoverishment and destitution when it is pointed out that the funds for local crisis support have taken a significant cut – spending on crisis support in 2017/18 was £3.8 million. This is over £15 million lower than spending under Crisis Loan and Community Care Grant provision in 2010/11. The number of successful applications for support through local schemes in Greater Manchester was just over 10,000 in 2017/18 compared to 123,000 Community Care Grants and Crisis Loan awards made in 2010/11 (Whitham, 2018: 13).

Universal Credit displacing austerity on to local authorities

UC has major impacts across the board on a variety of services delivered by LAs. The Joseph Rowntree Foundation has made a detailed assessment of the impact and cost of cuts on local government; its case studies highlight the crucial role LAs play in the growth agenda, as well as providing essential support to disadvantaged groups (Hastings et al, 2017). Gray and Barford (2018) argue that there are profound geographical impacts of LA cuts with those in the more deindustrialised and disadvantaged regions, where LAs are more reliant on central government, experiencing more disproportionate cuts.

Taking Manchester City Council as an example – the largest economy and source of employment within the city region – between 2011/12 and 2016/17 the Council had to deliver a massive £339 million of savings with a further £14 million required in 2017/18, following the cumulative effect of reductions in funding from central government (Manchester City Council, 2019b: 26). Despite these cuts and retrenchment, LAs are, in terms of 'their duty of care' having to manage the impact of the UC migration process. A key Manchester City Council source sums up the impact of UC on the city council services:

> Research identified the risk of welfare reforms pushing additional unmet costs on to local authorities and partners including voluntary and community sector (VCS) organisations, as they manage both the administrative and wider policy consequences of welfare reform creating significant workload pressures. Councils are uniquely placed to support families to adjust to changes brought about by wider welfare reforms. (Manchester City Council, 2019a: 11)

This raises an important question in terms of the city-regional roll-out implementation of UC in the context of austerity. At the time of writing, this has been stalled by the government but there will be thousands of workers transferred from Working Tax Credit to UC, which in turn will have major implications for in-work poverty and its impact on local welfare services.

The contested politics of devolution, austerity and welfare

We have attempted to capture the multiple civil society actors and their agendas in terms of negotiating and contesting welfare and employment policies in Table 3.1. Building on Chapter 1, our analysis of the role of actors and collective action includes trade unions, the voluntary sector, community organisations and representational structures such as local government which act as 'anchor institutions' in terms of engagement with unemployed and disadvantaged groups (see Hastings, et al, 2017; Etherington and Jones, 2018). As highlighted by the 'Just Work' programme (Johnson et al, 2017), it is important to understand

Table 3.1: Actor strategies for opposing labour market policies

Policy interventions	Tensions and conflicts	Key actors and sites of negotiation
Devolution deals	Growth versus distribution Inclusion, funding for devolution Deals, modes of representation	Trade unions, civil society, LAs; negotiating 'social dialogue' formalised in Greater Manchester; devolution and democracy; Inclusive growth politics via Inclusive Growth Analysis Unit
Employment rights	Low level of unionisation high levels of insecure work	North West TUC, Greater Manchester trade unions and GMCA Good Employment Charter
Welfare reform/ Universal Credit	Impact of austerity increasing labour market marginalisation Working poor, cuts in funding PBR model, negative impact Conditionality and sanctions, delays in benefit, tough claimant regime	Local authority employment and anti-poverty strategies and role of anti-poverty coalitions, disability rights Organisations advice services (Greater Manchester Law Centre, Greater Manchester voluntary sector) trade union/non-governmental organisation campaigns against welfare reform Links between non-governmental organisations and trade unions in Greater Manchester Negotiating with central government (submissions to Work and Pensions Select Committee)
Social, health and community support services	Impact of austerity on both LAs and disadvantaged groups Local authority conflicts with public sector trade unions	LAs, frontline services and WP providers, NHS providers, advice services; advocacy for benefit claimants trade unions Opposition to cuts in services and jobs
Apprenticeships and skills, area reviews	Cuts to skills funding, including adult skills budget, area-based reviews, phase out of European funded skills programmes, extent of employer buy-in in face of recession, quality of provision and engagement of limited access to advanced skills by disadvantaged groups to skills	Skills providers especially further education colleges (playing an advocacy role for disadvantaged groups), trade unions negotiating funding gaps in work representation around apprenticeship quality

Source: Adapted from Etherington (2020: 109)

the economic context in order to situate social and spatial agency and mobilisation. De-industrialisation has involved the loss of unionised work and led to the fragmentation of both the labour market and business structure, which creates significant challenges for trade unions to organise and coordinate collective action. This said, there exist active trade councils within the GMCR. The metropolitan geography and relatively strong interconnectedness from previous rounds of city-region building has provided a platform for social action to be networked across the city region.

There is an emerging agenda then, which recognises that quality of work and employment rights needs to be built into policy agendas. The North West TUC has outlined its own devolution employment charter (North West TUC, 2018) and the University of Manchester Inclusive Growth Analysis Unit has played an active role in shaping a discussion on 'responsible businesses' along with the GMCA, which has developed its own employment charter that seems to be broadly similar to that of the North West TUC (Rafferty and Jelley, 2018). The increasing awareness and discourse around representational gaps and lack of employment rights within the city-region economy has, therefore, brought to the fore campaigns around living wages and anti-poverty strategies.

One of the features of devolution under neoliberalism though is the tendency to marginalise trade unions and voluntary sector engagement within the devolution political process (see Smith Institute, 2017). In many respects this may explain why there have been tensions between the trade unions and the devolved authorities around the devolution process. This can be illustrated in the UNISON trade union response to the Greater Manchester Health and Social Care Plan, which goes to the heart of trade unions' lack of engagement with the devolution process and the way devolution embodies the implementation of privatisation:

> Our concerns include: the lack of employee and trade union involvement in the production of the Plan; the lack of focus on improving the quality of employment as a means of improving health outcomes and the absence of any plan to implement the living wage at a Greater Manchester scale; the implications on our members delivering public services of new delivery models. We believe that health service delivery and employment in Greater Manchester should be very much part of the National Health Service. (UNISON, 2016: 6)

Furthermore, the TUC argues (2014) that LEPs often do not recognise or understand the role that unions can play as agents for change. While it is recognised that LEPs should be held accountable for their development, there are no mechanisms currently in place for this to happen (see Pike et al, 2018). Furthermore, the devolution of employment policy tends to be taking place without any structural changes or adjustments that will allow the voice of disadvantaged groups to be heard within the city-region policy process, especially as there is no trade union representation on the Greater Manchester LEP. As GM has involved the devolution of major public services such as health and social care, it is of little surprise that some form of social dialogue has been established with the trade unions via the Greater Manchester Strategic Workforce Engagement Board and a Workforce Engagement Protocol. The election of a high-profile Labour mayor (Andy Burnham) in 2017 'was seen by the trade unions and voluntary sector organisations as an opportunity to contribute to a progressive agenda around poverty and inequality' (Johnson et al, 2017: 7). Within this context, Oldham Borough Council established its own Fairness Commission to track and monitor the impact of welfare reform. Salford Borough Council established its own inquiry into the impact of benefit sanctions. Of course, this is a contradictory process as they are also at the same time implementing public expenditure cuts.

The significance of LAs as 'anchor institutions' in terms of mitigating the impact of austerity and as a source of contestation in relation to negotiating and opposing austerity cannot be overstated. GM possesses a history of coordinated action across the different LAs, which has aided city-region wide network building within civil society (Hincks et al, 2017). There is evidence of this in the submissions and critical engagement with the welfare reform agenda, such as Manchester City Council's submission to the Work and Pensions Select Committee, Oldham Fairness Commission and the Tameside Poverty pledge. There are, however, tensions around these arrangements, as devolution involves devolving and managing austerity; devolution authorities efficiently administer centrally determined cuts. This means while there is greater (and formal) engagement of trade unions in the GMCR, this is tenuous given their opposition to the overall thrust of the devolved economic and social strategies (Nelson, 2017: 8).

Another pressing tension is the lack of control the devolved LAs have over the implementation of welfare reform, UC and skills policies. An example of this is the operation of advice organisations such as the Greater Manchester Law Centre, Greater Manchester Centre for Voluntary Organisation and TUC that provide some form of basis to negotiate and challenge regressive welfare policies. The Greater Manchester Coalition of Disabled People has responded to devolution by making demands on the mayor to shape a more progressive agenda:

> whilst the Greater Manchester Mayor does not have direct responsibility for delivering all of the services that we require to protect and promote our independence, the Mayor will have an important ambassadorial role and opportunity to promote best practice. This manifesto for disabled people has been produced to assist the Mayor in becoming our ally and champion in our fight for equality. (GMCDP, 2018: 3)

The forging of cross city mobilisation is also illustrated by the campaign against welfare reform and UC, as part of a national campaign, comprising a wide range of organisations across GM. The campaign, supported by the incumbent Mayor, has focused on resisting evictions due to non-payment of rent as a result of benefit cuts and delays built into the UC system (GMLC, 2018). Added to this, the upscaling or 'scale jumping' of engagement around the GMCR has proved to be a challenge for the likes of the Greater Manchester VCSE Devolution Reference Group, which has been historically embedded in localised civil society networks, and is consequently sub-regional in its mobilisations (see Chapter 1).

Conclusions

Manchester has been termed 'mythic Manchester' by some academics (Haughton et al, 2016) who cut through the hype of devolution to reveal a city region at breaking point, with cracks appearing in many services. As we have highlighted in this chapter, massive cuts in welfare benefits, leading to a depth and intensity of social problems, are pushing a series of critical capacity issues across civil society. Getting behind this and exposing its 'dynamics' (Shukaitis, 2013), we have argued that civil society 'precarity' is being reproduced through the GMCR labour market and economy through social struggles and the capital-labour relation, exhibited through the local politics of welfare-to-work – the 'new politics of austerity' (MacLeavy, 2011).

The growth model and trajectory of GMCR is pitted with multiple tensions as local and city-region institutions come to terms with the failure to redistribute the gains of 'growth'. The implementation of welfare reform and the UC benefit migration will only accentuate social and labour market inequalities because this is taking place within the context of major cuts in LA and welfare spending. Moreover, the austerity–neoliberal growth 'model' undermines democracy and system accountabilities. Devolution has an inbuilt democratic deficit in terms of the way local actors are highly constrained by central directives. As Finn (2015) has noted, the UK has one of the most centralised welfare-to-work systems within the OECD countries and this is reflected in the nature of the implementation of welfare reform. UC becomes a vehicle for downloading austerity and a source of contestation rather than negotiation and influence by local actors and institutions. City-region authorities, LAs and civil society institutions are acting as 'buffers' to mitigate the regressive impacts of austerity on poorer communities (Hastings et al, 2017).

The other element is the scope for influencing devolution policies by trade unions and civil society organisations. The institutional and governance changes have not in any way integrated social dialogue between those organisations representing trade unions and disadvantaged communities. This has major implications for the establishment of employment rights, fairness at work and bridge building between policymaking stakeholders and disadvantaged groups and communities. As Rubery et al (2018: 524) point out, the contradictions described in this chapter are not necessarily new, but there is a need to recognise through the introduction of city regions 'the state's political orientations towards work disciplining of the unemployed or allowing employers to renege on their traditional employment guarantees and responsibilities'.

4

Elite city deals

Introduction

As was stated by then Secretary of State for Wales, Ron Davies (1999), 'devolution is a process, not an event' – a sentiment deployed to express the dynamics and opportunities of devo-statecraft. In following this process within the context of Welsh devolution, this chapter seeks to highlight an interesting series of dynamics with regards to the development of city regions as the latest phase in a broader process of sub-national government restructuring under devolution. As stated throughout *City Regions and Devolution in the UK,* city regions have been vaunted as the appropriate scale for economic growth and this has informed the intentions of both the Welsh Government and the LAs of the CCR towards creating city regions in this context.

The chapter seeks to engage empirically and analytically with the broader body of literature on civil society vis-à-vis central–local relations in regional and local economic development. Particularly in the context of previous interventions by Duncan and Goodwin (1988), we show how the empirical case study of the CCR is actively recasting central–local social relations, and in doing so, building on Chapter 2, this raises interesting questions on the evolving dimensions of metagovernance. When Duncan and Goodwin formulated their ideas on states and uneven development during the 1980s, devolution in the UK, of course, did not exist. The chapter recasts central–local relations through devolution and suggests inter-scalar relationships increasingly coming to the fore. It suggests that notions of being scalar 'agent and obstacle' (Duncan and Goodwin, 1988) can provide an analytical lens in and through which to view the shifting and sticky relationships emerging between local state(s) and national state(s) in Wales. In particular, the chapter looks at how new territorial relations are being created within the devolved state of Wales through city regions. We suggest that this is recasting tensions between different governance institutions, as the local and national governments seek to legitimise different policy opportunities in the pursuit of economic growth.

The process of implementing the CCR has not been as straightforward as the successful signing of the city-deal on 15 March

2016 might suggest. This is because it raises several interesting empirical and theoretical concerns with regards to the implementation of sub-national economic policy in the wake of devolution and austerity (Waite, 2015). This reflects questions concerning: the historic difficulty in terms of local government structure in Wales (Pemberton, 2016) (and more broadly the UK); the process of deal making itself (O'Brien and Pike, 2015) – as an elite, technocratic process that was highly contested among elite actors (Ayres et al, 2017); the framing of the city region as a growth machine to enable specific actors within a city region (see Harding, 2007); and finally how such processes skew the representational regime of city region away from what could broadly be termed civil society. In short, we seek to expose some of the legislative contradictions of the Welsh state. Since devolution, the Welsh state has in various ways attempted to position civil society within processes of governance (see Chaney, 2016); however, the implementation of the city-region agenda suggests a more elitist approach is being taken in the pursuit of building a city region. This raises a series of questions with regards to social relations (MacLeod and Jones, 2007) within the development of the Welsh state and the representational regimes (MacLeod and Goodwin, 1999) of city regions (Beel et al, 2017).

In working through the above arguments, we first give further context as to why the city in Welsh policy is the 'go-to' scale for engendering economic growth and what in turn underpins its economic rationale. This section will also consider how city deals are made. Second, the chapter considers what underpins the CCR City Deal, how it was constructed and what it intends to do by looking at how such a policy is transformed when it is transferred over space (Peck and Theodore, 2015). Third, it will look at the process itself to delineate how central–local relations in Wales are being actively recast. Fourth, in highlighting these central–local processes of what can also be termed 'scalecraft' (Fraser, 2010; Pemberton, 2016), the chapter discusses how civil society and non-economic concerns are being positioned differently through the political geometry of devolution.

City regions and uneven development revisited

As we suggested in the Introduction, the UK Government has embarked on creating city regions within England through a deal-making process, which has sought to combine metropolitan LAs together via LEPs. LEPs and CAs are being presented as the 'natural' and 'functional' scale of economic activity around which each city region can strategically plan for future economic growth.

The process is asymmetric in its application due to waves of bespoke public-policy deals, which have devolved a variety of different competencies to CAs. This has meant central government policy has played out very differently in different places, as some city regions (such as GMCR, discussed in Chapter 3) have seen greater devolution granted to them, whereas other areas (such as the Leeds City Region) failed to get a deal until 2020. As such, a select number of city regions have (potentially) benefitted from being favoured by ministers to implement such deals and others have missed out (O'Brien and Pike, 2015). However, such processes have posed many problems for both city regions with devolution deals and those without, who are potentially striving to negotiate them for competitive advantage (Harrison, 2007). Surrounding these questions are several factors that have undermined the devolution process and weakened its potential to develop more inclusive forms of growth in city regions (Etherington and Jones, 2009).

Firstly, as noted above, austerity has undermined many of the deals put in place (see Davies and Blanco, 2017; Peck, 2012; Shaw and Tewdwr-Jones, 2017) before they have even been enacted. Austerity has consistently impacted heaviest on LAs where higher proportions of welfare claimants can be found. This often coincides with areas which have been granted deals such as GMCR and SCR; in GMCR this equates to around £6 billion and in SCR £1.1 billion to the constituent LAs (Etherington and Jones, 2016a, 2016b, 2017). This has meant real terms cuts to a variety of services and a harsher welfare environment for claimants as LAs have had to cut their budgets accordingly (Muldoon-Smith and Greenhalgh, 2015). Therefore, immediately, what has been potentially gained in terms of extra funding from a devolution or city deal is lost (see Beatty and Fothergill, 2016). As austerity impacts those most who have least as services are cut, it undermines any of the potential for devolution and city deals to move those people who are least skilled into the new city-regional economies they are trying to create (Penny, 2016).

The lack of a consideration to the social formation (Jonas, 2012) within city regions from austerity and the deals themselves, secondly, means a cycle of underachievement for city regions will be perpetuated, as LAs are both tasked with implementation of cuts to public services alongside developing the city region itself (Ward et al, 2015). This is then re-enforced by a growth model focused on agglomeration, the desired outcome that highlights the second missing connection. The agglomerative trickle-down model (Haughton et al, 2014), alongside historic spatially selective growth (Omstedt, 2016) and a stagnant economy at a national and local levels (Bailey and Budd, 2016), means that any potential growth will be undermined by a continuing process of uneven development, which will continue to play out within the city region (Etherington and Jones, 2009).

Thirdly, there has been a failure to address cultural and historical differences that exist across city regions and empower civil society in the process (see Breathnach, 2014). This relates most strongly to questions of accountability but also reflects concerns with regards to processes of depoliticisation (see Burnham, 2014; Etherington and Jones, 2018; Foster et al, 2014; Jessop, 2014). Due to the state centric nature of city and devolution deals, they have not involved a 'broader sense' of public, civil society or grassroots movements in the construction of new forms of governance (see Newman and Clarke, 2009). This has meant that city-region governance structures, such as the CA and LEP, have been somewhat distanced from public scrutiny and the spatial scales on which they operate seem to have little resonance with the publics they seek to serve. This means that the process of city-region building raises serious questions with regard to the governance structures created, due to the creation of a democratic deficit (Buser, 2013; Swyngedouw, 2009, 2018; Tomaney, 2016). As we noted in previous chapters, city-region institutions and mayors are supposed to partially address this, but with the creation of a variety of soft or fuzzy spaces of governance (see Haughton and Allmendinger, 2015; Hincks et al, 2017) such as LEPs and Transition Boards, this can be questioned. Within these spaces, only certain actors have agency, which suggests a skewing of city-regional social relations towards economic interests. The city-region building process then in itself is a purposeful act of 'depoliticisation' (see Burnham, 2014; Etherington and Jones, 2018; Jessop, 2014), whereby the 'elite/expert' growth model is presented as the only viable option and there is sparse opportunity to successfully contest this model within formal governance structures. We take forward these arguments in the next section, which examines city-region building and civil society in CCR.

Creating the Cardiff Capital Region

The above context concerning UK Government policy development is important, for in the process of creating the CCR a similar set of policy stimuli were cited by the Welsh Government and the city deal for CCR was negotiated directly with the UK Government. Because devolution is to the Welsh Government, an important differentiation for Wales, no devolution deal has been offered to the Cardiff City Region as a whole, only a CCR City Deal (see House of Commons Welsh

Affairs Committee, 2019). The following section highlights how this played out differently within the devolved structures of Wales. This is to highlight what Peck and Theodore (2015: 29) term 'policy transfer', whereby: 'Policies are not, after all, merely being transferred over space; their form and their effects are transformed by these journeys, which also serve continuously to remake relational connections across an intensely variegated and dynamic socioinstitutional landscape'. In following this transformation of the city region construct to fit the political geography of the CCR, we can trace how the city-region concept has been spatially deployed and geographically reshaped by its transference journey.

Fixing central–local relations in Wales

Wales has its own specific policy trajectory since devolution, which is both divergent and aligned to that of the UK and the development of city regions highlights this. Therefore, to create a bridge to the previous contextual section on city-region developments in England there is a need to consider how Wales has developed differently over a similar period. The consolidation of Wales as a regional/national space of social and economic governance, with increasingly sharp territorial definition since the introduction of devolved government in 1999, has refocused attention on the dynamics of spatial difference within Wales. Persistent uneven geographies of socioeconomic performance, as well as seemingly entrenched geographies of political and cultural difference, suggest the existence of 'locality effects' within Wales and present challenges for the delivery of policy. However, the shape of Wales's constituent localities is far from clear. Although Wales has a sub-regional tier of 22 LAs, these have only been in existence since 1995, when they replaced a two-tier local government system established in 1974. Moreover, the administrative map is overlain and cross-cut by a plethora of other governmental bodies including health boards, police authorities, transport consortia and economic development partnerships – to name a few – that work to their own territorial remits. An attempt to produce a more nuanced and process-led representation of Wales's internal geography was made with the WSP in 2004 (updated in 2008) – see Jones et al (2016).

Heley's (2013) insights reveal that this 'new spatial planning' for Wales attempts to create a more regional and relational approach to governance. Defined as uniquely Welsh by Haughton et al (2010) but reflecting a regional approach as had been adopted in England, it attempted to 'regionalise' the 22 Welsh LAs into reciprocal relationships of working together. As Heley adds:

> The WSP has six 'area visions' ... North-West (Eryi a Môn), North-East (Borders and Coast), Central Wales, Pembrokeshire (The Haven), Swansea Bay (Waterfront and Western Valleys), and South-East (The Capital Network). These 'areas' are not defined by administrative boundaries and this, it is suggested, enables partners to work together on common issues in a flexible way, to improve efficiencies, and to overcome problems associated with a limited local leadership base. These partners include the Welsh Assembly Government, its agencies, local authorities and private and voluntary/third sector organizations, and each area has a committee chaired by an Assembly minister and involving senior representatives of organizations working as part of the area network. (Heley, 2013, 1331–2)

The approach, therefore, built on pre-existing regional relationships and sought to foster these via what was termed a 'fuzzy' approach. Heley (2013) suggests the approach genuinely did shift the spatial imaginaries of policymakers towards a more relational approach; however, the inability to generate sufficient economic growth and the subsequent downturn in the global economy meant a new approach was desired (Jones et al, 2013). Added to this, efforts to align the initially 'fuzzy' boundaries of the WSP regions with the hard boundaries of LA areas demonstrates the accretional power of fixed institutional geographies in shaping the representation of localities (Haughton et al, 2010). With the removal of the WSP, focus shifted away from fuzzy, relational approaches to more territorial defined and metro centric approaches. Key here was the City Region Taskforce in Wales, headed by Elizabeth Haywood in 2012: it sought to develop two city regions in Wales following an agglomerative-growth logic. According to Government discourse at the time:

> The main factors in our decision to recommend recognition of two city-regions in south Wales were: critical mass; traffic flows; community identification; existing structures of governance, and the fact that our cities contribute less to the economy than cities anywhere else in the UK, and we need to ensure that contribution grows. (Welsh Government, 2012)

The above quote highlights the shift in spatial emphasis of the Welsh Government towards city regions and its alignment to approaches in England as led by the UK Government. This also then positioned both the Welsh Government and the LAs that sit within city regions surrounding Cardiff and Swansea with the task of implementing and building their respective city regions.

Alongside this as Pemberton (2016) highlights, the long history of LA restructuring in Wales, which has shifted between more 'regional' municipal areas historically to the more 'local' framework presently in use. The appropriate territorial-fix has also been difficult in Wales due to both major cities being in the south with a largely rural population in the north, which is fragmented by a difficult physical geography. It is this constitutional geography of the Welsh State and its local government structure that has therefore propelled the city region to produce CCR. This process is important as it highlights several important contextual issues: the actors involved; the process of negotiating multilevel governance; and the shifting relationship between local and national states, as both agents and obstacles to different policy regimes.

Alongside the development of the CCR was a concerted effort by the Welsh Government, via then Minister Leyton Andrews, to redraw the LA map of Wales. The purpose was to make a strategic move from twenty-two LAs to eight (see Jones et al, 2016). This failed due to resistance from Welsh LAs and territorially aligned Assembly Members, who did not wish to be forced so quickly into a process of consolidation:

> 'Similarly, before the recent – or last year's election in the Assembly when you had a very forceful approach from Welsh Government and they were looking to drive through a reorganisation, there was an awful lot of bad feeling, not only between political parties but within political parties because of that issue I just mentioned was heightened and I think a lot of authorities felt their numbers had been cut to pay for an increase in the Assembly and it was a shift in the balance of power.' (Interview, LA Rep Body, 2017)

This has led to a slowing of the pace of LA 'regionalisation' but, as the 'Reforming Local Government: Resilient and Renewed White Paper' (Welsh Government, 2017a) hints, this will not disappear as a possibility, especially within the context of continuing austerity. The unfolding of the above greatly shaped the relationships between ten

LAs in the CCR (see Figure 4.1) and the Welsh government, which led to two parallel processes of city-region building being put in place. Figure 4.2 represents this; in the left-hand box there is CCR Transition Board, which the Welsh Government created. This was to push through the development of the city region via a selection of local elites, primarily from business and education (not too dissimilar to the structure of a LEP board), with the purpose being to strategically plan the city region's implementation. To directly negotiate a city-deal with the UK Government, the LAs themselves, circumventing the Welsh Government, sidelined this approach:

> 'We'd had positive soundings from the UK Government, we had a bit more of a challenge to make the Welsh Government see the benefits of a City Deal, but as you know, a City Deal is in the ownership of local authorities, so we were leading on the concept. We had ten Leaders who ... some may have had a bit of scepticism about it, but were willing for us to explore it out, so we decided then that we would put together a bit, and we had some support in helping us to create what a City Deal bid ought to look like.' (Interview, Local Authority Leader CCR, 2017)

This created the governance structure on the right-hand side of Figure 4.2, which is continuing to evolve presently through the implementation of the city deal itself. The process of negotiating the city deal raises two interesting points: first, it was negotiated between LA leaders and the UK Government, whereby it circumvented the Welsh Government and had little public consultation. This raises both an issue of accountability due to little consultation being given and, second, it suggests that local government can be both agent and obstacle simultaneously in the implementation of central government policy – resistant to the city region via the Welsh Government, but accepting to it from the UK Government.

Cardiff Capital Region City Deal

The CCR City Deal was released on 15 March 2016; it is approximately worth £1.2 billion over 20 years and has a strong emphasis on the implementation of transport infrastructure. Also included within the deal are further opportunities in terms of developing digital infrastructure, improving skills and unemployment, delivering enterprise growth and strategic planning for future housing

Figure 4.1: Cardiff Capital Region local authorities

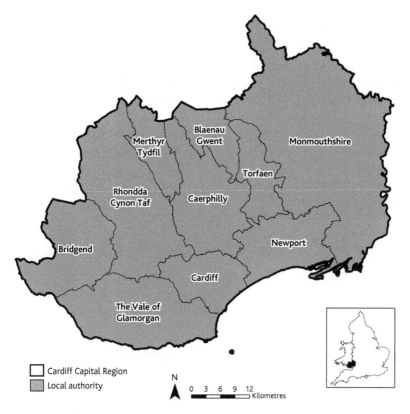

Source: Produced by Sam Jones, WISERD

and regeneration. It seeks to reflect the 'natural' economic footprint of the city-regional area: 'City-region boundaries must reflect economic reality and not political or administrative boundaries. Genuine engagement and meaningful collaboration across many LAs will be needed. This will certainly involve ceding power, funding and decision making to a more regional level' (Welsh Government, 2012: 7). Although the city deal reflects many of the same policy opportunities included in English city and devolution deals, as Figure 4.2 highlights, the structure stops short at devolving revenue generating powers to the region, hence no mayor is required. Instead, a 'CCR Cabinet' acts and comprises the leader from each LA, complemented by a 'CCR Economic Growth Partnership', or as it has been termed the 'CCR Business Council', which looks similar to a LEP, and the 'CCR Business Organisation', which will channel business investment for the city region (see HM Government, 2016; House of Commons Welsh Affairs Committee, 2019). Table 4.1 highlights

Figure 4.2: Shifting governance of the Cardiff Capital Region

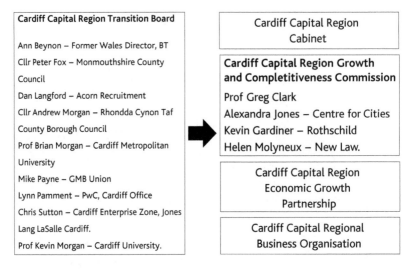

Cardiff Capital Region Transition Board	Cardiff Capital Region Cabinet
Ann Beynon – Former Wales Director, BT	**Cardiff Capital Region Growth and Completitiveness Commission**
Cllr Peter Fox – Monmouthshire County Council	Prof Greg Clark
Dan Langford – Acorn Recruitment	Alexandra Jones – Centre for Cities
Cllr Andrew Morgan – Rhondda Cynon Taf County Borough Council	Kevin Gardiner – Rothschild
Prof Brian Morgan – Cardiff Metropolitan University	Helen Molyneux – New Law.
Mike Payne – GMB Union	Cardiff Capital Region Economic Growth Partnership
Lynn Pamment – PwC, Cardiff Office	
Chris Sutton – Cardiff Enterprise Zone, Jones Lang LaSalle Cardiff.	Cardiff Capital Regional Business Organisation
Prof Kevin Morgan – Cardiff University.	

Source: Authors' analysis

Table 4.1: Business Council membership, 2018

Business Council for the Cardiff Capital Region
Neil Brierley, Faithful + Gould
Ann Beynon, Severn Trent Water and CBI
Katy Chamberlain, Business in Focus
Huw Lewis, Cardiff Airport
Heather Myers, South Wales Chamber of Commerce
Jo Rees, Blake Morgan
Grant Santos, Educ8 Group and FSB
Richard Selby, Pro Steel Engineering
Paul Webber, Arup
Karen Wenborn, SSE PLC, Cardiff
Huw William, University of South Wales

Source: Authors' analysis

the continuation of the privileging of 'business elites' in the process of city-region building, as the appointments to the CCR Business Council only engages active business leaders.[1] This again represents a further difference from the previous Transition Board, which included trade union representation.

The CCR City Deal, like other settlements, focuses its primary concern on strategies for generating economic growth within the city region and for the most part this aims to bolster the opportunities for agglomerative growth within the metropolitan centre of Cardiff.

Despite traversing into other areas, which are related to more social concerns such as skills and unemployment, the focus and success will largely be measured against GVA growth. This represents the overall framing of what a city region is meant to do, that is to generate economic growth, and this is made explicit within the city-deal document itself:

> This City Deal will provide local partners with the powers and the resources to unlock significant economic growth across the Cardiff Capital Region. It is a deal that builds on the region's sectoral strengths, its high skill base and three successful universities. The City Deal also provides an opportunity to continue tackling the area's barriers to economic growth by: improving transport connectivity; increasing skill levels still further; supporting people into work; and giving businesses the support they need to innovate and grow. (HM Government, 2016: 2)

The process of enabling 'local partners' is then central to the process of creating economic growth but the focus on economic growth alone hints at those it is specifically aiming to enable. Added to this, the surrounding media releases on the gov.uk website (see Table 4.2), by various actors involved in creating the deal suggest little else.

Ideologies of growth run deep though the press release statement and several discourse-analytic (Fairclough, 2010) points stand out with regards to the model of growth desired (Clarke et al, 2016) and the prescribed 'representational regime' (Rutherford, 2006) in and through which the city region is envisioned. Table 4.2 represents the order in which the statements were published online cascading from 1st to 5th. This is interesting because it highlights how geographical spatial scale and the production of an information-content hierarchy are deeply intertwined with each other; UK Government first, then Welsh Government, and finally local government and civil society actors last. Each of the statements opens the broader policy framework. Interestingly, the first four respondents all focus on very similar things with regards to: devolution to empowering local leaders; increased private sector investment; the city region as a growth engine to drive investment; more power to local decision makers for transport and infrastructure to aid further aid investment; and the importance of local leaders and authorities working together. Rather poignantly, it is only at the local territorial scale whereby we see a break in this discourse, as the City of Cardiff Council Leader suggests something

Table 4.2: City-deal cascading of representation

	Political actor	Quotation
1st	Chancellor of the Exchequer, George Osborne	'I want to create a devolution revolution around the UK and empower local leaders in Wales, so it's fantastic to announce a historic City deal in the Cardiff City Region worth over £1.2bn.' 'This landmark deal is expected to create up to 25,000 jobs and leverage £4 billion of private sector investment by handing real power to local decision makers that are best placed to ensure the welsh economy is fit for the future.'
2nd	Secretary of State for Wales Stephen Crabb	'Cardiff is one of Europe's youngest and most dynamic capital cities, with a growing international profile and a burgeoning reputation as a destination for businesses to invest.' 'The City Deal provides the springboard for Cardiff to emerge as a leading engine of growth in the UK. It will help transform Cardiff city region, expecting to unlock billions of pounds of private sector finance and deliver thousands of new jobs in South Wales.'
3rd	Chief Secretary to the Treasury, Greg Hands	'I'm very proud to be able to sign this historic deal – the first of its kind in Wales. The UK Government's £500m investment in the economy of South East Wales will help ensure that the infrastructure and transport links in the region come up to the standard that local people and businesses deserve.' 'It's vital that those making these decisions are local leaders, the people that know Cardiff and the wider region best.'
4th	The First Minister of Wales Carwyn Jones	'We have lobbied hard for a City Deal for the Cardiff Capital Region and put more than £500m on the table to support improving transport infrastructure within the region. Today's announcement sees that vision become a reality – it is a vote of confidence in the region and a huge economic boost.' 'Central to the success of a City Deal is the close collaboration and partnership between all ten LAs. It is a great example of what can be achieved by coming together for the greater good of our Capital region.'
5th	City of Cardiff Council Leader, Councillor Phil Bale	'We have worked long and hard to bring a City Deal to the Cardiff Capital Region and I'm delighted we've been successful. Financially we have secured a bigger deal for our residents than the Glasgow City Deal, but the real work starts now.' 'We want this Deal to make a real difference to people's lives, improving prospects for all our citizens. Today's signing means work can begin on creating a more inclusive and prosperous region.' 'I want everyone to know we are determined to deliver better opportunities for all our residents. Securing the City Deal can help us do this. We want to create better job opportunities for people and we want to enable them to take those job opportunities when they arise. At the end of the day we want to improve everyone's chances of enjoying a better future.'

Note: Names and title reflect those in post at the time.

Source: Press Release following the signing of the CCR City Deal, 15 March 2016, www.gov. uk/government/news/cardiff-capital-region-city-deal-signed

slightly more progressive in terms of how this will benefit the lives of people living in the CCR. Hence the 'shadow of hierarchy' (Jessop, 2016a) for these ideologies of growth is rather telling with regards to what is being envisioned in and through the city deal and then which actors it seeks to spatially select.

Placing civil society

The above discussion points towards the defining of what Jenson and Phillips (1996) have termed a 'new citizenship regime', where governance structures are designed in such a way that they legitimise some preferred groups over others. Accordingly: 'Who qualifies and is recognized as a model citizen is under challenge. The legitimacy of group action and the desire for social justice are losing ground to the notion that citizens and interests can compete equally in the political marketplace of ideas' (Jenson and Phillips, 1996: 112). In designing the city region to focus primarily on economic growth as its primary target, this suggests that concerns with regards to more social issues at city-region scale are not as important. Therefore, although each city region will implement its city deal differently, the 'rules of the game' appear to be shaped in one direction. This in turn, enables specific actors, such as those detailed in Figure 4.2 to be active in the process of building the city region. As Jessop (1990, 2008, 2016a) reminds us, the state has 'no power of its own'; state power is defined and aligned according to who has access to, and makes, the state apparatus, and the spatial contexts within which this occurs. In this case, business and political elites are effectively licensed social and civic capital (see Mohan and Mohan, 2002; Painter, 2005) to deliver the city-region neoliberal growth model. As is highlighted by the views of a Transition Board member:

> 'And equally, you don't get the benefit of sufficient quality of advice, because you need someone at a sufficient level where you can attract the right quality of person with the level of expertise across a wider area. So, my view is very much we need that more strategic focus, but we need to achieve economies of scale of delivery, and my view is that we should be having a more technocratic approach to delivery, with targets, and we should have a Regional Development Corporation.' (Interview, Business Leader, CCR, 2017)

This makes it difficult for those who would argue for more socially just or inclusive forms of growth to be implemented as they are distanced from being active in the new citizenship regime. In highlighting how economic growth is envisioned and will be enacted by CCR, the following sections will now discuss the ways in which this has been problematic for civil society members.

Struggling with the economic growth model

The key emphasis, as noted above, is to deliver and enable a governance scale which is best suited for economic growth above all other concerns. This means that other concerns such as social, cultural or environmental factors are considered less important in comparison to creating economic growth. For example, building on our arguments in Chapter 1, the insight below highlights how the agglomerative model of 'boostering' Cardiff may cause further uneven development elsewhere, if not appropriately managed:

> 'We are pushing for the Region as a whole in terms about how the impact will have on those communities furthest away from the nucleus, so you automatically think north in Cardiff's case, so the northern Valleys. It's probably not difficult to correlate the further north you go, then the worse the indices are in terms of deprivation, further away from the economic heartland ... I constantly talked about northern hubs, so actually, because you can't concentrate the economic investment purely into the centre of Cardiff, because we will have to invest billions into infrastructure to create the flow of people that we need to have and then we will stimulate more ghost communities, where people live further away from their caring needs in terms of where they have ageing parents, they have children that they're not close to where they work and they're not spending their money within those communities, so you don't get secondary spend within those communities.' (Interview, Welsh Civil Society Organisation, 2016)

But as has been highlighted above, city deals are not concerned with delivering a spatially even form of growth. They are looking to increase agglomerative growth in urban centres. Consequently, contesting the agglomerative growth logic that sees any growth as good (see Nathan and Overman, 2013) is difficult because this requires a deeply critical approach to the market itself, which is absent from policy discourse as this does not fit with the dominant growth logic presented in the city-deal approach. The quote below articulates this well as it suggests that environmental or social responsibilities sit in the background to economic growth and that raising such concerns makes you less relevant to the process of city-region building:

'My view is very much that it's about creating economic drivers within the region to regenerate and to challenge some of the key matters around things like employment, which in turn should impact on poverty etc. And I think one of the reasons that we're not at the table is we don't talk about the city-region … Certainly I've never picked up there being a sense of the city-region having a similar if not identical … responsibility towards things outside of the economic agenda, things like – environmental responsibilities or even more fundamental social responsibilities. In terms of that definition of it, we're probably seen as not having much of a voice. More likely to speak to businesses and get their views on what is good and what is right about city-region as opposed to the third sector.' (Interview, CCR/Welsh Civil Society Organisation, 2016)

This suggests that the neoliberal market driven approach contained within the CCR City Deal lacks the mechanisms to contest the historic failings of the region with regards to uneven development. The above and below quotes note this, as they suggest that the growth model is repeating the mistakes of the past due to the reliance on a 'trickle-down' approach:

'Well at the moment, we seem to be looking at measures for economic development, transport and a market-based model. What I would – I think it's that terrible phrase, in terms of the wealth that we generate 'trickling down' into other communities which again historically is not really showing there's much to be said for that.' (Interview, CCR/Welsh Civil Society Organisation, 2016)

Scale and accountability

Interviews with CCR civil society members also raised an ongoing tension between the concept of localism and the city region. The production of the city region changes the relationships of scale between civil society organisations and how they may engage with the 'local' state:

> 'All of a sudden we become completely insignificant so whereas at the moment locally we can lobby quite hard and push the direction on certain things, all of that power would go away and how to influence rather than power. So that for us would cause quite a significant problem. If we start working more collaboratively with other similar organisations then great, we can form a nice little consortium and then we can retain the same level of perceived power and all will be well with the world. But it doesn't fit well with how any of us work really; we work with quite defined communities, we do quite tailored things for them.' (Interview, CCR Housing Association, 2015)

As we noted in Chapter 1, the process of what Cox (1998) refers to as 'scale jumping', alluded to in the above quote, again represents a significant problem to civil society organisations working in the city region. As for the most part civil society organisations do not exist on a city-region scale and hence due to their size cannot scale up to address both the needs of the entire city region or contest its rhetoric: "In terms of the city-region stuff, I feel we've been stung in how we can engage. We've been very interested in engaging but I don't think organisations like ours are perceived as being a big enough hitter or having a big enough economic impact to interest them" (Interview, CCR Community, 2016). This means local voices can be marginalised through what Fraser (2010) and Pemberton (2016) call 'scalecraft' (the layered processes and practices of making geographical scale) as the governance structures of city region make them inactive and less relevant to the larger strategic plans for economic development. Pemberton adds:

> A focus on scalecraft highlights that a wider range of actors – including states, social and political groups and individuals – are all involved in scalar practices (Fraser, 2010: 334), and may be attempting to produce, restructure and rescale local government. In so doing, they seek to create competitive advantage or establish associations or connections to present their interests. (2016: 1309)

This is being employed through the city region to depoliticise its economic intentions (see Etherington and Jones, 2018). We have highlighted how contesting the economic model was difficult and this section compounds this by the process of shifting the governance regime on economic development away from democratic accountability at the local level. This intervention of state restructuring and the creation of soft space institutions (Haughton et al, 2013) that hold power chimes with others' observations of how urban governance regimes seek to displace dissent away from their activities as they build a hegemonic consensus to create economic development (Burnham, 2014; Etherington and Jones, 2016a; Foster et al, 2014; Jessop, 2014). In moving forward, this raises serious questions around the future of representation in soft institutional spaces such as growth boards especially if large proportions of civil society actors are placed outside the new citizenship regime. This has left civil society actors precariously positioned with regards to responding to new 'devolved' governance structures and reduced LA budgets. Wales, however, does operate differently to England and there is provision within law through the Wellbeing of Future Generations Act (Welsh Government, 2015a) that suggests local and civil society organisations are entitled to forms of representation.

Austerity geographies

Austerity in Wales has landed differently to the way it has been delivered in England, due to the Welsh Government passing on the cuts differently (see Jones et al, 2016). This has meant that LAs did not need to cut as deeply and as quickly, initially. Significant cuts have come later to LAs, as the respondents below suggest:

> 'Well obviously, we've seen massive, massive cuts in Welsh Government budget and that has been, in the main, passed on to local government so it's the local government, I would say, is probably the largest hit.' (Interview, CCR/National Level Trade Union, 2016)

> 'So, in my own view, just from what I can see, the impact of austerity, yes, it was back-loaded, but actually, when it came about, would have had a higher impact on those communities where we've got less private sector employment opportunities, so it would probably be very

similar within inner-city areas as well, if they've lost some
of their key services and they haven't been replaced with
jobs from the private sector.' (Interview, Welsh Civil Society
Organisation, 2016)

This has impacted civil society groups in a number of ways, but
primarily it has left them squeezed between reduced national and local
state funding opportunities, while at the same time facing increased
demand for the services they offer. For example, the phasing out of
Communities First has substantially affected several local community
groups (Dicks, 2014). Further to this, austerity has been viewed to be
shifting the relationships between 'civil society', 'state' and 'business'.

'Well that is a very interesting one; I think the tectonic plates
are changing. For us, the future in terms of being grant-aided
by government, that really isn't going to happen. We know
that the public sector and its days of supporting the third sector
in the way it has are coming to an end. We have to find, if we
are going to thrive and grow, new relationships and those new
relationships are probably going to have to be with business.'
(Interview, CCR voluntary and community sector, 2016)

The above insight is interesting because it suggests a changing set of
relationships between state, business, and civil society whereby as the
state reduces its support, civil society may potentially have to face a
difficult choice. Should it slot more deeply into the neoliberal growth
model, which makes it difficult for such actors to then contest the
economic rationale of the city region? The respondent reflects on this
further, suggesting a number of different possibilities into the future:

'Is there going to be businesses falling by the wayside? Will
there be more of a collaboration – a merger approach? Will
new business opportunities be sought and be successfully
sought, where the emphasis very much is on winning
new business opportunities rather than going for grants,
looking for investment? – are we going to have to move
to a low investment scenario which people haven't whole
heartedly embraced in the past? As I say, I do get a bit
focused on services, I do see social businesses working in
services, complementary to public services or non-statutory
public services of picking up services. I guess there hasn't
been a massive push for externalisation that there has been

in England.' (Interview, CCR voluntary and community sector, 2016)

Hence, as the above suggests, the terrain is shifting quickly and this is reshaping the very structure of civil society organisations and the way in which they will or will not have a role in to the future with regards to the building CCR.

Conclusions

This chapter has sought to traverse and situate the complexities of devolution, city-region building, and the (re)positioning of civil society through the development of the CCR. We have looked at the ways in which the UK state both defines and limits devolution and in this case frames the CCR City Deal. This is, of course, a geographical process, with existing geographies influencing the form and shape of any outcomes from deal-making public policy (Peck and Theodore, 2015).

In the context of building the CCR, a simplistic top down narrative of central government implementation and civil society reaction would not have addressed the complexity of the *realpolitik* in play. Hence, the historical legacy of economic and governance failures has created new geographies of governance and these are playing out differently in Wales. Welsh city-region building reflects this as devolution, with austerity and local government reorganisation creating different structures for city deals. Although on-the-surface city regions from the UK Government are the 'same policy', when filtered through scales of governance, the city region is being transformed differently. This reflects a recasting of central–local relations (Jones, 1999; Peck, 1995) at all scales of governance: LA – city region – Welsh Government – UK Government. Added to this, the city-region agenda has also attempted to construct nascent relationships of reciprocity between city regions. In the case of CCR, this means looking to the east and working with Bristol through the creation of the 'Western Powerhouse'.[2] Again this raises a series of further questions for the notion of 'scalecraft' for CCR and the Welsh state.

Specifically, this chapter has sought to empirically demonstrate how both an 'agent and obstacle' (Duncan and Goodwin, 1988) relationship has unfolded in Wales, as different governance institutions interact spatially. Therefore, despite their political manoeuvrings to secure a city deal, the CCR LAs are still greatly constrained by a lack of fiscal powers and in their subservience to both the Welsh and UK

Governments. This is highlighted by their inability to negate austerity and they are hence forced to deliver the necessary cuts as they are passed down to them while still implementing the city deal. Within these processes, we have revealed how civil society has been positioned outside the representational regime, but is also expected to play along in terms of engaging with the neoliberal growth model as austerity reshapes public service reform. This raises interesting questions with regards what role or influence civil society will have to shape a more progressive city region.

5

Beyond cities in regions

Introduction

This chapter questions where rural regions are being placed within the context of neoliberal growth strategies that posit agglomerative accumulation, that is policies to nurture value growth (primarily measured by GVA uplift), which is mainly aimed at the urban and more recently city-region spatial scale (Brenner and Schmid, 2011; Woods and Heley, 2017). The rural development question (Pemberton, 2019; Ward, 2006) is an enduring puzzle, which has eluded policymakers globally (Bock, 2016), while being consistently undermined by an urban bias (Hoggart, 2005). The global focus on the development of city regions and their implicit scalar, geopolitical and geoeconomic framing (Jonas and Moisio, 2018; Calzada, 2017), continues to reinforce this dynamic. Focusing on urban growth strategies, the chapter considers what this means for rural regions as they attempt to articulate growth strategies of their own, while being entangled within broader metagovernance processes surrounding economic development (Jessop, 2016b; see also Nelles, 2012; Winter, 2006). We highlight how rural regions struggle to create effective economic policy when they are cast as peripheral, or in the orbit, of major urban conurbations (Harrison and Heley, 2015), as such disparities have the potential to exacerbate the problems of combined and uneven development.

We have argued throughout this book that the UK is witnessing important 'state spatial restructuring' (Brenner, 2004, 2019) developments through the creation of 'city-region building state projects' (Jones, 2019a, 2019b). Since the election of the Coalition Government in 2010, UK policy on economic growth has shifted towards a 'city-first' approach (Deas, 2014). This can be seen in a multitude of city and devolution deals to UK city regions (see O'Brien and Pike, 2015). This has somewhat left non-core city (second-tier) and rural areas behind in policy terms, but attempts are being made to address this in more rural areas such as North Wales (see Harrison and Heley, 2015). With the development of two city regions in South Wales (CCR and SBCR), this has left the rest of Wales somewhat lacking with regards to the future of economic development outside its metropolitan areas. This has partly led to a process of 'region-making' within the rest of Wales as the remaining eight of twenty-two LAs have sought to find ways to collaboratively work together (Jones et al, 2016).

Alongside this has been an ongoing reform process of LAs in Wales that has sought to find ways for LAs to work more 'collaboratively' together (Welsh Government, 2015b). The North Wales region is advancing both agendas by signing a Growth Deal (NWGD) with the UK Government. This though raises several questions, which need to be addressed, if such a deal is to be compatible with the region's existing economic footprint and its continuing struggle to address issues of uneven development. The chapter highlights how policy discourses have been transferred from a primarily city region – metrocentric – approach to a rural, regional, approach that combines North Wales's LAs into a growth deal. This raises a series of tensions and challenges around how policy is transferred and transformed when it moves geographically. More critically, the chapter questions the mode of growth implied in such policy for North Wales as not addressing the spatial constraints already being placed on this region. Further, the 'tangled governance' (Jessop, 2016b) of the deal-making process itself, due to the often-misaligned policy intentions of the UK and Welsh Governments and the LAs themselves, raises a series of questions with regards to what policy options are viable. In turn, this reflects the significant tension with regards to what each stakeholder seeks from the growth deal process itself (see Economy, Infrastructure and Skills Committee, 2017).

North Wales consists of six LAs[1] along the A55 coastal corridor, from the island of Anglesey (Ynys Môn) in the north west (NW), to Flintshire in the north east (NE). The region could be described as a 'tale of two halves'; or alternatively, 'East, West and the bit in the middle' (Mann and Plows, 2016). The labour market of NE Wales is very different to NW Wales; essentially NE Wales is more industrial, with a strong manufacturing base, and greater existing connectivity to NW England; NW Wales is more rural, peripheral and de-industrialised, with a much higher percentage of its workforce in sectors such as tourism and agriculture, sectors of the labour market which are traditionally lower-paid and precarious – often seasonal and/or short term. Collectively, across the region, there is no main metropolitan centre, with the largest town being Wrexham (circa 60,000 people) in the NE.

It is within this majorly rural spatial context that the chapter considers the development of a Growth Deal for North Wales and the problems it has faced in attempting to transfer (urban) economic policy into the region. The chapter is divided into three main sections. It first, conceptually and in terms of policy interventions, considers what this means with regards to the transfer of policy from urban areas to rural ones – in particular, the transference of economic policy that is focused on creating agglomerative growth in a region with only small and dispersed centres of population. This places rural regions within the context of city-region building and due to a city-first approach, not only are rural areas often left behind, but there is also a lack of policy imagination being deployed to serve the economic needs of rural regions. Second, it unpacks the specifics of the NWGD and focuses on how this is seeking to generate economic growth and how this more broadly sits within the devolved nation of Wales as a whole. Wales is a devolved nation within the UK (alongside Scotland and Northern Ireland) and has its own policy trajectory within certain parameters, economic development being one such area (Heley, 2013; Jones et al, 2016). This is important to comprehend, because with the development of two city regions across South Wales, this has left a policy vacuum on economic development across the rest of Wales, which the chapter highlights within the devolved sub-national context of Wales. Third, it looks at how actors in North Wales are seeking to influence and shape a growth deal, replete with inbuilt tensions and challenges around this urban model for growth, set against the ground realities of the North Wales rural economy.

Making non-metropolitan spaces in a city-region world

As this book has suggested, the city region has been identified as the de facto scale for urban governance in contemporary economic development policy. We argued in the previous chapter that in the UK's devolved context, this has reflected the failure to deliver economic growth previously in Wales and a shift has taken place from the 'soft spaces and the fuzzy boundaries' of the WSP (Heley, 2013) to a more territorialised city-regional spatio-temporal fix (Waite et al, 2013; Waite, 2015). This, of course, has paralleled similar territorial shifts in England and Scotland, reflecting a dominant and 'triumphalist' city-first approach (Glaeser, 2012). Waite and Morgan (2019) refer to this as 'metrophilia', whereby it is seen as fashionable to uncritically embrace such approaches.[2] They suggest that:

> cities are the quintessential spaces where knowledge is generated and valorised because cities are the chief beneficiaries of agglomeration economies ... Although

exhibiting national variations, Metrophilia has international currency as we see governments, supported by think tanks and travelling bands of consultants, championing the metropolitan narrative regardless of spatial context. (2019: 384)

This, as the quote above suggests, means such processes move across (devolved) state boundaries as their application becomes scaled on the perceived problem in economic performance they are trying to fix (see Blackaby et al, 2018; Harrison, 2007; Waite and Bristow, 2019; Waite and Morgan, 2019). With such policy movements, there is only often a circumstantial evidence base to such 'successes' and the literature often has a habit of only picking the 'winners' to such strategies (Jonas and Ward, 2007). Rehearsing our argument again, the central tenant of this is theories of urban-scaled agglomeration (see Overman, 2012). The city region is nothing short of a crucible for creating economic growth, whereby through creating an agglomerating critical mass of economic activity in central urban areas, harnessed around public–private partnerships and involving civil society actors, economic development can be ubiquitously secured (see Ellison et al, 2007). This in turn helps to construct a specific 'spatial imaginary' for North Wales in relation to economic development, which attempts to construe a narrative or cultural hegemony for the North Wales region, in part reflecting on historic geographic differences to the rest of Wales and England, while at the same time ignoring differences that exist at the sub-regional level. As MacLeod (1998) has argued in the case of Scotland, 'historically contingent' specific administrative boundaries and regional spaces were created and imposed onto communities for whom these boundaries were perhaps less meaningful. Here, growth deals can also be seen to be a new type of region-shaping, whereby North Wales and its sub-regional geographies are policy-squeezed into a hegemonic construct for the purposes of economic development, where there is perhaps minimal consideration to the specificity of place or differences between rural and urban areas (Harrison and Heley, 2015).

All this raises critical questions for predominantly rural areas and regions (such as North Wales) due to the type, nature and geographic focus of growth being aimed for, which is also problematic to cities in a variety of ways (Jonas, 2012). Rural areas in this model of growth are either presented as the periphery to the city-regions urban centre (Pain, 2008) or are faced with finding ways to map onto their existing economic strategy more agglomerative strategies which may further increase uneven development (Etherington and Jones, 2009). Harrison and Heley (2015) highlight the normative nature in which this casts the relationships between urban and rural via city-regional policy. They suggest that this places the 'rural development problem' within the 'new territorial politics' of the city region, whereby the urban–rural divide can be overcome by 'functionally networked, not territorially-embedded administrative, geographies' (Harrison and Heley, 2015: 1114–15). For Ward (2006), alongside Harrison and Heley, this represents a regressive policy framework for rural areas:

> The city-region approach reproduces a rural development problem. It establishes and reinforces out-of-date notions of geographical centrality and hierarchies, and it actively marginalises places, consigning them to the periphery, dividing and polarising. City regions are taking root in regional economic development and spatial planning across the UK, and they are raising profound challenges for those involved in the economic development of rural areas. (Ward, 2006: 52)

The city-region agenda, therefore, applies a geographic concentration on urban areas while attempting to relationally network rural areas; the question then becomes does this approach lead to the empowerment of civil society and an even spreading of economic and social gains? As highlighted above and by others, such an approach potentially marginalises the rural due to the dominance of metropolitan centres, creating further uneven growth for rural areas (Shucksmith, 2008). It also fails to consider the ways in which areas external to the city region are capable of creating different models of economic growth that do not rely on urban agglomeration (Harrison and Heley, 2015; Haughton et al, 2016). The city-region agenda, therefore, shapes geoeconomic policy with a specific geopolitical focus and as Harrison and Heley suggest, this needs to be unpacked when looking at the building of rural regions, where a city-region building approach is dominant:

> This is due in large part to their different geo-political constructions of city-regionalism. In this way it also provides a revealing context from which to unpack how and why city-regionalism continues to be constructed geo-politically to the detriment of rural spaces and rural development needs, and to begin considering how to build these interstitial spaces between metropolitan areas into our theories of city-regionalism. (Harrison and Heley, 2015: 1116)

In the context of this chapter and developments within North Wales, we take several points of departure from the above discussion on rural development and city-region building. These include: a need to think through what rationales underpin the government(s) policy towards delivering economic growth in North Wales; the ways in which policies reflect the on-the-ground economic reality of North Wales, this includes existing successful economic growth in the region alongside problems of continuing combined and uneven development; and how policies for economic growth are transferred and shaped in different geographical settings. These points, therefore, allow for broader discussion to consider how policy should address 'interstitial spaces' in a city-region world. By interstitial spaces, we mean considering spatial formations that sit outside the dominant city-region discourse and how they form their own approaches to delivering economic development. Currently and what the following critique will suggest is that such interstitial spaces, like developing rural regions, still sit within an economic policy focus that is too heavily skewed towards and driven by a city-region approach. This fits with what Midmore (2018) comprehends as the economic 'myths' embedded in conventional economic thinking for rural regions, whereby the process of regionalisation gives credence to a discrete rural economy, that in reality does not exist. In the case of Wales, as we note in Chapters 4 and 6, the process of delivering city deals for the CCR and SBCR has partly driven the need to then address how to regionalise the regions to the North in the pursuit of economic growth (Blackaby et al, 2018). The chapter argues for the need to consider a new economic paradigm for rural regions – one that steps outside of the city-region approach.

Making interstitial spaces: the Growth Deal approach revisited

With the 'swing' (Jones, 2019a, 2019b) of UK sub-national policy moving towards city regions, and specifically a metropolitan focus post-2010, a variety of policy mechanisms have been deployed in an attempt to boost economic growth, with one of these being the 'Growth Deal' approach (BIS, 2011; HM Government, 2013). The policy of delivering Growth Deals by the UK Government began in England and has been a mechanism by which to fund and fuel LEPs. As noted in the Introduction, they have sat alongside various forms of deal-making public policy, which include both City Deals and Devolution Deals (see O'Brien and Pike, 2015). Growth, City and Devolution Deals, as the name(s) suggest, require negotiation, which takes place between the UK Government and the specific LA or CA (LEPs and LAs in England) (Etherington and Jones, 2018; Pugalis and Townsend, 2012). There have been several rounds of deal-making whereby in simple terms, collaborating LAs (in England) have progressed on a continuum from Growth and City Deals to Devolution Deals, although this has not been a linear or even process on speed and resources. There has also been a priority on granting such deals to metropolitan-combined LAs first (such as the Core Cities – see Deas, 2013), before deals are granted to less urban and more rural collaborating LAs. The metropolitan centres have consequently seen much larger and wide-ranging deals being granted (Shaw and Tewdwr-Jones, 2017).

In Wales, there have been City Deals to both the CCR and the SBCR (HM Government, 2017, 2016). These came later in the deal negotiating process (the CCR was signed in March 2016; the SBCR in March 2017) compared to those in England and Scotland, which were delivered much earlier in the Coalition Government's tenure (National Audit Office, 2016). This reflected a slow process of negotiation between the collaborating LAs and then a protracted negotiating period between those LAs, the Welsh Government and UK Government. Such deals though have only covered South Wales and this leaves the rest of Wales without any growth framework in place not counting Welsh Government and individual LA plans. This has led to the North Wales LAs, since late 2017, to seek and lobby for a Growth Deal to shape economic development practice outside of this urban context but constrained-by-design within the city-first policy frameworks (Blackaby et al, 2018). The UK and Welsh Governments, alongside the Welsh LAs all have different visions as to what this process of deal making is for. This is highlighted by the Welsh Assembly's Economy, Infrastructure and Skills Committee (2017), that reveals how the processes and practices of city and growth deal-making mean that respective governance institutions have very different ambitions. Its negotiation and the possible policy levers available are, therefore, constrained in potentially disparate directions (cf. Chapter 4, with its focus on the CCR City Deal). In the case of the NWGD, this has led to a slowing in the ability to close the growth deal and a protracted wrangle over funding contributions.[3]

Devolved regions in action: placing North Wales

Wales has a complicated and difficult geography, which reflects the main centres of population being in the south with the cities of Cardiff and Swansea, and a mountainous physical geography to the north, which makes for more rural and dispersed population demographics (Lovering, 1983). This impacts on how policy is applied in Wales with regards to governance (Pemberton, 2016) as the Welsh Assembly attempts to address the problems created by this difficult geography. This, therefore, influences how investment is spread and attracted to Wales as well as how services are provided across the nation. This has led to several overlapping governance territorialisations across Wales, as different actors exist on different footprints (Local Government, Health, Police, Fire Services and DWP). At a national level, since devolution, Wales has struggled to develop economically to the extent that proponents of devolution would have liked, and in comparison to the rest of the UK (Bristow, 2018; Blackaby et al, 2018; Gardiner et al, 2013). Added to this, since 2010, as in much of the UK, austerity has been an important factor impacting on the functioning of the Welsh Government and the LAs. This is reflected in how the Welsh Government has sought to restructure local government under a time of austerity, via the Williams Commission, whereby it has looked for LAs to find ways to consolidate services and, if desired, combine them (Welsh Government, 2017a). Current developments fall well short with regards to what was suggested by the Williams Commission, but highlight a rationalisation and collaboration direction of travel for the Welsh Government.

It is within this climate of joint working between LAs that, in South Wales, two city regions have been created via LA collaboration and in turn this has led to North Wales seeking a Growth Deal for. The 'region' of North Wales also reflects a complicated geography, highlighted by The WSP (Welsh Government, 2008), which identified the different regions of Wales as having extremely 'fuzzy boundaries', with stretched-out and relational public policy interventions occurring in some instances (see Orford and Webb, 2018). 'North Wales' stretches into what has been called the 'Deep Rural' (Wales Rural Observatory, 2009) of mid-Wales; for example, where southern Gwynedd (Meirionnydd), blurs into the mid-Wales LAs of Powys and Ceredigion. Then to the north and east, the Mersey Dee Alliance (MDA) reflects the cross-border relationships linking Flintshire and Wrexham with Cheshire and NW England (see Figure 5.1). 'North Wales', then, stretches and blurs across different borders and boundaries (Mann and Plows, 2016) and this blurring is reflected in policy initiatives such as the MDA. Further to this, North Wales is surrounded by a plethora of English City regions, particularly Liverpool and Greater Manchester. Importantly, North Wales is also made up of very distinctive and more territorially bounded sub-regions, or localities, with their own local

Figure 5.1: North Wales political geography

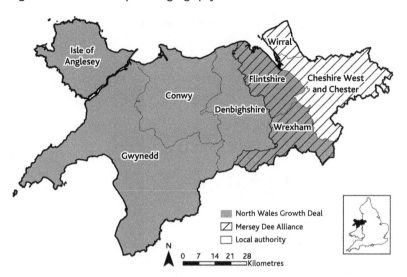

Source: Produced by Sam Jones, WISERD

characteristics and with very different labour market and other social demographics, such as the very marked difference in the percentage of Welsh language speakers in NE and NW Wales. These differences in local characteristics are important; they present locally specific challenges and opportunities.[4]

This is further reflected in a series of economic regional variations across North Wales. The differences highlight the variegated nature of the region and questions whether it exists as a truly economically functional region. The regional divergence, for instance, in the labour market is reflected in the GVA per head for North Wales (Figure 5.2).

These differences in the labour market are also reflected in the relative size of employers situated across North Wales. There is a marked regional split between NE and NW Wales, whereby larger firms predominate in the east, whereas small to medium enterprises are more significant in the west.

Collectively, this suggests a variegated economy across North Wales, as well as a region that does not have a functional economic area of its own (Lovering, 1983). This means that developing policy that enables economic growth across the region is difficult; different sub-regions require different forms of support to better enhance their economic performance. The aim of generating agglomerative economic growth for a metropolitan centre then means that sub-city regional and peripheral differences do not matter if the centre is growing (see

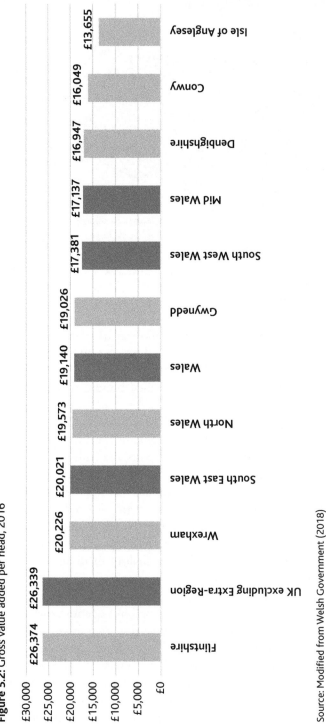

Figure 5.2: Gross value added per head, 2016

- Isle of Anglesey £13,655
- Conwy £16,049
- Denbighshire £16,947
- Mid Wales £17,137
- South West Wales £17,381
- Gwynedd £19,026
- Wales £19,140
- North Wales £19,573
- South East Wales £20,021
- Wrexham £20,226
- UK excluding Extra-Region £26,339
- Flintshire £26,374

Source: Modified from Welsh Government (2018)

Fujita and Krugman, 1995; Krugman, 1998; Overman, 2012). In a rural region such a centre does not exist, therefore, there is no focal point for growth. The labour market and firm composition differences between NE and NW Wales, therefore, will affect the likely impacts and uptake of economic development opportunities in the region. This is because as growth stimuli is applied and if successful, it will have uneven impacts across an already unevenly developed regional space. It is important though to note here that the Welsh Index of Multiple Deprivation shows that there are micro localities (Lower Layer Super Output Areas, LSOAs) with very high levels of deprivation within LAs across North Wales, so the picture is much more complex than simply one of an 'affluent NE Wales versus a struggling NW Wales'.

This means the NWGD faces a series of challenges that are quite different to that faced by most urban areas, which to date have benefitted from Growth Deals. For North Wales, we identify a series of key challenges facing the region which are: the before mentioned regional imbalances; the lack of a Welsh 'Mittelstand' and supply chain capacity (CRESC, 2015); the potential impact of Brexit; and a lack of quality employment opportunities and the related skills gap. These also sit alongside the considerable challenges of continuing austerity; lack of infrastructure (although problematic in itself); various health challenges related to geography and deprivation; and the changing demographics of the region. There is, therefore, a critical question moving forward – does the NWGD tackle these issues of rural development or exacerbate them?

The North Wales Growth Deal

In attempting to deal with these difficult and overlapping geographies, LAs have sought to develop a Growth Deal for North Wales with the UK Government via the North Wales Economic Ambition Board (NWEAB). This is because local and national actors are promoting the growth deal framework as the *only* opportunity available to the region to address its economic needs, whereby, the collective effort of North Wales LAs could deliver growth for the region: "The North Wales county councils are proud to have submitted a growth bid for North Wales. The region is unified in recognising the need to transform the way the region's economy is structured" (Interview, Wales Leaders Group for Economic Growth, 2017). The NWGD and its negotiation reproduces the 'spatial imaginary' of North Wales as a bounded region, which can then be connected to other spatial imaginaries such as the Northern Powerhouse (see Berry and Giovannini, 2018). This is important because, despite the differentiated nature of the region, the narrative of a collaborative, functioning and bounded regional entity is essential to giving sufficient scale to make a potential growth deal plausible. To date, a deal has not been finalised but the direction of travel for the deal is relatively clear. This is because, like other Growth, City and Devolution Deals at this regional scale, only certain competencies are offered to LAs in pursuit of economic development (O'Brien and Pike, 2015).

The six LAs have pitched to the UK Government a deal worth £1.3 billion (with leveraged finance) with £383.4 million coming directly from UK and Welsh Governments. With regards headline figures, this aims to create an uplift in GDP for the region from around £12 billion (2015) to £20 billion by 2035 and to create 5,000 jobs (NWEAB, 2018). The bid has three main themes: 'Smart North Wales', focusing on innovation in high value sectors; 'Connected North Wales', addressing transport and digital infrastructure; and 'Resilient North Wales', seeking to retain young people, raise employment levels and improve skills to achieve inclusive growth (NWEAB, 2018: 3). Broadly, this includes focusing on low carbon and nuclear energy – including regeneration at Trawsfynydd; university research; better transport links; growing digital businesses; and increasing skills and opportunities to keep more young people in the area. Several stakeholders interviewed are hopeful that the Growth Deal could help with regard to political and economic 'clout': "It's a new way of working ... we need to be more like the private sector ... they don't recognise [LA] borders" (Interview, Anglesey Council, 2016).

Several stakeholders are of the opinion that this approach could help a 'parochial and inward-looking' (Interviewee, Anglesey Council, 2017) NW Wales to become more outward facing. Partnership working is seen as potentially facilitating additional 'clout' because all LAs and different agencies are 'speaking with one voice'. It is clear that the stimulus of the Growth Deal has already catalysed a significant amount of regional partnership working – 'Team North Wales'. According to one commentator:

> 'Economic leaders across the region are agreed on a collaborative approach, and are driving the work collectively on a singular regional approach to the Growth Bid – this is supported by regional leaders and key politicians, and is to be further developed and promoted as an inclusive approach that delivers "Team North Wales".' (Interview, NWEAB, 2017)

The NWGD is aimed to strategically enhance the impact and value of independent but strategically linked inward investment/economic development initiatives, some of which are well developed (such as Parc Adfer, Deeside, and HMP Berwyn prison and others at least under way or stalled – such as a new nuclear plant on Anglesey-Wylfa Newydd). The NWEAB's *Growth Vision* report (2016) sets out a very comprehensive 'roadmap' of these inward investment projects, which are (strategically and discursively) linked to the region's three Enterprise Zones (manufacturing in Deeside, energy on Anglesey and ICT and aerospace in Snowdonia).

Several of the stakeholders interviewed are understandably 'bullish' and optimistic about these projects, which are described as being 'significant opportunities' (Interview, 2017) for the region's economy and labour market, with positive impacts on employment and for developing supply chain opportunities. There was a great deal of optimism from the stakeholders most closely involved with strategic planning and delivery of these initiatives, who have built additional capacity as a result of learning from the economic shocks of the recession, de-industrialisation and associated mass redundancies: "there is a sense of real opportunity for change and growth in the region [which] is aspiring to grow … The impacts and implications of mass redundancies of the past has resulted in the growing, aspirational economy that North Wales is today" (Interview, NWEAB, 2017). One of the primary focuses to the NWGD is on transport infrastructure, which aims to do two things: to better connect the region internally and then externally to NW England. With specific reference to bordering English LAs, such as those contained within the MDA, this reflects the existing 'functional economy' of the region, which sits across the Wales/England border. Added to this, is also the pre-existing 'spatial imaginary' of the Northern Powerhouse, which is also seen as a strategic opportunity for the North Wales economy due to its geographical positioning and relative ease of commuting:

> The North Wales Growth Bid will be aligned to the strategies for the Northern Powerhouse and the immediate North West of England, specifically the strategy of the Mersey Dee Alliance and close partnerships including the Cheshire and Warrington Local Enterprise Partnership … The work is strongly aligned to the national aims of the UK Industrial Strategy and the WG [Welsh Government] Economic Plan. (NWEAB, 2018: 12)

The NWGD, therefore, seeks to align itself towards the North (West) of England and the developing agglomeration economies of two city regions. This interestingly focuses the NWGD away from South Wales and Cardiff (see Economy, Infrastructure and Skills Committee, 2017). This has meant strong emphasis has been placed on the development of road and rail infrastructure, which is especially focused on the north east of the region, with the North East Metro cited as a key infrastructure development (Welsh Government, 2017c).

The NWGD also seeks to address what is seen as the underperformance of the region due to its peripheral location in both the UK and Welsh economies. This seeks to unite actors at all levels (LA, Welsh Government and UK Government) in wishing to negotiate such a deal and highlights the economic rationales that are in play with regards to how best secure growth:

> A North Wales growth deal will revolutionise the way our towns and villages in North-Wales govern themselves – shifting powers down from London and Cardiff to local leaders who are better placed to take decisions that affect their communities. The Northern Powerhouse, coupled with a growth deal represents our best chance to bring transformational change to North Wales. (Welsh Government, 2017b, quoting Guto Bebb, Wales Office Minister)

Approximately, the NWGD hoped to secure a £335.5 million split between the Welsh and UK Governments, with a further £219 million coming from universities and colleges and around £109 million upfront from businesses. The NWGD, therefore, hoped to secure around £3.1 billion of private sector funding alongside this over the long-term of the growth deal. Signed in November 2019, this was negotiated down to a £240 million package, split equally between the UK and Welsh Government, with the private sector and other partners committing to make up the rest of the investment (see HM Government and Welsh Government, 2019).

Discussion: Does the Growth Deal 'fit'? Critiques and caveats

The chapter turns to consider whether such a deal is appropriately framed to address the needs of North Wales and in what ways the Growth Deal is deeply problematic in its approach for addressing those locality needs.

Drawing on the interviews, stakeholders voiced concerns about the lack of evidence for the (urban-transferred) growth deal model, in relation to cross-border working relationships; the focus on infrastructure and skills; the 'city deal' trickle-down approach; and the evidence base for 'cluster' approaches. Further concerns were raised around the potential for these approaches to have negative impacts, such as displacement and disruption, particularly at the periphery. The following section, therefore, seeks to raise a series of concerns that the Growth Deal approach creates, as the proposed growth policies shift to a rural setting.

Policy discourse versus geographical reality

'There's a disconnect between these big schemes and peripheral economic wellbeing ... the jury's out on city deals and growth deals; there's patchy evidence at best ... no data to say it's contributing positively.' (Interview, Colegau Cymru, 2017)

One of the central problems with the Growth Deal approach is the circumspect evidence on which it is built. Ward and Jonas (2004) suggest that such approaches often have a habit of only focusing on areas that have been successful for their evidence base, while neglecting areas that have failed in the implementation of such strategies. Interviewees, in several contexts where they perceived evidence gaps to be present, further highlight this. Examples given include: little evidence on the successful working of cross-border economic partnerships with few examples of what 'best practice' is, or an understanding of what the pitfalls to this approach could be; the viability of the 'trickle-down' effect of inward investment and infrastructure development to local suppliers, local economy, the periphery; and whether infrastructure and skills investment actually delivers sustainable and evenly spread economic growth and quality employment or whether it exacerbates uneven growth. On the 'what, why and how' of micro businesses and self-employment, which make up the bulk of businesses especially in rural (North) Wales, there has also been little attempt to find out more about what they need/want, particularly regarding their willingness and capacity to 'scale up'. Throughout, possible impacts of 'Brexit' on current/planned initiatives and policies run deep as concerns. Added to this, the viability of North Wales as a functional economic area is questioned, due to the region's divergent east/west split. Therefore, the NWGD continues to perpetuate a 'spatial imaginary', which may be geographically defined, but is poorly connected in economic terms – especially when the importance of cross border relationships defines more accurately the functional economy of the region. This, therefore, suggests that for North Wales the Growth Deal will deliver at best very uneven benefits for the region.

The key proposals of the NWGD are more likely to deliver enhanced economic development for NE Wales than for NW Wales. This is an issue of existing capacity and connectivity; stakeholders note that Flintshire/Wrexham is already 'more aligned' with Cheshire and Warrington, as embodied in the MDA; NE Wales LAs 'already work with Manchester, Liverpool'; this cross-border work is 'business as usual' for NE Wales. While the hope is that improving connectivity will provide opportunities, which penetrate to the peripheral areas of NW Wales, several stakeholders felt that the benefits were realistically more likely to accrue to NE Wales.

> 'On a certain level its already happening – the Mersey/ Dee Alliance – Wrexham/Flintshire – they are currently able to access cross border relationships ... [there are further developments of cross border schemes which are] aspirational at the moment ... I think some of the NE industries, chamber of commerce [are more likely to] see the opportunities.' (Interview, NWEAB, 2017)

For example, in terms of infrastructure, several stakeholders felt that there are 'real benefits' with regards to improving transport connections between the already closely connected regions of NE Wales and Manchester/Crewe (NW England), but that this would not necessarily help NW Wales.

Several stakeholders also felt that it is uncertain and unproven that cross-border growth and development in NW England and NE Wales will stimulate or facilitate supply and demand side capacity in peripheral NW Wales, to any significant extent.

> 'I don't think that you get trickle down/spin out to the periphery ... culturally and politically that's very difficult to do ... it's wishful thinking [that the periphery will benefit] ... capital infrastructure accrues capital to areas, which are already strong.' (Interview, Colegau Cymru, 2017)

> 'We want to grow the whole of North Wales as a region [of Wales] rather than suck people into the NE ... we shouldn't rely on [cross border growth] as the only growth deal for

N Wales ... there's a danger of hype which could turn the NW Wales population off. There are regional opportunities, which are immediate and current.' (Interview, Civil Society Stakeholder, 2017)

The labour market differences between NE and NW Wales outlined earlier were identified as central to some interviewees' concerns about the NWGD as it currently stands. A concern raised by several interviewees is, therefore, that the emphasis on big infrastructure projects does not sufficiently address the locally specific characteristics of the North Wales region. This raises a series of questions with regards to the Growth Deal approach to address the needs of an economically unaligned region such as North Wales, with urban, semi-urban, rural, deep rural and an East/West geographic split. This suggests from the outset that any economic benefit from the Growth Deal is going to be deeply uneven when delivered to the region.

Agglomeration and spatial displacement

Several interviewees raised concerns that NW England and NE Wales investment projects and cross-border capacity growth, while designed to simultaneously boost capacity in NW Wales, could actually have the opposite effect and could catalyse displacement in NW Wales (see Figure 5.1). Peripheral areas could lose human and financial capital, which could 'leak out' from Wales; this is agglomeration essentially. According to one perspective:

'[T]he problem with agglomeration is that it doesn't happen equally around the region ... does North [West] Wales have the human capital to win the agglomeration battle? ... Liverpool/Manchester is a massive gravitational force pulling things in ... dark matter ... pulling resources in rather than sending resources spinning out ... its where the financial capital, and consequently the human capital, lies ... it's a myth that there are no casualties.' (Interviews, Colegau Cymru, 2017)

Therefore, whether transport infrastructure improvements will provide economic benefits to NW Wales or not is a contentious issue; there are significant differences of opinion between stakeholders on this issue. There has, of course, been a number of studies which have questioned the economic benefits of such transport focused approaches (see Melia,

2018) and the actual economic benefit they bring to the populations they serve. Several stakeholders suggest that the focus on infrastructure, particularly transport infrastructure, may be misplaced. Transport improvements are important, but it depends on the context, such as where and what sort of business you are. Transport and infrastructure improvement can: "cut both ways ... could actually exacerbate an outflow of capacity ... it depends what the infrastructure is connected to ... infrastructure doesn't necessarily take you anywhere ... [when] there are more efficient nodes elsewhere" (Interview, sustainability consultant, 2016). Several interviewees made this potential for transport connectivity and infrastructure improvements to 'cut both ways' and potentially catalyse displacement. This is an area of significant disagreement between those promoting the NWGD and the interviewee stakeholders above, who felt that there was little evidence to show that transport infrastructure brought economic benefits; instead, exacerbating a long-history of out-migration/displacement, particularly at the periphery. Whereas the LAs who are developing and driving strategic initiatives (informing the NWGD) argue that investment in transport infrastructure is key to developing the region's economic potential.

Conclusions

> 'The Northern Powerhouse model is a good brand, a hook even, but a lack of tangible investment runs deep ... how will it actually translate in terms of opportunities for Anglesey and North Wales is limited.' (Interview, Anglesey Council, 2017)

This chapter has discussed non-metropolitan city-regional alternatives in the context of the (academic and policy) city-regional debate. It has specifically sought to raise a number of concerns based on the imposition of an urban 'spatial imaginary' through city-region building. The city-region agenda, although not transported and dropped into a rural region per se, shapes the possibility of what a rural region can become when aligned to a city-region policy prescription (in both discursive and material terms). We have highlighted how such an approach potentially marginalises 'the rural' due to the dominance of metropolitan centres in this policy approach. The chapter has demonstrated the way in which the NWGD has been constructed in order to align with city-region developments, though this is revealed to be deeply problematic for rural regions. The NWGD, premature in its evolution, is being implemented with little or no acknowledgement of the various concerns raised above. We have questioned the rural viability of the implied and applied urban growth model. This approach to economic development also has the potential to create further uneven growth for rural areas, by failing to consider the ways in which areas external to the city region are capable of creating different models of economic growth, which do not rely on urban agglomeration. All this said, a Mid-Wales Growth Deal is being prepared, which is also without a core city context to drive economic development and experience could mirror some of pitfalls and dilemmas of the NWGD.[5]

North Wales's unique selling point is its natural resources and unique identity as a bio-diverse region with important cultural heritage, which arguably chimes uncomfortably with a hegemonic discourse of partnership-based inward investment. Only specific actors from the local business communities, the LAs and the two national governments have agency to enact what a growth deal should or could be. There is limited evidence that such a model can and will succeed; and certainly limited 'periphery proofing' has been undertaken. With infrastructure and skills lagging over time, based on limited rounds of investment, the jury is out on whether the growth deal model will exacerbate historic patterns of displacement (out-migration) and skills capacity to sustain any growth within economic development. There is a dire need to improve the quality of jobs and the strategic roles played by the cultural heritage and agriculture tourism sector, as well as community level economic development possibilities around green energy. As two commentators point out:

> 'We know the kinds of activity that will persist ... the kinds of economic activity that are geographically bound ... Welsh language tourism, green infrastructure.' (Interviews, Colegau Cymru, 2017)

> 'We are not an industrial powerhouse, but we have an extraordinary landscape based on our environmental credentials ... there is an opportunity to develop the image of North Wales; successful businesses do (re)locate here for lifestyle reasons.' (Interview, sustainability consultant, 2016)

In addressing this and offering new knowledge, future research in this rural vein can contribute to the emerging literature on inclusive growth via city-region building (see Bevan Foundation and Joseph Rowntree Foundation, 2017; Lee, 2019; Vickers et al, 2017). This is seeking out a new economic model and for the likes of the Royal Society of Arts (2016, 2017), with regards to social and economic policy, reducing inequality and deprivation can itself drive growth. This requires investment in social infrastructure, including public health, early years support, skills and employment services, which should go hand in hand with investment in physical infrastructure, and in business development. This will have a first order impact on productivity and living standards. This sits within a broader framing of events whereby the context of Brexit has stimulated: a new Shared Prosperity Fund with potential for regional actors; increased demands for greater devolution; and a strengthening of calls for Welsh independence (see Welsh Government, 2017b). The rural challenges of delivering on this in the context of the NWGD have never been so pressing and the need for alternative economic development approaches, sensitive to the geographies of rural localities, has never been so urgent.

6

City-region limits

This City Deal will provide the region and its partners with the new ways of working and resources to unlock significant economic growth across the Swansea Bay City Region. It is a Deal where both Welsh and UK Governments have committed to jointly invest, subject to the submission and approval of full business cases in relation to the eleven identified projects and the agreement of governance arrangements for the deal, up to £241 million on specific interventions which seek to support and further build on the region's strengths which include health, energy and manufacturing sectors and are underpinned by a world-class digital infrastructure, successful universities and innovative health boards. (HM Government 2017: 3)

Introduction

In this chapter, we consider the implications of applying the city-region concept to a medium-sized city and whether such an application of a spatial and governmental policy is appropriate when the central city in question is also not necessarily economically dominant or connected to its wider city region. Building on the previous chapter, this raises the wider question that, within the process of sub-nation state restructuring, how can the city-region construct a deal with its application in what are often 'relational' and 'stretched' (MacLeod and Jones, 2007) polycentric city-regional contexts. We focus on the case of the SBCR, based in South West Wales, observed through the lens of Welsh devolution and through the concept of the city region as a scalar narrative for the delivery of economic development.

This chapter suggests that as a concept for delivering economic growth in Wales, the 'fit' of the city-region concept to Swansea Bay pushes the very essence and dynamics of the economic model in question to its spatial limits, hence the title. This is questioned via comprehending how and why the scale and differences across the SBCR stretch the spatial construct of city-region building. Swansea as a smaller, geographically peripheral UK metropolitan centre, lacks economic dominance over a city region, which is polycentric and porous in its social and spatial nature. This means it struggles to embed the dynamics of the city-region neoliberal growth machine model, outlined in the Introduction, into a coherent centric local growth framework. This, in turn, suggests that with regards to sub-national state spatial restructuring in Wales, a different model may well be much better to suited to this region in question. Our critique, then, is not just applicable to Swansea Bay, but also to other medium and smaller-sized city regions attempting to deliver a city-region agenda. The transference of the city region as a geopolitical policy footprint for economic growth (Jonas and Moisio, 2018), therefore, needs to be more carefully thought through in its implementation. Its usage, whereby a city-first or urban centric model is deployed without a dominant agglomerative centre, becomes mired in the difficulties of the more complex and diverse economic geographies.

To address our wider conceptual arguments with regards city regions, as well as the implementation of the SBCR, the chapter is organised in three sections.

The first section develops further some of the conceptual arguments in the book with regards to city-region building, to situate Swansea within its nuanced contexts. The second details the SBCR within the City Deal Approach being deployed by the UK and Welsh Governments. The third section looks at the emerging caveats and critiques of this approach to local and regional economic development in this part of South Wales.

The city-regional world revisited

With the city region becoming the dominant discourse in urban development policy and the appropriate scale on which economic actors can position themselves within the global economy as 'scalarly' sufficient to react to changes, we have suggested throughout this book that agglomeration tendencies privilege economic growth on centralised urban areas. Here, the consensus relates to the idea that if you centralise as much of your economic activity as possible, greater economic returns follow from spatial proximity and in turn, cumulation causation can operate (see Nathan and Overman, 2013; Overman et al, 2007). The city-region model has thus shaped economic growth policy as a metropolitan scale concern, which as we highlighted in Chapter 5, lends itself to the critique of 'metrophilia' – the 'sweeping tendency' to present cities as panaceas for a myriad of economic and social challenges, in the process ignoring the needs of 'marginalised strata' within the city and of 'non-metropolitan places' *beyond* the city (Waite and Morgan, 2019: 384).

The critical approach to metrophilia is useful in the context of this chapter as it highlights the way in which despite the vaunted 'bespoke' nature of the city-region building process, it is underpinned by a city-first agenda, which places far more emphasis on the importance of the urban. This in the context of some city regions may posit some forms of success, but as this policy framework is applied to ever more varied cities and regions, the underpinning approach becomes much less applicable and plausible. Building on the arguments in the Introduction, the economic rationale of defining city regions by their 'functional' or 'natural' economic area draws attention to the need to also examine the spaces of economic and social flows vis-à-vis Travel to Work Areas around the city region. This can sometimes cross pre-existing and historic administrative and cultural boundaries, as well as reflect the different spatial structures of settlements and the geographies of urban and rural economic growth. In the case of Swansea Bay, as the chapter will develop, as a medium-sized city in an enlarged geographical city region, it lacks the agglomerative pull economically to make the city-region function as, for example, Storper (2013) would suggest. This means that due to weak economic ties alongside a polycentric makeup of other settlements such as Llanelli, Carmarthen, Neath and Port Talbot, the city-region model for economic growth is both ill-conceived and ill-fitted in its application on Swansea Bay. This does not, however, stop a process of city-region building taking place, in what Haughton et al (2016: 356) would suggest is informed by 'decontextualized economic theory that uses abstract economic laws to develop problematic policy prescriptions focused on the assumed potential of large cities to generate growth'. Haughton et al are taking aim at agglomeration as a model for growth directly as well as the city-region concept more broadly and it is within this critique that we see parallels to the SBCR's attempt to implement and harness such policy concepts. This follows with Waite and Morgan (2019) above, in that the city-region concept is mistakenly being applied as a 'panacea' for a series of economic problems. This means it is ill equipped to actually address them, to fit the pre-existing geography or to provide any real 'inclusive growth' (see Lee, 2019); in many respects, through agglomeration, it has the potential to exacerbate uneven development.

Swansea Bay City Region and City Deal

The city region as a policy construct for economic development is built on a variety of factors that attempt to institutionalise an agglomeration economy over time and across space. As we suggested in Chapter 5, the opportunity to territorialise this city region came through city deals, which create a bounded SBCR, but in doing so, also create the conditions for a series of contradictions and tensions within this mode of state intervention. These tensions reflect the relatively small economic foot print of Swansea, as the metropolitan centre in a wider region (see Figure 6.1), but also refuel the difficult and competitive geographies of the Welsh state, whereby the two primary cities of Wales (Swansea and Cardiff) are relatively close in geographical proximity, contain collectively the largest proportion of the Welsh population, and have historically been deeply competitive with each other (see Gooberman, 2017). This makes delivering a sub-nation state structure for Wales and particularly South Wales difficult. Therefore, piecing together that perceived sense of scale for Swansea Bay is difficult, as it is required to stretch into a rural hinterland and it is constrained to the east by the CCR and its own economic footprint.

The SBCR consists of the four LA Areas that make up what could loosely be called 'South West Wales'. The city region includes

Figure 6.1: Swansea Bay City Region

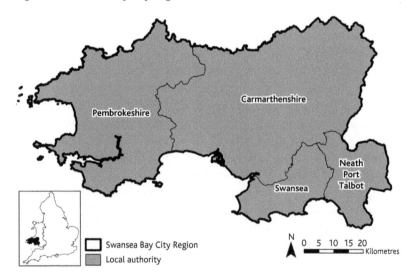

Source: Produced by Sam Jones, WISERD

Pembrokeshire, Carmarthenshire, Neath Port Talbot and Swansea itself, with the latter two being more distinctively urban. This urban/rural split between the LAs is considerable and the economic footprint of Swansea itself, as the metropolitan centre across the region, is relatively small. Using Travel to Work Areas data as a proxy for the economic connectedness of the city region, Swansea has relatively weak connections to its rural hinterlands. Figures 6.2 and 6.3 highlight this picture, suggesting that there is little in the way of flow between Swansea and the rural parts of Carmarthenshire and Pembrokeshire. There is little travel between these LAs to Swansea for work, alongside there being relatively weak infrastructure connections (whether road or rail) to even facilitate this, which over time has significant impact on patterns of economic development and settlement growth.

Figure 6.2: Swansea travel-to-work flows

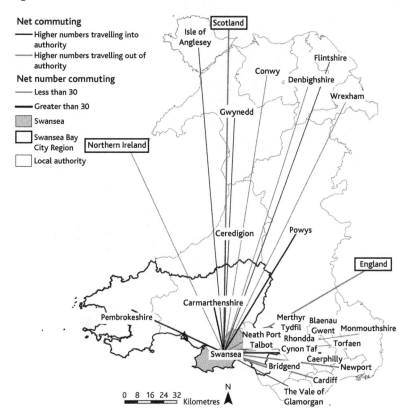

Source: Produced by Sam Jones, WISERD

Figure 6.3: City region travel times

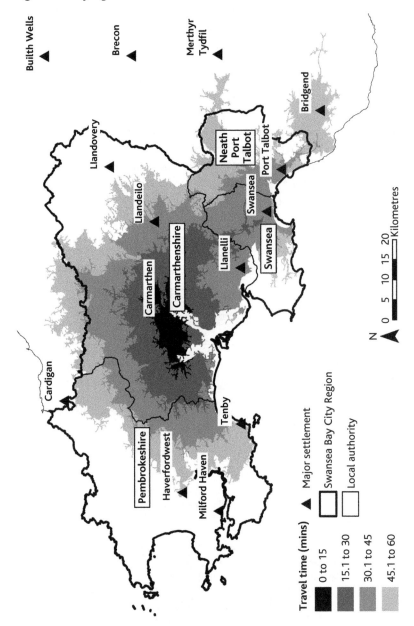

Source: Produced by Sam Jones, WISERD

Table 6.1: Swansea Bay City Region descriptive statistics

Local authority	Employment (%)	Unemployment (%)	Inactivity (%)	GVA per head (£)	Ave. earnings per week (£)	Enterprises per 10,000 people
Swansea	68.3	4.9	21.3	19,300	506.90	454
Pembrokeshire	71.9	5.6	22.1	18,400	457.30	644
Carmarthenshire	73.1	3.1	21.5	15,900	495.70	560
Neath and Port Talbot	72.7	4.0	22.1	16,200	586.70	363

Source: Welsh Government (2019)

This reflects an economic reality of the city region with areas possessing very different economies and, therefore, somewhat divergent economic interests. This variable picture at the LA level is also reflected in the descriptive statistics for the city region (see Table 6.1), which suggest further patterns of divergence. This divergence and urban/rural split, paints a mixed picture for the city region, whereby there is reduced employment in Swansea and less businesses per 10,000 people in Swansea and Neath Port Talbot (with higher populations) but there are higher incomes in the more urban LAs and Swansea achieves a higher GVA per head than its surrounding LAs.

This is compounded by a relatively weak economic performance for the city region as a whole, when compared to the rest of Wales and the UK. Using Welsh Government (2019) statistics, it has the lowest employment rate (71.1 per cent), the second highest employment rate (4.4 per cent), the highest inactivity rate (21.7 per cent), the lowest GVA per head (£17,600) and the lowest gross disposable household income per head (£15,600).

It is on this mixed and varied economic picture that the city deal was negotiated between the four LA areas, the UK Government and the Welsh Government (see Figure 6.1). This presented a complicated process for negotiation and much like the CCR City Deal (discussed in Chapter 4) was a product of tensions between LAs and the Welsh state in the context of potential local government restructuring plans, alongside tension between the Welsh and UK Governments in terms of delivering the city-region concept (see Pemberton, 2016). The delivery of the city deal was proceeded by the Swansea Bay Transition Board, which was led by Sir Terry Matthews (a leading private-sector elite and Wales' first billionaire), and this initiated as a process of city-region building by the Welsh Government (Swansea Bay City Region, 2016). The initial plans were based on the ambitious concept of an Internet Coast to secure 5G digital capability for South Wales and bring about an upward shift in the productivity capability of Swansea's advanced manufacturing base through 'catapulted' technology. The SBCR City Deal document, signed in March 2017 (HM Government, 2017), though reflected the product of negotiations between the LAs themselves over their immediate (rather than forward looking) priorities and the UK Government over what was permissible Treasury expenditure at that time. This complicated deal-making structure, alongside the economic geography of Swansea Bay, therefore, greatly reflects what was delivered and supports the claims made by Scott that 'city-regions are always at the same time conditioned by idiosyncrasies related to local material, social, and cultural circumstances' (Scott, 2019: 574).

In summation, the SBCR City Deal secured £1.3bn of funding for its 11 proposed projects, whereby £637m was projected to be leveraged finance from the private sector and with the Welsh and UK Governments having committed in principle to £241m of that total. The city deal further aims to deliver a 'collective focus' for the city region. The signed version notes that:

> The City Deal provides clarity of purpose, consistency of approach and absolute focus on collective action over the next two decades. We aim to tackle the structural challenges holding back our economy and reduce the gap between our performance and the rest of the UK in terms of wealth creation to the benefit of both. (Swansea Bay City Region, 2016: 2)

The deal was to be implemented over the next 15 years, aiming to boost the regional economy by £1.8 billion and generate almost 10,000 new, high-quality jobs. It was split into four main themes: Internet of Economic Acceleration; Internet of Life Science & Well-being; Internet of Energy: and Smart Manufacturing. These four themes were then further split into eleven different projects, of which, only three operate on across the city-region scale as a whole (see Figure 6.4).

The lack of operation across the city region as a whole highlights the lack of economic convergence, as well as the need, in political terms for each LA, to see some aspect of the deal landed in their area for the purposes of political legitimacy. Despite this, the deal makes

Figure 6.4: Swansea Bay City Deal project map

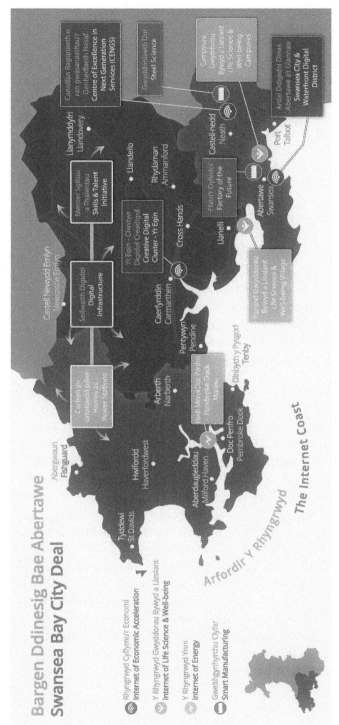

Source: Carmarthenshire County Council

clear that it is about ensuring economic growth for the city region and widening its economic footprint:

> The Deal provides an opportunity to continue tackling the area's barriers to economic growth through: developing higher value sectors and higher value employment opportunities to match; increasing the number of businesses within these sectors to widen the economic base; and improving the region's GVA level against the UK average. As well as taking forward programmes to drive economic growth the City Deal commits local leaders and partners to implementing effective leadership across the City Region. (Swansea Bay City Region, 2016: 3)

The deal, therefore, attempts to improve a struggling city-region economy following specific markers of success such as GVA uplift. It attempts to do this via attracting, or creating in situ, high-end businesses primarily related to health, improving digital infrastructure and in the specific regeneration of parts of Swansea's urban core.

Quite a city-regional stretch: emerging critiques

The above SBCR City Deal, despite the bombast and optimism of local elites involved in its implementation, papers over a number of structural and strategic weaknesses within the South Wales economy and its 'geo-constitution' (Wills, 2016). Not least, there was a breakdown in the governance of the city deal implementation itself due to gross misconduct, which resulted in several high-level suspensions from public office and later criminal investigations by the Regional Crime Unit for Southern Wales over the misuse of public money to support private business interests in the controversial Llanelli Wellness and Life Science Village project.[1] These were ongoing during the period of our research and are outside the scope of this chapter, but needless to say they do not support the argument that devolution through localist city-region building represents a role model of democracy, the basis for civil society awakening, or virtuous economic and social renewal more broadly. The scope of this chapter is not the governance of the SBCR City Deal per se, but with the deeper concern with applying the city-region framework and its limits.

Conflicting aspirations

As has been alluded to, the city region has been negotiated between a set of conflicting aspirations, which are presented via each of the key institutional actors' concerns as to what they wish to see developed from the city-region building process. This is reflected in the views of the Welsh Assembly's Economy, Infrastructure and Skills Committee which suggests that:

> It is clear that Deals and the investment that follows them have given the UK Government a role in economic development that (as a devolved area) would normally be the preserve of the Welsh Government. If this joint working is harmonious, then there is strong potential for it to benefit all parties. However, there is a history of fractiousness and finger-pointing between the two governments, particularly when it comes to economic development and infrastructure projects in areas where devolved responsibilities are not 100% clear. (Economy, Infrastructure and Skills Committee, 2017: 18–19)

From this grounding for conducting and delivering a city deal, a deal that keeps all groups happy was always going to be difficult and to require significant compromise. This is especially pertinent in terms of thinking through what sort of economic growth is wanted and who does it benefit. For example, there are differing legislative approaches to economic development from the UK and Welsh Governments; for the UK Conservative Government there is an emphasis on 'city-first' agglomerative growth. This fits well with perhaps what local elites in Swansea would emphasise as important too, as it places emphasis on the city itself and the search for urban wealth creation. Whereas, the Welsh Government (Labour), although not ideologically against agglomeration per se, supports an alternative ideological model of economic development predicated more on achieving spatial justice (see R Jones, 2019; Welsh Government, 2015a) via the Wellbeing of Future Generations Act (2015). This is reflected in the below quote:

> 'I guess strategically where we were and in the four months of negotiations strategically we had to fulfil the ambitions of both governments and as you say you've got a Labour Government here, a Conservative Government in Westminster, so we had to have the capability really of knowing what both governments' agendas were and

how to marry those two agendas and we're still doing it post-negotiation. We still have to marry two strategic ambitions together but I guess it helps that officials from Welsh Government and UK Government can come to an agreement themselves and have one path forwards.' (Interview, Local Government Leader, 2018)

This implies the need to integrate the desires of both governments in terms of what they consider to be appropriate economic growth, but it also positions the divergent rural and urban LAs away from more long-term strategically planned approaches. As we suggested above, local political legitimacy becomes important. This is because for the city region as a whole, partners are required to deliver a deal from which they derive some form of benefit. This, in turn, localises policy away from city-region wide projects and concerns, which are unable to be integrated with local territorial concerns. This, in empirical terms, also points to the need to consider the dynamics of 'metrophilia', which we now turn to examine.

Dealing with metrophilia

'You've got an opportunity here as a region, Swansea is known globally now because of the football, you've got to use that brand to reach out to the world to attract people to come here.' He said, I think that was accepted. And on top of that then, if you accept Swansea is "As much as we would like to describe Carmarthenshire and Pembrokeshire and all the other great areas within the region, Swansea is your brand. That's why it's Swansea Bay ..." the engine of the region, the major urban centre, the major economic centre of the region, then if you get the engine running well you are going to disperse that wealth out into the other parts of the region.' (Interview, Local Authority Leader, 2018)

The logic of the above LA leader gets to the nub of the point – *"Swansea is your brand"* – not the 'South West Wales City Region' or any other name, but Swansea itself is front and centre. The emphasis is also made on the city being the major economic and urban centre, in short the metro-centre for making the city region 'work'. The quote also highlights the belief in a trickle-down effect from the development of Swansea itself but as has been noted, the weak economic ties of the city region and the unevenness of agglomerative growth, suggest this will struggle. This argument is shared by actors in the region:

> 'Now Pembrokeshire was not keen on the city-region approach I think because of our experience of city-regions. When we're sitting on the periphery of it the Region looks very different sitting in West Wales than it does sitting in Swansea. So, if you're sitting in Swansea the City Region Deal looks like a pretty good thing, but we're a long way from Swansea.' (Interview, Civil Society Leader, 2018)

The positioning here of Pembrokeshire as the most peripheral (and rural) to Swansea is key to the discussion and the comprehension of what a city-region economy will bring. For the SBCR, then, this is the 'construal' (Jessop, 2016a) within the city-region building narrative; that for underperforming and smaller metropolitan centres, any form of trickle-out to the rest of the city region is highly unlikely to surface. Metrophilia is clearly not the answer here for ensuring city-region wide economic and social development. This is further compounded by genuine rural development question for the city region and the arguments rehearsed in the previous chapter on North Wales also apply to the SBCR.

As we have noted above (Figure 6.1), a large proportion of the region can be defined as rural and has minimal economic connection to Swansea itself. It also presents a series of other and differing development needs. The quote below highlights this in terms of health:

> 'Well we're very, very concerned about it. Whilst the City Deal will concentrate on health and life science as a major investment, rural health is not being taken care of ... It's also got the issue of attractiveness, we've got this shift from rural areas into urban areas which leaves a vacuum then in terms of skills and the linguistic skills in that rural area so health is a growing issue ... That's where I believe an English city-region has got the advantage in that it is an urban area, good communication links, high volume of people, good learning resources distributed. We haven't got that; we've got this rural aspect, which is difficult.' (Interview, Former SBCR Board Member, 2018)

Within the city deal, there are a variety of projects that look to develop aspects of the city region's health economy, but the specific rural needs are not addressed. Added to that, the above participant highlights a growing issue for rural areas due to the emphasis on projects that are urban: this in turn creates the reverse of agglomeration in rural areas, as people leave. Interestingly, the SBCR does not differentiate its policy interventions along rural and urban lines. Again, the overly metrocentric focus is not the answer to rural problems – it exacerbates them.

Austerity and financialisation

Further problems are aggravated by the ongoing impact of austerity and the question as to how the city region will be sustainably financed. As noted in Chapters 4 and 5, austerity has landed differently in Wales to England, with the Welsh Government buffering some of the impact, but this has still impinged on Welsh LAs severely. In the quote below, the continuing effects of austerity against the LA are even cited as a reason to not continue with the city-region process.

> 'We were going into a time of … well we're in a period of austerity, we cannot afford extra expenditure on things that are not known. This, to me, was opening the doors – could be a series of unknowns, so I was very, very, very cautious, yes … I go back to my point at the beginning; in these days of austerity we've not got the funds. We are being cut back, cut back, cut back for the last five, six years. And we shouldn't, councils should not be relied upon as a charity for business expansion. There are programmes that are grants, if your business plan stacks up, there are banks that will lend you money. What I'm saying is, I think, that the Assembly and the English Government could be … forming their own bank, if you like, just allowing businesses to borrow cheaper money. That's the only reason that these schemes want in on this because it's borrowing cheap money, they can't get it the same rates from the banks or the private sector so of course they want a part of it.' (Interview, Local Authority Leader, 2018)

Here, the interviewee links the two projects, city-region building and austerity together, but also more fundamentally questions the role of what a LA should be doing in relation to supporting business.

Chapters 1, 2 and 3 indeed highlighted this Janus-faced nature of city-region devolution in England. Against a backdrop of austerity, based on these insights, a similar devo-dynamic is in play. This is further reflected in an uneasiness surrounding the financing of a city deal too and the risk each LA faces in supporting it (in the wake of austerity). Below, the discussion as to whether the city deal is based on 'capital or revenue' is illuminating, particularly as to how stretched LAs are and the actual value placed on the city deal. According to one perspective:

> 'And then there's the issue around what is the nature of the funding in the City Deal, if you read it, it says two different things; on one page it says that it's "funding", so that could be capital or revenue, over the page it says it's capital. Now I need revenue for one or two of the projects so I'm asking them to clarify, essentially. They started off saying it's all capital and I said, "oh dear". And now they are starting to back-track a bit, so it's all part of the negotiation. But of the – we've got a revenue requirement of thirty-four million quid, on two main projects, one of which is here and the other one is the regional skills programme and a few bits and pieces elsewhere, but basically there's a deliverability issue around the projects if we can't get the clarity.' (Interview, Local Authority Official, 2018)

For the LA official, the city deal being financed via capital funding is untenable, due to the upfront cost of project delivery. The vagueness in the city deal documents does not help and in turn, with stretched resources, has meant the need to negotiate further before the deal can be implemented is a stark reality of this devolution through city-region building process. Here, austerity and the process of negotiating the deal between multiple actors, and the requirement of the state to support businesses with funding, raise a series of difficult questions for the ongoing implementation of the city deal.

Trickle-out ...

The possibility of around £1.3 billion in funding being available for investment does offer a number of opportunities to deliver the projects in the SBCR City Deal and this level of funding is, of course, attractive to private investment. Therefore, as the LA leader below suggests, the scale of this interest is genuinely global in its offering:

'I think the investment from both governments is just giving us the profile that private sector want to invest and it's the catalyst. Because both governments want to invest in the region. We're already seeing global investors wanting to talk to us ... there are companies talking to us now that we've never seen in Carmarthenshire but they're here now because of the City Deal and what that offers and that's great to see.' (Interview, Local Government Leader, 2018)

Although there are questions as to whether the projects outlined in the city deal will have their desired effect over time, as city-region actors hope for, is very much open to debate, but with such 'global' external interest, another fundamental question opens up. How much of the proposed £1.3 billion investment will remain in the city region, to be appreciated by the regional civil society of the Swansea Bay? For some, this is another failing of city-region building process itself, whereby not enough attention has been concentrated on city-regional welfare capture, to influence the politics of distribution thereafter. According to one source:

'I had probably three or four objectives the biggest one being fair procurement. Probably the second one a voice for construction and hopefully probably lining up with "yours localism" as well. I wanted to get the local point across that construction is the first rung on the ladder when it comes to investment and so on ... Obviously a lot of people didn't agree with my views. I did bang on all the time about procurement and it needed to start with Smart Fair Procurement but I've written there that was totally lost to be honest with you. I couldn't get it written into the City Region Deal and I think that's the most important. The enabler for the whole of the City Region Deal is the construction so whether or not the project is on infrastructure or it's on life science, wellness centre as one is or it's on the city centre regeneration it starts with construction.' (Interview, Former SBCR Board Member, 2018)

The above quote highlights how as a Board Member participant within the process of developing the city region, there is an inability to guarantee that the funding coming to Swansea Bay will remain with its economy. Again, this highlights a further critique to the city-region policy construct as it is currently premised; this spatio-temporal fix cannot find ways to ensure that, even if it creates an agglomerative effect from investment, that investment may not necessarily remain within the city-region crucible. This instead represents a form of trickle-out, whereby infrastructure, new buildings and so on maybe built, but with an increasingly fragmented or even 'dismembered' (Toynbee and Walker, 2017) local state, little of its economic footprint will ultimately remain in the city region.

Conclusions

'You could call it the hegemony of a laissez faire – the neo-liberal hegemony. To use that phraseology: it's the dominant philosophy, isn't it? And I don't think that has been challenged. You've got Jeremy Corbyn and John MacDonald coming in but even there I suspect that's more about macro-economic policy and it really strikes me again that, in my experience of politicians, they know very little about this area so they tend to assume what (hacks it) in terms of economic development is big buildings and roads, something tangible. I come back to my point, in economic development terms in Wales there's too much development and not enough economics.' (Interview, Health Board Chair, 2018)

This chapter has sought to expose the immense difficulties of instituting a city-regional model of economic and social development for the SBCR, which is a collection of polycentric medium-sized urban entities, historically battling for recognition as nodes in the increasing globalisation of capital networks. We have highlighted the pre-existing economic tensions in this locality of South Wales, namely an agglomerative economy riddled with weak links and connections within and between the towns and cities. The city deal does nothing short of replicating and extenuating these economic and social problems. Over time, the LA and city-centric dominated strategy has led to the lack of a city-region wide spatial strategy, with emphasis being placed on too many geographically discreet projects, which are used to both secure political legitimacy and partially plug the gaps left behind by the decade of austerity. In the words of one influential academic commentator:

Dylan Jones-Evans … reportedly said that the deal had gone away from 'investing in infrastructure and people' towards

Figure 6.5: Swansea Bay City Deal revised project map

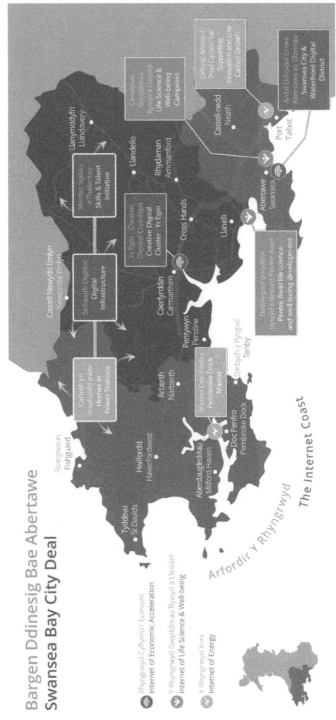

Bargen Ddinesig Bae Abertawe
Swansea Bay City Deal

Source: Carmarthenshire County Council

'building more buildings'. He argued that the strategy taken had 'been discredited by economic development organisations around the world'. Professor Jones-Evans criticised the deal for moving away from funding and skills for business by no longer having an infrastructure or investment fund and claiming that less than 1% of the budget specifically earmarked for skills. In addition, he argued that the emphasis on new digital technologies, which was at the heart of the proposition document, had been cut back to a single funded project. Most worrying, he argued, was the absence of any funding to support the proposed installation of a new transatlantic cable from North America into Oxwich Bay. This project, Professor Jones-Evans argued 'has the potential to totally transform the economic fortunes of the whole of South Wales'. (Quoted in House of Commons Welsh Affairs Committee, 2019: 19)

Within this context of political capture by certain local state elites, Figure 6.5 captures the current (August 2020) status of the SBCR City Deal projects. Essentially, three projects in the original vision (Centre of Excellence in Next Generation Services, Factory of the Future and Steel Science) have been replaced by the Supporting Innovation & Low Carbon Growth project in the Neath Port Talbot area.[2] Economic development officers within the supporting LAs are at pains to point out that steel science and smart manufacturing elements are now contained within the Supporting Innovation & Low Carbon Growth project. Critics point to this being more about protecting the initially allocated funding parameters and safeguarding the interests of steel production in Port Talbot than providing the basis for increased economic productivity and shared prosperity across the SBCR.

As the city-region building 'round of institutional investment' (Peck, 1995), then, has been rolled-out over this existing complex geography, we would argue that in years to come, this (curtailed) model of economic development will indeed exacerbate combined and uneven development, and furthermore it will not lead to the empowerment of civil society actors to be able to 'formulate an agenda, act and make change' (Wills, 2016: 13). This raises questions with regards to what an appropriate 'growth' strategy would be for places like the Swansea Bay. We turn to this in the next chapter.

Conclusions: City-regional futures

Learning from a civil society perspective has great value, especially very early on before decisions are made. Firstly, it broadens the set of knowledge available for the deliberative stages before any pens are put to paper. As already noted, it does so in a way that is as close to communities and their localities as feasible at this stage. Secondly, it is a step towards making connections and having good communication with potential future partners. (UK2070 Commission, 2020b: 6, emphasis added)

The building of a spatially balanced and inclusive form of growth is a task that Westminster and Whitehall have failed to fully embrace. That has got to, and looks set to, change. As the Government sets about its task, it is right to invest in towns (and cities). But places will be helped rather than profoundly changed by the policies on offer thus far. This is because the economic forces that are making some towns more prosperous and hollowing out others are much more powerful, more poorly understood and harder to change than we are yet as a country ready to acknowledge. That said, the link between towns and successful cities is a good start for building successful policy in many places. (Emmerich, 2020a: 6)

Introduction

The first quotation is taken from civil society perspectives within the UK2070 Commission, which as noted in the Introduction, is investigating spatial inequality and proposes an agenda for strategy long-term action. The study examines experiences in 'left behind' places, by looking at perspectives on inequality of those civil society organisations who are already working in these contexts. This chimes with *City Regions and Devolution in the UK: The Politics of Representation*, which has probed on the 'symptoms' rather than the 'prevalence' of the phenomenon and the role of civil society actors therein. We have provided an overview of city-region building and considered how local governance restructuring shapes political, social and cultural landscapes.

Reviewing the GMCR, SCR, SBCR, CCR and the NWGD, we have exposed the tensions and opportunities for local elites and civil society actors. Moreover, the nature of the economic development that civil society actors are expected to work within is contradictory. We have identified the tension between civil society autonomy at the margins of city-region devolution and the abrogation of responsibility at the centre. Like the social economy localism debates that preceded this wave of devolution, dependent on state and its agents, city-region building with civil society is 'a vehicle by which social and economic risks can be moved away from the state and on to local communities, which are expected to assume responsibility' for economic governance (Leyshon and Lee, 2003: 19–20). We maintain a position, then, that to conceptualise and understand the dynamics of civil society within city regions requires, firstly, close attention to the state and its spatial manifestations and, secondly, to the links between the state and the mainstream economy. In short, this spatially selective incorporation of civil society only moderates the city-regional effects of capitalism and certainly does very little to actually reform or replace the prevailing growth model.

A new approach is clearly needed that recognises and empowers the 'agency of those who are facing disadvantage directly, and brings insights about how civil society offers assistance' (UK2070 Commission, 2020b: 3). Nothing short of a 'fundamental shift is needed to address the deep-rooted or structural problem of regional inequality'. Yet, as this book has highlighted, inequality is also a problem that is directly experienced – communities live with it and 'have agency in making changes' (UK2070 Commission, 2020b: 3). This implies that policymakers and communities must work together in order to define the problem and work out solutions to it. An era of 'civic repair' is emerging in the UK on the back of a series of economic, cultural, political and technological upheavals that collectively and individually are reshaping patterns of social cohesion and stratification and the dynamics of inclusion and exclusion in communities, labour markets and the practice of citizenship. Civil society is central to these dynamics, as a site in which change is negotiated and responses developed and implemented, but also the need for further study. Chapter 3 noted and warned though that relational and empathic aspects of civil society mobilisations vis-à-vis the economy and city-regional governance should not be inadvertently seen as an excuse to *further* roll-back or displace state socioeconomic duties.

This chapter looks at two pathways for the development of city regions in the UK. The first is the current preoccupation with city regions as agglomeration nodes in neoliberal networks – the 'giantist' (Lefebvre, 1976: 103) trickle-down sentiments expressed by Emmerich and others (see Katz and Nowak, 2017). Founder of the consultancy Metro-Dynamics and former HM Treasury and 10 Downing Street policy guru, Emmerich has played a key role in developing devolutionary momentum, advancing the agglomeration arguments in the Introduction (see Emmerich, 2017a), and specifically being central to the Greater Manchester devolution deals. The idea that 'levelling-up' (see King and Ives, 2019; Pitt, 2020; Tomaney and Pike, 2020) is a geographic issue though is misplaced and skews focus by putting emphasis on 'regional investment' (Emmerich, 2020b), rather than challenging the overall economic elite model, which remains overly driven by financialisation and the marginalisation of civil society actors. The chapter highlights a depoliticising condition being coined 'the post-political', where an array of players, stakeholders and organisations are playing active roles in the transformation of relations between state and market economy by also involving and increasing the influence of corporate interests and the privatisation of public services (Haughton et al, 2013; MacLeod, 2013). Related to this, power is often being transferred to, or captured, by an elite formation in terms of political, social and cultural influences (Crouch, 2004, 2020). Rather than promoting democracy and civil society empowerment, this new 'regime' of politics can undermine it; governance per se has bypassed direct elected and representative democracy (Swyngedouw, 2010: 6).

The second is an alternative socioeconomic model of economic governance being called the 'foundational economy', which encompasses those goods and services, together with the economic and social relationships that underpin them, that provide the everyday infrastructure of civilised life (Foundational Economy Collective, 2018). A non-exhaustive list includes gas and electricity, water, waste sewerage, retail food supply, telecommunications, health and social care, housing, education and public transport. Over the past 50 years or so, many of these goods and services have been increasingly incorporated within market logics by policies that promote commodification, privatisation and financialisation. Previously this would have be placed in the domain of civil society and subsequently a central–local nationalising state (see Duncan and Goodwin, 1988). The failure of these unfettered market policies and their impact on the daily lives of citizens in city regions is evident throughout the pages of this book, and the series of economic and social events that unravelled across the world in early 2020. The chapter concludes by looking at the opportunities for *instituting* a 'foundational city-regional economy'.

Post-political city regions and the depoliticisation of civil society

According to 'post-political' approaches a 'regime' of governance, which operates at different spatial scales and territorial reaches, is increasing the actors in policy implementation. Accordingly, the 'status, inclusion or exclusion, legitimacy, system of representation, scale of operation and internal or external accountability of such actors takes place in non-transparent, ad hoc, context dependent ways and differs greatly from those associated with egalitarian pluralistic democratic rules and codes' (Swyngedouw, 2010: 6). One of the key elements to this approach is the parallel role of *depoliticisation* – the narrowing of the boundaries of democratic politics, the displacement strategies used by the state to frame engagement, and the emergence of technocratic and delegated forms of governance (see Wood and Flinders, 2014). In the context of neoliberalist city-regional agglomerations, this process reinforces dominant ideologies and imaginaries around what is possible and required, restricting or foreclosing avenues for debate around alternative and critical discourses (Darling, 2016; Deas et al, 2020).

Extending Jessop's analysis in the Introduction, depoliticisation is an increasingly important governing strategy for exercising state power, removing the political character of decision making by privileging certain elite interests in the state-making process, in turn framing politics and shaping political opportunities. The existence of the state being, among other things, a 'political' sphere, which presupposes the possibility of a depoliticisation of civil society, makes it 'clear that the depoliticisation of civil society could only be achieved through bloody legislation against the expropriated – producing a "class" free from the means of production and "free" to sell their labour power – a process that could not in essence be more political' (Burnham, 2014: 191). This is contemporised by Wood and Flinders (2014: 152), who emphasise that depoliticisation is a contingent neoliberal political strategy for managing conflicts and rationalising urban governance, which exhibits three forms:

- *Governmental depoliticisation*: focusing on the switching of issues from the governmental sphere through the 'delegation' of those issues by politicians to arm's-length bodies, judicial structures or technocratic rule-based systems that limit discretion;

- *Societal depoliticisation*: involving the transition of issues from the public sphere to the private sphere and focusing on the existence of choice, capacity deliberation and the shift towards individualised responses to collective challenges;
- *Discursive depoliticisation*: the role of language and ideas to depoliticise certain issues and through this, define them as little more as elements of fate.

State agents deploy three patterns of intervention across these forms for deferring, displacing, and transferring the political moment and containing, albeit temporarily, crises further. By *deferring* the political, the state can enact strategies of deferral of conflict to some future point in time. By *displacing*, the state can shift political problems to other arenas and groups. By *transferring* the political, conflict can be removed from immediate community and representative processes into new, fuzzy communities of interest and democratic processes that may not align or map onto experiences of change 'on the ground' (Allmendinger and Haughton, 2015: 44).

In short, depoliticisation characterises the neoliberal political-administrative state system, the operation of which requires a careful unpacking of the 'organizational form and sociopolitical bases of the state' (Jessop, 1990: 345). In this approach though there is a need to not only examine where it takes place (such as sites of government and governance), but also how policy and politics are defined by their contents and in situations where choice, capacity for agency, deliberation and social interaction prevail. In short, depoliticisation, as Jessop points out, can only be guaranteed through a process of 'repoliticisation' and an assertion of the 'political' in and through the state – underlying the point that both are integral to each other (Jessop, 2014). Moreover, these 'attempts may involve reorganising the integral state in the shadow of hierarchy and, indeed, serve to enhance state power by exercising influence indirectly and/or at a distance from the state' (Jessop, 2014: 214).

City Regions and Devolution in the UK has accordingly sought to demonstrate how the city region–state nexus operates not just in relation to the state's organisation form and sociopolitical bases, but also how crises, contradictions, depoliticised politics, and struggles can emerge within a devolved governance framework and create opportunities for civil society. In effect, through depoliticisation as a governing strategy, state managers are also able to spatially reorganise the state apparatus to retain arm's-length control over crucial economic and social processes, while simultaneously benefiting from the distancing effects of depoliticisation. As a form of politics, depoliticisation also seeks to change market expectations by rationalist assumptions regarding the effectiveness and credibility of policymaking in addition to shielding the government from the consequences of unpopular policies. Depoliticisation, then, draws attention to the representational regimes of state-making through civil society: those social forces outside the political system.

Depoliticisation operates through hegemony-seeking 'discursive institutions' (Fuller, 2017), which establish semantic links between the discursive aims of those seeking to control, and the pragmatics of the everyday lives of those subject to such institutions. The various chapters of this book have highlighted these processes at work through the creation of precarious city regions in the context of a central–local politics of austerity fiscal localism. In short, as argued throughout the book, 'ideologies of growth' (Lefebvre, 1976: 102) and devolved forms of austerity are being reproduced through city regions and the ability of civil society groups to set the agenda, including proposing alternatives to the urban regime, is limited. The perceived post-political consensus around the 'local growth agenda' though implies that to critique this is not in the spirit of being a city-region team-player and 'scuppering social progress' (Emmerich, 2017b: 6; cf. Etherington and Jones, 2016a). There is, indeed, to further paraphrase Lefebvre (1976: 102) on the politics of growth poles, almost blind-trust agglomeration ideologies hiding reality: 'an idyllic picture of the economic situation, ignoring the clouds on the horizon ...'

Civic repair and the foundational economy

One alternative to this growth model starts with a reconsideration of the socioeconomic foundation of the city-regional economy and offers a more 'constitutional' political economy for promoting 'place-based social innovation' (Morgan, 2018). The FE rejects the traditional focus city-region based agglomeration and productivity in favour of 'that part of the economy that creates and distributes goods and services consumed by all (regardless of income and status) because they support everyday life' (Bentham et al, 2013: 7). FE draws on Braudel's (1981) tripartite architecture of society, where the economy is conceptualised in three layers: the world economy of large companies and institutions engaged in global export markets; the local market economy of anchor institutions, SMEs and the self-employed addressing local needs; and a subsistence economy of informal activities (see Haughton, 1999: 9). Whereas conventional sector-based city-region economic development foregrounds the first, most visible layer, the FE draws attention to the latter layers – those more mundane and overlooked, yet fundamental, economic activities that constitute the foundation of everyday life and as Lefebvre argues, 'the critique of everyday life' and its reconstitution holds the future for understanding and challenging capitalism (see Brenner and Elden, 2009; Whitehead, 2005).

Reflecting Polanyi's (1957) concept of embeddedness, the FE presents public services and civic infrastructure – frequently delivered 'outside' the economy by the state and third sector – as much a part of the economy as the 'world economy' of marvellous export industries. Foundational sectors are seen not as some unproductive drag on the 'real' economy, paid for out of tax receipts from 'productive' sectors, such as high-tech and knowledge-intensive industries, but as the real foundation of our economy generating social value and providing the majority of jobs (at least 50 per cent in some city regions). FE scholars, then, posit the 'grounded city' as an alternative to the free-floating and disconnected agglomerative 'competitive city' – 'the city as a space of collective civic provision, which meets social needs' and whose economy is 'grounded' in its locale and local population (Engelen et al, 2017: 408). 'Grounded' means three things: a city's development is inter-dependent with, and rooted in, its metropolitan regional hinterland of resource and labour inputs; that one of the major 'accelerators' of urban-economic growth is rising land values; and grounded in the sense that cities are built on their FE, acting as a 'stabiliser'. While accelerators provide opportunities for (inclusive) growth, stabilisers help 'ground' a city, acting as a 'buffer' to the vagaries of changing market dynamics. With the FE, city-regional growth can refocus on more controllable and locally embedded 'accelerators' of growth balanced by 'stabilisers' of provision of essential services. Thompson et al (2020) cite grassroots innovation and entrepreneurship at a local level as an important accelerator, in capturing 'unearned social increment'. Rather than rely on large corporations from elsewhere to drive economic growth (and extract wealth created rather than re-investing locally), this involves incubating SMEs, social enterprises and entrepreneurs in ways that not only generate economic value through new business activity but also connect local labour markets with large-scale 'innovation assets' and 'growth sectors' (Thompson et al, 2020: 1177). Focusing on Greater Manchester, Folkman et al build on this to suggest a 'new civic offer' based on:

> the city and economy as it is. With 80,000 on the housing waiting lists of the ten GM boroughs, the first priority should be social housing; with so many on low wages, the

first priority in transport should be much lower public transport fares; with so much employment in sectors like retail and hospitality, the first priority should be to ensure that all chain based operators in these sectors pay the GM Living Wage. The Brexit result is a warning to Greater Manchester politicians who need now to reconnect with their voters, by renewing the civic offer. Instead of relying on property development as the accelerator in the centre, they need to rely on the foundational economy as the stabiliser in all ten boroughs. Because the quantity and quality of foundational goods and services is the social precondition of civilized life, and in activities like adult care the GMCA could start out on the road of social innovation and radical experiment to benefit all citizens. (Folkman et al, 2016: 3)

Enacting and embedding this strategy, of course, requires a fundamental challenging of the logic of indefinite agglomeration and rebalancing of the priorities between the market economy and social economy. Deas et al's research on Greater Manchester's 'agglomerationist growth model' notes the arrival of FE discourses in policy interventions, with some 27 references in key documents pertaining to spatial and industrial strategies, but 'it is merely used as a loose signifier for low wage sectors such as retail and social care, *rather than concerns over subsistence economies and alternative coping strategies*' (Deas et al, 2020: 9, emphasis added). Much research is still to be done on the ways in which civil society organisations have emerged as key players in the delivery of public services with consequences for civic gain and loss. The challenge, of course, is upscaling, as a 'perennial issue' this is how 'the influence of these groups and the lessons learned from them can spread beyond their immediate locality'. An 'urban platform' mechanism is often needed to allow for the 'integration and deliberation of these multiple concerns' (Hodson et al, 2020: 213). Moreover, advancing Deas et al (2020) and previous research on the social economy and civil society (Amin et al, 2002, 2003), strategies and their interventions need to move beyond mitigating against the effects of capitalism and make that shift towards fundamentally challenging and replacing the current growth model.

In Wales, FE thinking is beginning to address some of these difficult questions, by focusing on underpinning policies and action plans as part of the proactive 'governance of the future' (R. Jones, 2019) agenda within civil society. In the context of the Wellbeing of Future Generations Act (Welsh Government, 2015a), which as noted in Chapter 5 is central to new narratives of justice, the Welsh Government has been supporting and developing the FE as part of a desire for a better and more socially and spatially just Wales by the year 2050 (see Davidson, 2020). State strategy since 2019 has focused on three areas.

First, a £4.5 million Foundational Economy Challenge Fund has been established to support a series of experimental projects that test how the Welsh Government can best support the FE and which government interventions work best. Second, a renewed focus has occurred, growing the 'missing middle' to increase the number of grounded firms in Wales and establish a firm base of medium-sized Welsh firms, which are capable of selling outside Wales but have decision making firmly rooted in communities. Third, spreading and scaling best practice follows this by looking at social value within procurement. Critical here are the strengthening of local supply chains and changes to local governance within city regions via the recently created Public Service Boards. These have been designed to renew local state democracy, but suffer the initial problem of adding to 'regional partnership complexity' (WLGA, 2017: 2) and alongside city-regional governance, not linking with the more progressive Future Generations Act interventions on spatial justice (Axinte, 2020). Monitoring these developments and their impact on civil society will prove critical for assessing if, how, and where the FE is being translated from theory, to manifesto, then into geographical practice.

Postscript: Landing the foundational economy post-COVID-19

CORONAVIRUS ALERT. New rules in force now: you must stay home. More info & exemptions at gov.uk/ coronavirus Stay home. Protect the NHS. Save lives. (Text message from UK Government to all UK mobile phones, 15 March 2020)

It's important for me to level with you – we know things will get worse before they get better. But we are making the right preparations, and the more we all follow the rules, the fewer lives will be lost and the sooner life can return to normal. (Letter sent by Prime Minister Boris Johnson to all UK homes, 8 April 2020)

At the time of writing, there is a coronavirus global pandemic (COVID-19) outbreak. This started in Wuhan, China, possibly originating in a seafood wholesale market as the original source of transmission from bats to humans. As of 1 February 2021, there have been over 2.1 million confirmed worldwide deaths and 101 million confirmed cases. The pandemic has resulted in mobility restrictions and nationwide 'lockdowns' to slowdown the rates of infection and ease the pressure on national health and other services.

The lockdown has created the conditions for a worldwide recession by exposing the 'frailty of the social contract' (*Financial Times*, 2000: 10) and the 'imbalances in contemporary society' (Elliott, 2020: 2). With productivity slowing and large groups of individuals on either short-terms contracts and or unable to work from home, millions have been forced out of work and onto a series of welfare benefits such as (in the UK) UC. In the early months of lockdown, for instance, the UK unemployment count rapidly increased with over 1.5 million new benefit claims and predictions of 8 million (25 per cent of the workforce) jobs being at risk (McKinsey & Company, 2020). This has impacted disproportionality on civil society, heavily reinforcing existing patterns of labour market inequality and precarity. Weak labour markets dependent on low skills and localities of poverty within the areas of multiple deprivation have taken the brunt of intense economic restructuring (compare the accounts of Berry et al, 2020; Centre for Cities, 2020; Etherington, 2020; Guinan et al, 2020; Local Trust, 2020). Moreover, COVID-19 related death rates in the most deprived areas are more than double those of the less deprived and the socioeconomic gap in COVID-19 mortality is larger than the general mortality gap (ONS, 2020).

Economic recovery and growth models

The political economic geography of (de)growth and recovery is critical, with predictions of economic contraction being at least 20 per cent for the UK economy, compared to an OECD average of nearly 10 per cent, with time periods being modelled and supply-chain critical sectors (such as advanced manufacturing) being hit hardest (see Gregory and Arnold, 2020; Midlands Engine, 2020). In March 2020, with a Coronavirus Act, the UK Government stepped in to rescue the economy with an unprecedented £350 billion financial package to support jobs, incomes and businesses, acting in nothing short of a 'wartime ... do whatever it takes' measure by the Conservatives. The stimulus package, which included a Job Retention Scheme for 'furloughing' 8 million jobs (covering one-third of all private sector employees), a massive new government loan guarantee scheme for businesses and a three-month mortgage holiday, was worth around 15 per cent of the UK's total GDP and far exceeds the scale of the rescue measures taken in the wake of the 2008 financial crash. There is limited provision for contingent workers identified by zero-hour or seasonal work and those in rented accommodation (see Etherington, 2020; Thomas et al, 2020). In short, the spectre of Lefebvre looms: '[t]he reproduction of the relations of production, both as a concept and as a reality, has not been "discovered": it has revealed itself' (Lefebvre, 1976: 7).

At the local level, LAs were asked by the government to 'make things happen' to prevent societal collapse, particularly for older and disabled people at risk. Councils were to be given 'the resources they need[ed] to do the job' (Jenrick, 2020: 1). The Local Resilience Forums, created under civil contingency planning legislation, were activated and previous discourses of 'big community' and 'self-contained social units' (Senior, 1969: 46) deployed at LA spatial scales in England and the city-region scale in Wales to provide the conditions for multi-agency strategic and operational responses. Gaps immediately emerged between the metagovernance rhetoric of planning (see Haughton et al, 2020) and the continued march of austerity and its impact on the local state. A study undertaken by the Special Interest Group of Municipal Authorities estimated, for England's 343 LAs, a financial shortfall of £8 billion for 2020 – caused by increased emergency expenditure (food packages, social care, and so on) not covered by central government and lost revenues from business rates, council tax and commercial activity (Butler and Syal, 2020: 6; see also LGA, 2020). In the case of Greater Manchester, the city-regional 'comeback kid' (Williams, 2020a: 3), government intervention initially covered only 12 per cent of the forecast financial impact of COVID-19. This produced a shortfall of £541 million, putting Manchester City Council 'on the brink of ruin' (Williams, 2020b: 2). With civil society actors claiming locality experiences of 'nothing like this since 1930s' (Williams, 2020a: 3), wider claims of the fracturing and even 'collapse of central–local relations' in the wake of this crisis have been made (Harris, 2020; Williams, 2020c).

The 'COVID-19 crisis' exemplifies what many who have made arguments around the FE and more broadly the concept of Social Reproduction (Bhattacharya, 2017) have been outlining. In simple terms, the functioning of the economy is fundamentally built on these concepts and when these foundations are rocked, the entire economy very quickly starts to shake and crumble (see Berry et al, 2020). In this context, as we noted in the Introduction, the state is forced to reconcile an ongoing tension between the neoliberal necessity to maintain the expansion of surplus value, the accumulation strategy of the economy at large, with the need to sustain social harmony and its own legitimation during the crisis. This is most prescient in the context of care, healthcare being obvious, but also broader notions of social care (including childcare, disability care, care for the elderly and so on; see Askew, 2009). Many currently working from home have discovered this for themselves; without the support of nurseries, schools and home caring services, their ability to complete a day's labour has become increasingly difficult. Added to this, has been an awareness of what industries really matter in a crisis by what is comprehended as 'key work/worker'; those who have had to keep going despite obvious risk represent the parts of economy and society that cannot be allowed to stop in order to not only maintain the current economy, but the fabric of society itself. There are also parts of the economy and society that simply cannot afford to stop or cannot work remotely from home. This is either due to the nature of their employment, particularly those self-employed, or the nature of the work they do, which has meant COVID-19 has increased their precarity.

The need for and belief in a FE solution to the contemporary crisis, however, has not been reflected in the policy choices of the past 10 to 15 years. Whereby, the focus shifted towards the maintenance and recovery of the neoliberal accumulation strategy, for the UK state, following the 2008 global financial crisis. This coincided with an ideological attack on the functioning of the state (especially the local state) via austerity, as we have outlined here. 'Austerity localism' (Griggs et al, 2017), which we have identified through this book, and associated with austerity plus the devolution of risk and responsibility away from the state to protect both state and market from undue demands on their resources, defines this retrenchment of the local state and has greatly undermined a whole series of foundational institutions therein. This means austerity, combined with multiple waves of privatisation, in the years prior to the COVID-19 crisis has routinely stripped sectors (particularly those around health, social care, worker support, police and LAs themselves) of their capacity to act with, or without, the current crisis, while focusing spending on other sectors of the economy (Monbiot, 2020). Yet, it is these underfunded parts of the economy, the state and more broadly civil society that are now most crucial to dealing with the crisis. Summarising these manifold economic and social concerns across the UK:

The Covid-19 pandemic has caught the United Kingdom woefully underprepared. The present crisis has revealed the distressed state of our local economies and the brittle condition of the local public sector, following decades of underinvestment and disrespect. At the same time, this dual public health and economic emergency has underscored the centrality of community to our everyday lives. As we ready ourselves to rebuild and reconstruct within the shattered post-Covid-19 landscape, we must strive to make the economic recovery the starting point for economic reform and *a new birth of community in this country*. (Guinan et al, 2020: 3, emphasis added)

The redistributive switching of the UK state under austerity has also, in a deeply contradictory sense, sought to empower the 'local' via devolution to city regions. This has been a very specific form of 'empowerment' (Amin et al 2002, 2003; Bailey and Wood, 2017), that should be viewed as a broader metagovernance state strategy, which is 'spatially selective' (Jones, 1997) and seeks to only give agency to certain strategically-significant actors. As we have demonstrated in this book, this economy-first narrative with an emphasis on agglomerative growth (often measured in terms of GVA uplift) has been written through the process of building city regions. This agenda has focused on high-end growth, while simultaneously ignoring the foundational aspects of the economy on which it is built (see Jonas, 2012; Schneider and Cottineau, 2019). This further distances 'non-economic' actors from positions of agency and through the creation of institutions such as LEPs, alongside devolution, city, and growth deals, new 'citizenship regimes' (see Jenson and Phillips, 1996) are collectively instilled. As our chapters have revealed, this positions civil society on the *outside*, whereby they have to contest (with some albeit limited success,) the prevailing direction of city-region building.

The cumulative consequences of the above have, of course, resulted in an unbalanced form of economy being developed. We have argued that the paralleled or entwined processes of austerity and city-region devolution have disempowered, depoliticised and weakened the structures of social reproduction in favour of a neoliberal growth model. This means that during the COVID-19 crisis itself, the state is and has been less well equipped to deal with the strains that are being placed on it (Berry et al, 2020; Dodds et al, 2020; Etherington, 2020). This could have catastrophic effects in the short to medium term with regards to how the crisis will develop, but it also grants an opportunity to think through what next and what sort of economy should be built post-the-crisis.

Research agendas on foundational economy city regions

Commentators are talking about the need for 'Local Marshall Plans' to guide the economy in and through a period of 'multifaceted recovery' (Localis, 2020). In the coming months and years, it is hoped that the mistakes of austerity in the context of the COVID-19 crisis, as well as the increased awareness to what the FE does as a vital service for people's lives and livelihoods, pushes societal and governmental thinking towards a new way of conceptualising the economy that places these needs first. The FE is that part of the economy which produces essential goods and services consumed by all (regardless of income and status). This part of the economy is well suited to developing new models of co-production for the design and delivery of public services such as education, care for the elderly and housing, where LAs need to work with civil society. This different approach to areas of our lives, such as the provision of food in schools and social care, requires politicians to leave behind the austerity agenda and instead tap the power of purchase in more strategic and transformational ways to promote public health, social justice and ecological integrity. The Foundational Economy Collective (2018: 7–11) accordingly points to a ten-point plan for post-crisis restructuring and renewal, which we feel provides city-region building with new opportunities and challenges:

1. Start the extension of collective responsibility for foundational basics with health and care.
2. After health, housing and energy are the other immediate foundational priorities.
3. Food is altogether more complex but needs tackling.
4. Introduce social licensing: regulation which imposes social and environmental obligations on all corporate providers of foundational services.
5. Reform taxes on income, expenditure and wealth to greatly increase the capacity of government to raise revenue.
6. Disintermediate investment from pension funds and insurance company bailouts so that it goes directly into provision of material infrastructure.
7. Shorten fragile long supply chains in foundational commodities while recognising the futility of local autarchy.

8. Every city, town and peripheral rural area should develop a live/work transition plan within nation state and EU enabling frameworks.
9. Rebuild technical and administrative capacity at all levels of government.
10. Finally, the European countries need to accept some responsibility for completely inadequate foundational systems like health care in adjacent regions.

This extensive list points to a very different conception as to how to form governmental city-regional infrastructures and what their priorities should be. In short, it seeks to rebuild the capacities of the economy and the state (many lost through austerity) to give the support needed for citizens to live better lives in all places. This deviates greatly from the direction of travel perpetuated by the UK Government and development of city regions discussed throughout this book. City regions, if they are to have a future post-COVID-19, need to be reconstituted to embrace the foundational aspects of the economy and be opened up towards more politicised and open forms of democratic participation. A repoliticisation project is urgently needed, which 'attempts to rekindle political debate, whether by engaging with formal democratic institutions or by fusing "soft" institutions with mechanisms through which ideas and antagonisms can play out' (Deas et al, 2020: 4). Finally, as the COVID-19 crisis in the UK and globally deepens, the unprecedented response, which has required, at high speed, increased investment in foundational aspects of the economy, as well as for new forms of financial support to be given, hints at what could and should be maintained after the crisis period. Whether this happens is a very different question.

A future research agenda for civic expansion and 'civic repair' (Lockwood, 1999) city regions should be concerned with action and other research in specific FE sectors. This should draw on heterodox conceptions in which social innovation, place-based innovation, smart cities and mission-led innovation oblige us to reconsider what 'innovation' actually means today and who are its principal agents. The 'foundational turn' points to the following questions: to what extent are local and regional growth policies focusing on foundational sectors? Are they addressing inclusive growth through social innovation in specific sectors? What forms of social innovation are being adopted in different regional contexts? How can interventions in FE sectors contribute to regional growth and civic gain? Addressing these points will deliver significant theoretical and empirical findings of relevance to academics and policymakers addressing the area of city-regions research. These include: economic development (broadly), smart cities, regional studies, urban studies and place-based innovation in the contemporary crisis and beyond. In the UK context, 50 years on, a key question raised by the Royal Commission on Local Government in England remains for civil society and city-region building endeavours, with a contemporary reminder offered by Cumbers on democratic structures now being urgently needed to underpin economic life:

> If one wants the interests of a region as a whole to prevail through the democratic process, *one must create a structure which enables these interests to find effective expression in action.* If one creates a structure that gives only sectional interests the power to take positive action, it is no use expecting the electoral process to negate itself in order to avert the natural consequences of one's folly. To do so is not an act of faith in human altruism: it is an act of sabotage to democracy. (Senior, 1969: 22, emphasis added)

> A functioning democracy, in a stable and civilized society, is one that respects the rights of individuals, citizens and communities to *participate on equal terms in the public and civic realms of society.* Given the central importance of the economy in providing the resources necessary for a society to flourish, the decision making around these resources should be a matter for public engagement and democratic debate. (Cumbers, 2020: 3, emphasis added, see also Cumbers, 2012)

Notes

Chapter 2

[1] See www.libdemvoice.org/devo-sheffield-announced-transport-skills-business-support-housing-no-mayor-43737.html

Chapter 4

[1] See www.walesonline.co.uk/business/appointments/cardiff-capital-region reveals-board-14299732

[2] See www.bbc.co.uk/news/uk-wales-42737949

Chapter 5

[1] Anglesey, Conwy, Denbighshire, Flintshire, Gwynedd and Wrexham.

[2] In its original sense 'metrophilia' refers to a fetish for poetry, but is used in this context to refer to a fetish for narratives that valorise the metropolis.

[3] See www.bbc.co.uk/news/uk-wales-46031434; www.bbc.co.uk/news/uk-wales-politics-46482907

[4] In 2011, the percentage of people aged 3+ who can speak Welsh in Gwynedd (NW Wales) was 65.4 per cent, whereas in Wrexham (NE Wales) it was 12.9 per cent.

[5] See www.countytimes.co.uk/news/17684963.mid-wales-growth-deal-minister-pleased-with-progress-in-powys/

Chapter 6

[1] See www.walesonline.co.uk/news/wales-news/police-reveal-project-centre-swansea-16679624

[2] www.swanseabaycitydeal.wales/news/regional-green-light-for-587-million-neath-port-talbot-programme/

References

Allen, M. and Ainley, P. (2013) *The Great Reversal: Young People, Education and Employment in a Declining Economy*, Radicaled, London.

Allmendinger, P. and Haughton, G. (2012) 'Post-political spatial planning in England: a crisis of consensus?' *Transactions of the Institute of British Geographers*, 37: 89–103.

Allmendinger, P. and Haughton, G. (2015) 'Post-political regimes in English planning: from third way to big society' in J. Metzger, P. Allmendinger and S. Oosterlynck (eds) *Planning Against the Political: Democratic Deficits in European Territorial Governance*, Routledge, London, 29–53.

Amin, A., Cameron, A. and Hudson, R. (2002) *Placing the Social Economy*, Routledge, London.

Amin, A., Cameron, A. and Hudson, R. (2003) 'The alterity of the social economy' in A. Leyshon, R. Lee and C.C. Williams (eds) *Alternative Economic Spaces*, Sage, London, 27–54.

Askew, L.E. (2009) ' "At home" in state institutions: the caring practices and potentialities of human service workers' *Geoforum*, 40: 655–63.

Atkinson, R. and Flint, J. (2001) 'Accessing hidden and hard-to-reach populations: snowball research strategies' *Social Science Update*, 33, Department of Sociology, University of Surrey.

Axinte, L.F. (2020) 'Regenerative City Regions? A Case Study of Cardiff Capital Regions and its Future Generations' Thesis submitted for the degree of Doctor of Philosophy in City and Regional Planning, Cardiff University.

Axinte, L.F., Mehmood, A., Marsden, T. and Roep, D. (2019) 'Regenerative city-regions: a new conceptual framework' *Regional Studies, Regional Science,* 6: 117–129.

Ayres, S., Sandford, M. and Coombes, T. (2017) 'Policy-making "front" and "back" stage: assessing the implications for effectiveness and democracy' *The British Journal of Politics and International Relations*, 19: 861–876.

Bailey, D. and Budd, L. (ed) (2016) *Devolution and the UK Economy*, Rowman & Littlefield, London.

Bailey, D. and Wood, M. (2017) 'The metagovernance of English devolution' *Local Government Studies*, 43: 655–663.

Bailey, N. and Turok, I. (2001) 'Central Scotland as a polycentric urban region: useful planning concept or chimera?' *Urban Studies*, 38: 697–715.

Bakker, K. (2010) *Privatising Water: Governance Failure and the World's Urban Water Crisis*, Cornell University Press, New York.

Barber, B.R. (2014) *If Mayors Ruled the World: Dysfunctional Nations, Rising Cities*, Yale University Press, New Haven, CT.

Beardmore, E. (2015) 'No choice over mayor in £900m historic deal' *The Star*, 3 October, 8–9.

Beatty, C. and Fothergill, S. (2014) 'The local and regional impact of the UK's welfare reforms' *Cambridge Journal of Regions, Economy and Society*, 7: 63–79.

Beatty, C. and Fothergill, S. (2016) *The Uneven Impact of Welfare Reform*, Sheffield Hallam University, Sheffield.

Beatty, C. and Fothergill, S. (2017) *Jobs Welfare and Austerity: How the Destruction of Industrial Britain Casts a Shadow Over Present Day Public Finances*, CRESR, Sheffield Hallam University, Sheffield.

Bedale, C. (2016) 'Health and Social Care Reform in Greater Manchester' Presentation to Greater Manchester Association of TUCs Conference, 24 September.

Beel, D., Jones, M., Jones, I.R. and Escadale, W. (2017) 'Connected growth: developing a framework to drive inclusive growth across a city-region' *Local Economy*, 32: 565–75.

Bell, A. and Hindmoor, A. (2009) *Rethinking Governance: The Centrality of the State in Modern Society*, Cambridge University Press, Cambridge.

Bentham, J., Bowman, A., De la Cuesta, M., Engelen, E., Ertürk, I., Folkman, P., Froud, J., Johal, S., Law, J., Leaver, A., Moran, M. and Williams, K. (2013) 'Manifesto for the Foundational Economy' CRESC Working Paper 131, Centre for Research on Socio-Cultural Change, Manchester.

Berry, C. (2016) 'Industrial policy change in the post-crisis British economy: policy innovation in an incomplete institutional and ideational environment' *The British Journal of Politics and International Relations*, 18: 829–47.

Berry, C. and Giovannini, A. (eds) (2018) *Developing England's North: The Political Economy of the Northern Powerhouse*, Palgrave Macmillan, London.

Berry, C., O'Donovan, N., Bailey, D., Barber, A., Beel, D., Jones, K., McDaniel, S. and Weicht, R. (2020) *The Covidist Manifesto: Assessing the UK State's Emergency Enlargement*, Future Economies UCRKE, Manchester Metropolitan University, Manchester.

Bevan Foundation and Joseph Rowntree Foundation (2017) *Everyone Better Off: Why Cardiff Capital Region's Growth Must be Inclusive*, Cardiff Capital Region Commission on Growth and Competitiveness, Cardiff.

Bhattacharya, T. (2017) *Social Reproduction Theory: Remapping Class, Recentering Oppression*, Pluto, London.

BIS (2010a) 'Understanding local growth' BIS Economics Paper, Number 7, Department for Business, Innovation and Skills, London.

BIS (2010b) *Skills for Sustainable Growth*, Department for Business, Innovation and Skills, London.

BIS (2011) *The Plan for Growth*, Department for Business, Innovation and Skills, London.

BIS (2015) 'Evaluation of the employer ownership of skills pilot, round 1: initial findings' BIS Research Paper, Number 221, Department for Business, Innovation and Skills, London.

Blackaby, D., Drinkwater, S., Murphy, P., Leary, N.O. and Staneva, A. (2018) 'The Welsh economy and the labour market' *Welsh Economic Review*, 26: 1–12.

Blanco, I., Griggs, S. and Sullivan, H. (2014) 'Situating the local in the neoliberalisation and transformation of urban governance' *Urban Studies*, 51: 3129–46.

Bock, B.B. (2016) 'Rural marginalisation and the role of social innovation: a turn towards exogenous development and rural reconnection' *Sociologia Ruralis*, 56: 552–73.

Bogdanor, V. (1999) *Devolution in the UK*, Oxford University Press, Oxford.

Bogdanor, V. (2019) *Beyond Brexit: Towards a British Constitution*, IB Tauris, London.

Bowman, D., Froud, J., Joha, S., Law, J., Leaver, A., Moran, M. and Williams, K. (2014) *The End of the Experiment: From Competition to the Foundational Economy*, Manchester University Press, Manchester.

Braudel, F. (1981) *The Structure of Everyday Life, Civilization and Capitalism*, Volume 1, Harper and Row, New York.

Breathnach, P. (2014) 'Creating city-region governance structures in a dysfunctional polity: the case of Ireland's national spatial strategy' *Urban Studies*, 51: 2267–84.

Brenner, N. (2004) *New State Spaces: Urban Governance and Rescaling of Statehood*, Oxford University Press, Oxford.

Brenner, N. (2019) *New Urban Spaces: Urban Theory and the Scale Question*, Oxford University Press, Oxford.

Brenner, N. and Elden, S. (eds) (2009) *State, Space, World: Selected Essays*, University of Minnesota Press, Minneapolis, MT.

Brenner, N. and Schmid, C. (2011) 'Planetary urbanisation' in M. Gandy (ed) *Urban Constellations*, Jovis, Berlin, 10–13.

Brenner, N., Peck, J., and Theodore, N. (2012) *Afterlives of Neoliberalism: Civic City Cahier 4*, Bedford Press, London.

Bristow, G. (2018) 'Reflections on the Welsh economy: remanence, resilience and resourcefulness' *Welsh Economic Review*, 26: 13–20.

Bristow, G. and Healy, A. (2015) 'Crisis response, choice and resilience: insights from complexity thinking' *Cambridge Journal of Regions, Economy and Society*, 8: 241–56.

Burn, C. (2017) 'How station saga helped to derail devolution hopes' *Yorkshire Post*, 22 September, 17.

Burnett, K. (2016) 'Northern Powerhouse, northern politics' in 'Powering on: The Northern Powerhouse, two years in' *New Statesman*, 19–25 February, 22.

Burnham, P. (2014) 'Depoliticisation: economic crisis and political management' *Policy and Politics*, 42: 189–206.

Buser, M. (2013) 'Democratic accountability and metropolitan governance: the case of South Hampshire, UK' *Urban Studies*, 51: 2336–53.

Butler, P. and Syal, R. (2020) 'Coronavirus crisis may leave English councils with £5bn funding shortfall' *The Guardian*, 26 April, 6.

Callinicos, A. (2012) 'Contradictions of austerity' *Cambridge Journal of Economics*, 36: 65–77.

Calzada, I. (2017) 'Metropolitan and city-regional politics in the urban age: why does "(smart) devolution" matter?' *Palgrave Communications*, 3, SSRN, London.

Centre for Cities (2015) 'Northern Powerhouse' Factsheet, 2 June, Centre for Cities, London.

Centre for Cities (2020) 'Coronavirus: feature' Briefing, 27 April, Centre for Cities, London.

CESI (2014) *The Work Programme: How Is It Performing?* Centre for Economic and Social Inclusion, London.

Chaney, P. (2016) 'How does single party dominance influence civil society organisations engagement strategies? Exploratory analysis of participative mainstreaming in a "regional" European polity' *Public Policy and Administration*, 31: 122–46.

Clarke, G.R., Martin, R. and Tyler, P. (2016) 'Divergent cities? Unequal urban growth and development' *Cambridge Journal of Regions, Economy and Society*, 9: 259–68.

Cochrane, A. and Massey, D. (1989) 'Developing a socialist urban policy' in P. Alcock, A. Gamble, P. Lee and A. Walker (eds) *The Social Economy and the Democratic State: A New Policy Agenda for the 1990s*, London, Lawrence and Wishart, 132–54.

Conservative Party (2015) *Conservative Election Manifesto 2015*.

Cox, K. (1989) 'The politics of turf and the question of class' in M. Dear and J. Wolch (eds) *The Power of Geography: How Territory Shapes Social Life*, Unwin Hyman, London, 61–90.

Cox, K. (1998) 'Spaces of dependence, space of engagement and the politics of scale, or: looking for local politics', *Political Geography*, 17: 1–14.

CRESC (2015) 'What Wales could be', Report for FSB Wales, Centre for Research on Socio-Cultural Change, Manchester.

Crouch, C. (2004) *Post-Democracy*, Polity, Cambridge.

Crouch, C. (2020) *Post-Democracy After the Crisis*, Polity, Cambridge.

Cumbers, A. (2012) *Reclaiming Public Ownership: Making Space for Economic Democracy*, ZED Books, London.

Cumbers, A. (2020) *The Case for Economic Democracy*, Polity, Cambridge.

Cumbers, A., Helms, G. and Swanson, K. (2010) 'Class agency and resistance in the older industrial city' *Antipode*, 42: 46–73.

D'Arcy, C., Gardiner, L. and Rahman, F. (2019) *Low Pay in Greater Manchester*, Resolution Foundation, London.

Danson, M., MacLeod, G. and Mooney, G. (2012) 'Devolution and the shifting political economic geographies of the United Kingdom' *Environment and Planning C: Government and Policy*, 30: 1–9.

Darling, J. (2016) 'Privatising asylum: neoliberalisation, depoliticisation and the governance of forced migration' *Transactions of the Institute of British Geographers*, 41: 230–43.

Davidson, J. (2020) *#Futuregen: Lessons from a Small Country*, Chelsea Green Publishing, London.

Davidson, M. and Ward, K. (2018) *Cities Under Austerity: Restructuring the US Metropolis*, SUNY Press, New York.

Davies, J.S. and Blanco, I. (2017) 'Austerity urbanism: patterns of neoliberalisation and resistance in six cities and the UK' *Environment and Planning A*, 49: 1517–36.

Davies, P. (2011) *The Role of Local Enterprise Partnerships in Tackling Skills Needs*. 157 Group, London.

Davies, R. (1999) 'Devolution: a process, not an event' *The Gregynog Papers*, Cardiff.

Dean, J. (2009) *Democracy and Other Neoliberal Fantasies: Communicative Capitalism and Left Politics*, Duke University Press, Durham, NC.

Dear, M. and Wolch, J. (1987) *Landscapes of Despair: From Deinstitutionalisation to Homelessness*, Polity, Cambridge.

Deas, I. (2013) 'Towards a post-political consensus in urban policy? Localism and the emerging agenda for regeneration under the Cameron Government' *Planning Practice and Research*, 28: 65–82.

Deas, I. (2014) 'The search for territorial fixes in subnational governance: city-regions and disputed emergence of post-political consensus in Manchester, England' *Urban Studies*, 51: 2285–314.

Deas, I., Haughton, G. and Ward, K. (2020) 'Scalar postpolitics, inclusive growth and inclusive economies: challenging the Greater Manchester agglomeration model' *Cambridge Journal of Regions, Economy and Society*, https://doi:10.1093/cjres/rsaa022

DeVerteuil, G. (2016) *Resilience in the Post-Welfare Inner City: Voluntary Sector Geographies in London, Los Angeles and Sydney*, Policy Press, Bristol.

Devin, D., Bickerstaffe, T., Nunn, A., Mitchell, B., MacQuaid, R., Egdell, V. and Lindsay, C. (2011) *The Role of Skills from Worklessness to Sustainable Employment with Progression*, UKCES, Wath-upon-Dearne.

Dicks, B. (2014) 'Participatory community regeneration: a discussion of risks, accountability and crisis in devolved Wales' *Urban Studies*, 51: 959–77.

Dodds, K., Castan Broto, V., Detterbeck, K., Jones, M., Mamadouth, V., Ramutsindela, M., Varsanyi, M., Waschsmuth, D. and Yuan Woon, C. (2020) 'Covid-19 pandemic: territory, politics, governance dimensions of the crisis' *Territory, Politics, Governance*, 8: 289–98.

Donald, B., Glasmeier, A., Gray, A. and Lobao, L. (2014) 'Austerity in the city: economic crises and urban service decline' *Cambridge Journal of Regions, Economy and Society*, 7: 3–15.

Dore, J. (2020) 'Message from the Leader of Sheffield City Council: Council Tax 2020–21' Sheffield City Council, Sheffield.

Dromey, J. and McNeil, C. (2017) *Skills 2030: Why the Adult Skills System Is Failing to Build an Economy for Everyone*, IPPR, London.

Duncan, S. and Goodwin, M. (1988) *The Local State and Uneven Development: Behind the Local Government Crisis*, Polity, Cambridge.

Economy, Infrastructure and Skills Committee (2017) *City Deals and the Regional Economies of Wales*, National Assembly for Wales, Cardiff.

Ekosgen (2012) *Skills Enhancement Fund: Skills Research in the Sheffield City Region*, Ekosgen, Sheffield.

Elliott, L. (2020) 'The coronavirus has exposed the imbalances in modern Britain' *The Guardian*, 3 May, 2.

Ellison, G., Glaeser, E.L. and Kerr, W. (2007) 'What causes agglomeration? Evidence from coagglomeration patterns' Working Paper, No. 07-13, Centre for Economic Studies, US Census Bureau, Washington.

Emmerich, M. (2017a) *Britain's Cities, Britain's Future*, London Publishing Partnership, London.

Emmerich, M. (2017b) 'Rejecting devo will scupper social progress', *Local Government Chronicle*, 2 October, 6.

Emmerich, M. (2020a) 'Important choices lie ahead', *The Municipal Journal*, 2 March, 6.

Emmerich, M. (2020b) *Levelling Up: Making Investment Appraisal Fit for Purpose*, Metro-Dynamics, London.

Engelen, E., Froud, J., Sukhdev, J., Salento, A. and Williams, K. (2017) 'The grounded city: from competitivity to the foundational economy' *Cambridge Journal of Regions, Economy and Society*, 10: 407–23.

Etherington, D. (2020) *Austerity, Welfare and Work: Exploring Politics, Geographies and Inequalities*, Policy Press, Bristol.

Etherington, D. and Jones, M. (2009) 'City-regions: new geographies of uneven development and inequality' *Regional Studies*, 43: 247–65.

Etherington, D. and Jones, M. (2016a) 'The city-region chimera: the political economy of metagovernance failure in Britain' *Cambridge Journal of Regions, Economy and Society*, 9: 371–89.

Etherington, D. and Jones, M. (2016b) 'Devolution and disadvantage in the Sheffield City-Region: an assessment of employment, skills, and welfare policies' Sheffield Solutions Policy Briefing, September, Faculty of Social Sciences, The University of Sheffield, Sheffield.

Etherington, D. and Jones, M. (2017) 'Devolution, austerity and inclusive growth in Greater Manchester: assessing impacts and developing alternatives' Policy Brief, Staffordshire Business School, Staffordshire University, Stoke-on-Trent.

Etherington, D. and Jones, M. (2018) 'Restating the post-political: depoliticization, social inequalities, and city-region growth' *Environment and Planning A*, 50: 51–72.

EWERC (2017) *Just Work in Greater Manchester,* European Work and Employment Research Centre, Manchester Business School, Manchester.

Fairclough, N. (2010) *Critical Discourse Analysis: The Study of Language*, Routledge, London.

Fall, K. (2020) 'My life in No 10' Interview with Andrew Billen, *The Times Magazine*, 29 February, 44–7.

Fawcett, P., Flinders, M., Hay, C. and Wood, M. (eds) (2017) *Anti-Politics, Depoliticization, and Governance*, Oxford University Press, Oxford.

Financial Times (2000) 'Virus lays bare the frailty of the social contract' *Financial Times*, 4 April, 10.

Finegold, D. and Soskice, D. (1988) 'The failure of training in Britain: analysis and prescription' *Oxford Review of Economic Policy*, 4: 21–53.

Finn, D. (1987) *Training Without Jobs*, Macmillan, London.

Finn, D. (2015) *Welfare to Work Devolution in England*, Joseph Rowntree Foundation, York.

Florida, R. (2014) *The Rise of the Creative Class, Revisited*, Basic Books, New York.

Folkman, P., Froud, J., Johal, S., Tomaney, J. and Williams, K. (2016) *Manchester Transformed: Why We Need a Reset of City Region Policy, Centre for Research on Socio-Cultural Change*, The University of Manchester, Manchester.

Foster, E., Kerr, P. and Byrne, C. (2014) 'Rolling back to roll forward: depoliticisation and the extension of government' *Policy and Politics*, 42: 225–41.

Foundational Economy Collective (2018) *The Foundational Economy: The Infrastructure of Everyday Life,* Manchester University Press, Manchester.

Fraser, A. (2010) 'The craft of scalar practices' *Environment and Planning D: Society and Space*, 42: 332–46.

Fujita, M. and Krugman, P. (1995) 'When is the economy monocentric? Von Thünen and Chamberlin unified' *Regional Science and Urban Economics*, 25: 505–28.

Fuller, C. (2017) 'City government in an age of austerity: discursive institutions and critique' *Environment and Planning A*, 49: 745–66.

Fuller, C. (2018) 'Entrepreneurial urbanism, austerity and economic governance' *Cambridge Journal of Regions, Economy and Society*, 11: 565–85.

Gardiner, B., Martin, R., Sunley, P. and Tyler, P. (2013) 'Spatially unbalanced growth in the British economy' *Journal of Economic Geography*, 13: 371–89.

Glaeser, E. (2012) *Triumph of the City*, Macmillan, London.

GMCA (2018) *Welfare Reform and Universal Credit in Greater Manchester*, Greater Manchester Combined Authority, Manchester.

GMCDP (2018) *Disabled People's Manifesto*, Greater Manchester Coalition for Disabled People, Manchester.

GMLC (2017) 'ESA Claims' A study by Paul Cosier, Great Manchester Law Centre, Manchester.

GMLC (2018) 'Universal Credit roll-out: the end of social security' Press Release 18 April, Greater Manchester Law Centre, Manchester.

Gooberman, L. (2017) *From Depression to Devolution: Economy and Government in Wales, 1934–2006*, University of Wales Press, Cardiff.

Goodwin, M., Duncan, S. and Halford, S. (1993) 'Regulation theory, the local state and the transition of urban politics' *Environment and Planning D: Society and Space*, 11: 67–88.

Goodwin, M., Jones, M. and Jones R. (2005) 'Devolution, constitutional change and the geographies of economic development: explaining and understanding the new institutional geographies of the British state' *Regional Studies*, 39: 421–36.

Goodwin, M., Jones, M. and Jones, R. (2012) *Rescaling the State: Devolution and the Geographies of Economic Governance*, Manchester University Press, Manchester.

Goodwin, M., Jones, M. and Jones, R. (2017) *Rescaling the State: Devolution and the Geographies of Economic Governance*, Manchester University Press, Manchester. (New Preface for the paperback edition.)

Gough, J. (2014) 'The difference between local and national capitalism, and why local capitalisms differ from one another: a Marxist approach' *Capital and Class*, 38: 197–210.

Gramsci, A. (1971) *Prison Notebooks*, Lawrence and Wishart, London.

Granqvist, K., Sarjamo, S. and Mäntysalo, R. (2019) 'Polycentricity as spatial imaginary: the case of Helsinki City Plan' *European Planning Studies*, 27: 739–58.

Gray, M. and Barford, A. (2018) 'The depth of the cuts: the uneven geography of local government austerity' *Cambridge Journal of Regions, Economy and Society*, 11: 541–63.

Gregory, M. and Arnold, P. (2020) 'Understanding the potential economic impacts of Coronavirus' Briefing, Ernst & Young, London.

Griggs, S., Howarth, D. and MacKillop, E. (2017) 'The meta-governance of austerity, localism, and practices of depoliticization' in P. Fawcett, M. Flinders, C. Hay and M. Wood (eds) *Anti-Politics, Depoliticization, and Governance*, Oxford University Press, Oxford, 195–216.

Guinan, J., Leibowitz, J., McInroy, N. and McKinsey, S. (2020) *Owning the Future: After Covid-19, a New Era of Community Wealth Building*, The Democratic Collective and the Centre for Local Economic Strategies, Manchester.

Hadjimichalis, C. and Hudson, R. (2014) 'Contemporary crisis across Europe and the crisis of regional development theories' *Regional Studies*, 48: 208–18.

Hall, P. (2009) 'Looking backward, looking forward: the city region in the mid-21st century' *Regional Studies*, 43: 803–16.

Hall, P. and Tewdwr-Jones, M. (2010) *Urban and Regional Planning*, 5th edition, London, Routledge.

Hall, S. (2011) 'The march of the neoliberals' *The Guardian*, 12 September, 6–7.

Harding, A. (2007) 'Taking city regions seriously? Response to debate on "City-regions: new geographies of governance, democracy and social reproduction"' *International Journal of Urban and Regional Research*, 31: 443–58.

Harris, J. (2020) 'The pandemic has exposed the failings of Britain's centralised state' *The Guardian*, 25 May, 3.

Harrison, J. (2007) 'From competitive regions to competitive city-regions: a new orthodoxy, but some old mistakes' *Journal of Economic Geography*, 7: 311–32.

Harrison, J. (2014) 'Rethinking city regionalism as a production of new non-state spatial strategies: the case of Peel Holdings Atlantic Gateway strategy' *Urban Studies*, 51: 2315–35.

Harrison, J. and Heley, J. (2015) 'Governing beyond the metropolis: placing the rural in city-region development' *Urban Studies*, 52: 1113–33.

Harvey, D. (2011) 'Roepke lecture in economic geography – crises, geographic disruptions and the uneven development of political responses' *Economic Geography*, 87: 1–22.

Harvey, D. (2016) *Abstract from the Concrete*, Sternberg Press, Cambridge, MA.

Hastings, A., Bailey, N., Bramley, G. and Gannon, M. (2017) 'Austerity urbanism in England: the "regressive redistribution" of local government services and the impact on the poor and marginalised' *Environment and Planning A*, 49: 2007–24.

Hatcher, R. (2017) 'The West Midlands Combined Authority has turned its back on inclusive economic growth to tackle inequality' Mimeograph, Birmingham City University, Birmingham.

Haughton, G. (1999) 'Community economic development: challenges of theory, method and practice' in G. Haughton (ed) *Community Economic Development*, Routledge, London, 3–22.

Haughton, G. and Allmendinger, P. (2015) 'Fluid spatial imaginaries: evolving estuarial city-regional spaces' *International Journal of Urban and Regional Research*, 39: 857–73.

Haughton, G., Allmendinger, P., Counsell, D. and Vigar, G. (2010) *The New Spatial Planning: Territorial Management with Soft Spaces and Fuzzy Boundaries*, Routledge, London.

Haughton, G., Allmendinger, P. and Oosterlynck, S. (2013) 'Spaces of neoliberal experimentation: soft spaces, postpolitics, and neoliberal governmentality' *Environment and Planning A*, 45: 217–34.

Haughton, G., Deas, I. and Hincks, S. (2014) 'Making an impact: when agglomeration boosterism meets anti-planning rhetoric' *Environment and Planning A*, 46: 265–70.

Haughton, G., Deas, I., Hincks, S. and Ward, K. (2016) 'Mythic Manchester: Devo Manc, the Northern Powerhouse and rebalancing the English economy' *Cambridge Journal of Regions, Economy and Society*, 9: 355–70.

Haughton, G., White, I. and Pinto, N. (2020) 'Planning the post-pandemic era' *Town and Country Planning*, April-May, 138–40.

Healey, P. (2009) 'City regions and place development' *Regional Studies*, 43: 831–43.

Heinrich, V.F. (2005) 'Studying civil society across the world: exploring the thorny issues of conceptualization and measurement' *Journal of Civil Society*, 1: 211–28.

Heley, J. (2013) 'Soft spaces, fuzzy boundaries and spatial governance in post-devolution Wales' *International Journal of Urban and Regional Research*, 37: 1325–48.

Henderson, G., Schuemaker, K. and Baker, R. (2013) *Northern Skills for Northern Prosperity: The Rationale for Localising the Skills System in England*, IPPR, London.

Henderson, J. and Ho, S.Y. (2014) 'Re-forming the state' *Renewal: A Journal of Social Democracy*, 22: 22–41.

Hincks, S., Deas, I. and Haughton, G. (2017) 'Real geographies, real economies and soft spatial imaginaries: creating a "more than Manchester" region' *International Journal of Urban and Regional Research*, 41: 642–57.

Hitchings, R. and Latham, A. (2020) 'Qualitative methods I: on the current conventions in interview research' *Progress in Human Geography*, 44: 389–98.

HM Government (2010) *Local Growth: Realising Every Place's Potential*. Cm 7961, HM Government, London.

HM Government (2011) *Localism Bill*, HM Government, London.

HM Government (2013) *Growth Deals*, HM Government, London.

HM Government (2014) *Sheffield City Region Agreement on Devolution*, HM Government, London.

HM Government (2015a) *Cities and Local Government Devolution Bill*, HM Government, London.

HM Government (2015b) *Sheffield City Region Devolution Agreement*, HM Government, London.

HM Government (2016) *Cardiff Capital Region City Deal*, HM Government, London.

HM Government (2017) *Swansea Bay City Region: A City Deal*, HM Government, London.

HM Government (2018) *Civil Society Strategy: Building a Future that Works for Everyone*, HM Government, London.

HM Government and Welsh Government (2019) *North Wales Growth Deal: Heads of Terms Agreement*, Welsh Government, Cardiff.

HM Treasury (2007) *Review of Sub-National Economic Development and Regeneration*, HM Treasury, London.

HM Treasury (2016) *Northern Powerhouse Strategy*, HM Treasury, London.

HoC Library (2018) 'Further education: Post-16 Area Review' Briefing Paper 7357, 21 May, House of Commons Library, London.

Hodson, M., McMeekin, A., Froud, J. and Moran, M. (2020) 'State-rescaling and re-designing the material city-region: tensions of disruption and continuity in articulating the future of Greater Manchester' *Urban Studies*, 57: 198–217.

Hoggart, K. (2005) *The City's Hinterland: Dynamism and Divergence in Europe's Peri-Urban Territories*, Ashgate, London.

Hoole, C. and Hincks, S. (2020) 'Performing the city-region: imagineering, devolution and the search for legitimacy' *Environment and Planning A*, 52: 1583–601.

House of Commons Welsh Affairs Committee (2019) *City Deals and Growth Deals in Wales: Second Report of Session 2019,* House of Commons, London.

Hunt, T. (2015) 'Comparing the post-crisis performance of the Sheffield, Brighton and Oxford city-region economies' SPERI British Political Economy Brief, No. 17, The University of Sheffield, Sheffield.

IFS (2019) *Inequalities in the Twenty-First Century: Introducing the IFS Deaton Review*, London, IFS.

Imrie, R. and Raco, M. (2003) *Urban Renaissance? Community and Urban Policy*, Policy Press, Bristol.

Jenrick, R. (2020) 'Communities Secretary's statement on coronavirus (COVID-19)' Speech, 18 April, Ministry of Housing, Communities and Local Government, London.

Jenson, J. and Phillips, S.D. (1996) 'Regime shift: new citizenship practices in Canada' *International Journal of Canadian Studies*, 14: 111–36.

Jenson, J. and Saint-Martin (2010) 'New routes to social cohesion?' Citizenship and the social investment state' *Canadian Journal of Sociology*, 28: 77–99.

Jessop, B. (1990) *State Theory: Putting Capitalist States in their Place*, Polity, Cambridge.

Jessop, B. (2000) 'Governance failure' in G. Stoker (ed) *The New Politics of British Local Governance*, Macmillan, London, 11–32.

Jessop, B. (2002) *The Future of the Capitalist State*, Polity, Cambridge.

Jessop, B. (2008) *State Power: A Strategic-Relational Approach*, Polity, Cambridge.

Jessop, B. (2011) 'Metagovernance' in M. Bevir (ed) *The Sage Handbook of Governance*, Sage, London, 106–123.

Jessop, B. (2012) 'Economic and ecological crises: green new deals and no-growth economies' *Development*, 55: 17–24.

Jessop, B. (2014) 'Repoliticising depoliticisation: theoretical preliminaries on some responses to the American fiscal and eurozone debt crises' *Policy and Politics*, 42: 207–23.

Jessop, B. (2016a) *The State: Past, Present, Future*, Cambridge, Polity.

Jessop, B. (2016b) 'Territory, politics, governance and multispatial metagovernance' *Territory, Politics, Governance*, 4: 8–32.

Jessop, B. (2020) *Putting Civil Society in its Place: Governance, Metagovernance, and Subjectivity*, Policy Press, Bristol.

Jessop, B. and Sum, N.L. (2013) *Towards a Cultural Political Economy: Putting Culture in its Place in Political Economy*, Edward Elgar, Cheltenham.

Johnson, M., Lucio, M.M., Cartwright, J., Mustchin, S. and Grimshaw, D. (2017) *Just Work in Greater Manchester. Report 2*. Manchester University of Manchester/Alliance Business School, Manchester.

Jonas, A.E.G. (2012) 'City-regionalism' *Progress in Human Geography*, 36: 822–9.

Jonas, A.E.G. and Moisio, S. (2018) 'City regionalism as geopolitical processes: a new framework for analysis' *Progress in Human Geography*, 42: 350–70.

Jonas, A.E.G and Ward, K. (2007) 'Introduction to a debate on "City-regions: new geographies of governance, democracy and social reproduction"' *International Journal of Urban and Regional Research*, 31: 169–78.

Jonas, A.E.G. and Wilson, D. (eds) (1999) *The Urban Growth Machine: Critical Perspectives, Two Decades Later*, SUNY Press, Albany, NY.

Jonas, A.E.G and Wood, A. (eds) (2012) *Territory, the State and Urban Politics*, Ashgate, Farnham.

Jones, G.R., Meegan, R., Kennet, P. and Croft. J (2015) 'The uneven impact of austerity on the voluntary and community sector: a tale of two cities' *Urban Studies*, 53: 2064–80.

Jones, L., Mann, R. and Heley, J. (2013) 'Doing space relationally: exploring the meaningful geographies of local government in Wales' *Geoforum*, 45: 190–200.

Jones, M. (1997) 'Spatial selectivity of the state? The regulationist enigma and local struggles over economic governance' *Environment and Planning A*, 29: 831–64.

Jones, M. (1999) *New Institutional Spaces: Training and Enterprise Councils and the Remaking of Economic Governance*, Routledge, London.

Jones, M. (2001) 'The rise of the regional state in economic governance: "partnerships for prosperity" or new scales of state power? *Environment and Planning A,* 33: 1185–211.

Jones, M. (2019a) *Cities and Regions in Crisis: The Political Economy of Sub-National Economic Development*, Cheltenham, Edward Elgar.

Jones, M. (2019b) 'The march of governance and the actualities of failure: the case of economic development twenty years on' *International Social Science Journal* 227/228: 25–41.

Jones, M., Orford, S. and Macfarlane, V. (eds) (2016) *People, Place and Policy: Knowing Contemporary Wales Through New Localities*, Routledge, London.

Jones, R. (2012) 'State encounters' *Environment and Planning D: Society and Space*, 30: 805–21.

Jones, R. (2019) 'Governing the future and the search for spatial justice: Wales' Well-being of Future Generations Act' *Fennia*, 197: 8–24.

Katz, B. and Bradley, J. (2014) *The Metropolitan Revolution: How Cities and Metros Are Fixing Our Broken Politics and Fragile Economy*, Brookings Institution Press, Washington DC.

Katz, B. and Nowak, J. (2017) *The New Localism: How Cities Can Thrive in the Age of Populism*, Brookings Institution Press, Washington DC.

Katz, B. and Wagner, J. (2014) 'The rise of innovation districts: a new geography of innovation in America' *Brookings*, May, 1–33.

Keating, M., Loughlin, J. and Deschouwer, K. (2013) *Culture, Institutions and Economic Development: A Study of Eight European Regions*, Edward Elgar, Cheltenham.

Keep, E. (2014) *What Does Skills Policy Look Like Now the Money has Run Out?* Association of Colleges, London.

Keep, E. (2016) *The Long-Term Implications of Devolution and Localism for FE in England*, Association of Colleges, London.

Kennett, P., Jones, G., Meegan, R. and Croft, J. (2015) 'Recession, austerity and the great risk shift. Local government and household impacts and responses in Bristol and Liverpool' *Local Government Studies*, 41: 622–44.

King, N. and Ives, E. (2019) *A Rising Tide: Levelling up Left-behind Britain*, Centre for Policy Studies, London.

Krugman, P. (1998) 'What's new about the new economic geography?' *Oxford Review of Economic Policy*, 14: 7–17.

Le Galès, P. (2016) 'Neoliberalism and urban change: stretching a good idea too far?' *Territory, Politics, Governance*, 4: 154–72.

Lee, N. (2017) 'Powerhouse of cards? Understanding the "Northern Powerhouse"' Regional Studies, 51: 478–89.

Lee, N. (2019) 'Inclusive growth in cities: a sympathetic critique' *Regional Studies*, 53: 424–34.

Lefebvre, H. (1976) *The Survival of Capitalism: Reproduction of the Relations of Production*, Allison & Busby, London.

Leyshon, A. and Lee, R. (2003) 'Introduction: alternative economic geographies' in A. Leyson, R. Lee and C.C. Williams (eds) *Alternative Economic Spaces*, Sage, London, 1–26.

LGA (2020) *Re-thinking Local*, Local Government Association, London.

Lindbolm, C.E. (1968) *The Policy-Making Process*, Prentice Hall, Englewood Cliffs, NJ.

Lindsay, C., Canduela, J. and Raeside, R. (2013) 'Polarization in access to work-related training' *Economic and Industrial Democracy*, 34: 205–25.

Local Trust (2020) *Communities at Risk: The Early Impact of Covid-19 on 'Left Behind' Neighbourhoods*, Local Trust, London.

Localis (2020) *Vital Signs: Building Regional Economic Resilience in the COVID Age*, Localis, London.

Lockwood, D. (1999) 'Civic integration and class formation' *British Journal of Sociology*, 47: 531–50.

Logan, J.R. and Molotch, H.L. (1987) *Urban Fortunes: The Political Economy of Place*, University of California Press, Berkeley, CA.

Lovering, J. (1983) 'Gwynedd: a county in crisis' *Coleg Harlech Occasional Papers in Welsh Studies*, No. 2, Coleg Harlech, Harlech.

Lovering, J. (1999) 'Theory led by policy: the inadequacies of the new regionalism (illustrated from the case of Wales)' *International Journal of Urban and Regional Research*, 23: 379–95.

Lovering, J. (2007) 'The relationship between urban regeneration and neoliberalism: two presumptuous theories and a research agenda' *International Planning Studies*, 12: 343–66.

Lyall, S., Wood, M. and Bailey, D. (2015) *Democracy: The Missing Link in the Devolution Debate*, New Economics Foundation, London.

MacKinnon, D. (2020) 'Governing uneven development: The Northern Powerhouse as a "state spatial strategy"' *Territory, Politics, Governance* https://doi.org/10.1080/21622671.2020.1743202

MacLeavy, J. (2011) A 'new politics' of austerity, workfare and gender? The UK coalition government's welfare reform proposals' *Cambridge Journal of Regions, Economy and Society*, 4: 355–67.

MacLeod, G. (1998) 'In what sense a regional problem? Place hybridity, symbolic shape, and institutional formation in (post-)modern Scotland' *Political Geography*, 17: 833–63.

MacLeod, G. (2001) 'New regionalism reconsidered: globalization and the remaking of political economic space' *International Journal of Urban and Regional Research*, 25: 804–29.

MacLeod, G. (2013) 'New urbanism/smart growth in the Scottish Highlands: mobile policies and the post-politics in local development planning' *Urban Studies*, 50: 2196–21.

MacLeod, G. and Goodwin, M. (1999) 'Reconstructing an urban and regional political economy: on the state, politics, scale, and explanation' *Political Geography*, 18: 697–730.

MacLeod, G. and Jones, M. (1999) 'Reregulating a regional rustbelt: institutional fixes, entrepreneurial discourse, and the "politics of representation"' *Environment and Planning D: Society and Space*, 17: 575–605.

MacLeod, G. and Jones, M. (2007) 'Territorial, scalar, networked, connected: In what sense a "regional world"?' *Regional Studies*, 41: 1177–91.

Manchester City Council (2017) 'Roll out of Universal Credit' *Resources and Governance Scrutiny Committee*, 9 November, Manchester City Council, Manchester.

Manchester City Council (2019a) 'The impact of welfare reform and Universal Credit on the Manchester economy' *Economy Scrutiny Committee*, 6 March, Manchester City Council, Manchester.

Manchester City Council (2019b) 'The Council's 2019/2020 budget paper pack' Documentation to be considered at the Resources and Governance Scrutiny Committee on 25 February and Budget Council on 8 March, Manchester City Council, Manchester.

Mann, R. and Plows, A. (2016) 'East, west and the bit in the middle: localities in North Wales' in M. Jones, S. Orford, and V. Macfarlane (eds) *People, Place and Policy: Knowing Contemporary Wales Through New Localities*, Routledge, London, 95–117.

Martin, R. (2015) 'Rebalancing the spatial economy: the challenge for regional theory' *Territory, Politics, Governance*, 3: 235–72.

Martin, R., Sunley, P., Tyler, P. and Gardiner, B. (2016) 'Divergent cities in post-industrial Britain' *Cambridge Journal of Regions, Economy and Society*, 9: 269–99.

Massey, D. (1979) 'In what sense a regional problem?' *Regional Studies*, 13: 233–43.

Massey, D. (2015) 'Vocabularies of the economy' in S. Hall, D. Massey and M. Rustin (eds) *After Neoliberalism? The Kilburn Manifesto*, Lawrence & Wishart, London, 3–18.

McCann, P. (2016) *The UK Regional-National Problem: Geography, Globalisation and Governance*, Routledge, London.

McKinsey & Company (2020) 'Covid-19 in the United Kingdom: assessing jobs at risk and the impact on people and places' 11 May, McKinsey & Company, London.

McNeil, C. (ed) (2010) *Now It's Personal: The New Landscape of Welfare-to-Work*, Institute of Public Policy Research, London.

Meegan, R., Kennett, P., Jones, G. and Croft, J. (2014) 'Global economic crisis, austerity and neoliberal urban governance in England' *Cambridge Journal of Regions Economy and Society*, 7: 137–53.

Melia, S. (2018) Does transport investment really boost economic growth? *World Transport Policy and Practice*, 23: 118–28.

Midlands Engine (2020) 'Economic impact of COVID-19' Editorial 1, 28 April, Midlands Engine, Nottingham.

Midmore, P. (2018) 'Rural development in Wales: looking backwards, looking forwards' *Welsh Economic Review*, 26: 21–8.

Mohan, G. and Mohan, J. (2002) 'Placing social capital' *Progress in Human Geography*, 26: 191–210.

Monbiot, G. (2020) 'Privatisation to blame for our tragic Covid-19 response' *The Guardian*, 27 May, 3.

Morgan, K. (2018) 'Experimental governance and territorial development' Paper delivered at the OECD Seminar on Experimental Governance, 14 December. Cardiff University, Cardiff.

Muldoon-Smith, K. and Greenhalgh, P. (2015) 'Passing the buck without bucks: some reflections on fiscal decentralisation and the business rate retention scheme in England' *Local Economy*, 30: 609–26.

Nathan, M. and Overman, H. (2013) 'Agglomeration, clusters, and industrial policy' *Oxford Review of Economic Policy*, 29: 383–404.

National Audit Office (2013) *Funding and Structures of Local Economic Growth*, Stationery Office, London.

National Audit Office (2016) *English Devolution Deals. HC 948*, Stationery Office, London.

Nelles, J. (2012) *Competitive Metropolitan Policy: Governing Beyond Local Boundaries in the Imagined Metropolis*, Routledge, London.

Nelson, K. (2017) *Devolution in Greater Manchester: Explanations, Responses, Concerns*, Public Services International Unit, University of Greenwich, Greenwich.

New Economy Manchester (2015) *Welfare Reform in Greater Manchester Impact on People, Services, Housing, and the Economy*, New Economy, Manchester.

Newman, J. (2014) Landscapes of antagonism: local governance, neoliberalism and austerity, *Urban Studies*, 51: 3290–305.

Newman, J. and Clarke, J. (2009) *Publics, Politics and Power: Remaking the Public in Public Services*, Sage, London.

NIACE (2012) *The Work Programme: What is the Role of Skills?* Leicester, NIACE.

Normington, D. and Hennessy, P. (2018) *The Power of Civil Servants*, Haus Publishing, London.

Norris, E. and Adam, R. (2017) *All Change: Why Britain is Prone to Policy Reinvention and What Can Be Done About It*, Institute for Government, London.

North Wales Economic Ambition Board (NWEAB) (2016) *Growth Vision for the Economy of North Wales*, NWEAB, Conwy.

North Wales Economic Ambition Board (NWEAB) (2018) *A Growth Deal for North Wales: Smart, Resilient and Connected*, NWEAB, Conwy.

North West TUC (2018) *A City Region Employment Charter*, North West TUC, Liverpool.

O'Brien, P. and Pike, A. (2015) 'City deals, decentralisation and the governance of local infrastructure funding and financing in the UK' *National Institute Economic Review*, 233: R14–R26.

O'Brien, P. and Pike, A. (2019) ' "Deal or no deal?" Governing urban infrastructure funding and financing in the UK City Deals' *Urban Studies*, 56: 1448–76.

Offe, C. (1984) *Contradictions of the Welfare State*, Hutchinson, London.

Offe, C. (1985) *Disorganized Capitalism: Contemporary Transformations in Work and Politics*, Polity, Cambridge.

Omstedt, M. (2016) 'Reinforcing unevenness: post-crisis geography and the spatial selectivity of the state' *Regional Studies, Regional Science*, 3: 99–113.

ONS (2020) 'Deaths involving COVID-19 by local area and socioeconomic deprivation: deaths occurring between 1 March and 17 April 2020' Statistical Bulletin, 1 May, Office for National Statistics, Newport.

Orford, S. and Webb, B. (2018) 'Mapping the interview transcript: identifying spatial policy areas from daily working practices' *Area*, 50: 529–41.

Otten, J. (2014) 'Devo Sheffield announced: transport, skills, business support, housing, no mayor' *Liberal Democrat Voice*, 12 December.

Overman, H. (2012) 'Investing in the UK's most successful cities is the surest recipe for national growth' Politics and Policy Blog, LSE, London.

Overman , H. (2014) 'Making an impact: misreading, misunderstanding, and misrepresenting research does nothing to improve the quality of public debate and policy making' *Environment and Planning A*, 46: 2276–82.

Overman, H., Rice, P. and Venables, A.J. (2007) *Economic Linkages Across Space*, Centre for Economic Performance, London.

Pain, K. (2008) 'Examining "core-periphery" relationships in a global city-region: the case of London and South East' *Regional Studies*, 42: 1161–72.

Painter, J. (2005) 'Governmentality and regional economic strategies' in J. Hillier and E. Rooksby (eds) *Habitus: A Sense of Place*, Aldershot, Ashgate, 131–57.

Painter, J. and Goodwin, M. (2000) 'Local governance after Fordism: a regulationist perspective' in G. Stoker (ed) *The New Politics of British Local Governance*, London, Macmillan, 33–53.

Payne, J. and Keep, E. (2011) *One Step Toward, Two Steps Back? Skills Policy in England Under the Coalition Government*, SKOPE, Cardiff.

Peck, J. (1995) 'Moving and shaking: business élites, state localism and urban privatism' *Progress in Human Geography*, 19: 16–46.

Peck, J. (2012) 'Austerity urbanism' *City*, 16: 626–55.

Peck, J. (2014) 'Pushing austerity: State failure, municipal bankruptcy and the crises of fiscal federalism in the USA' *Cambridge Journal of Regions, Economy and Society*, 7: 17–44.

Peck, J. and Theodore, N. (2000) 'Work first: welfare-to-work and the regulation of contingent labour markets' *Cambridge Journal of Economics*, 24: 119–38.

Peck, J. and Theodore, N. (2015) *Fast Policy: Experimental Statecraft at the Thresholds of Neoliberalism*, University of Minnesota Press, Minneapolis, MN.

Peck, J. and Tickell, A. (1994) 'Jungle law breaks out: neoliberalism and global-local disorder' *Area*, 26: 317–26.

Peck, J. and Tickell, A. (2012) 'Apparitions of neoliberalism: revising "Jungle law breaks out"' *Area*, 44: 245–9.

Pemberton, S. (2016) 'Statecraft, scalecraft and local government reorganisation in Wales' *Environment and Planning C: Government and Policy*, 34: 1306–23.

Pemberton, S. (2019) *Rural Regeneration in the UK*, Routledge, London.

Pemberton, S. and Shaw, D. (2012) 'New forms of sub-regional governance and implications for rural areas: evidence from England' *Planning Practice & Research*, 27: 441–58.

Penny, J. (2016) 'Between coercion and consent: the politics of "cooperative governance" at a time of 'austerity localism' in London' *Urban Geography*, 38: 1–22.

Perraudin, F. (2016) 'Sheffield region's bid to absorb Chesterfield faces legal setback after ruling' *The Guardian*, 22 December, 16.

Pidd, H. (2020) 'Go big or go home to heal UK divide, report tells No 10' *The Guardian*, 27 February, 15.

Pike, A., Rodriguez-Pose, A., Tomaney, J., Torrisi, G. and Tselios, V. (2012) 'In search of the "economic dividend" of devolution: spatial disparities, spatial economic policy, and decentralisation in the UK' *Environment and Planning C: Government and Policy*, 30: 10–28.

Pike, A., Marlow, D., McCarthy, A., O'Brien, P. and Tomaney, J. (2015) 'Local institutions and local economic development: the local enterprise partnerships in England, 2010-' *Cambridge Journal of Regions, Economy and Society*, 8: 185–204.

Pike, A., MacKinnon, D., Coombes, M., Champion, T., Bradley, D., Cumbers, A., Robinson, L. and Wymer, C. (2016) *Uneven Growth: Tackling City Decline*, Joseph Rowntree Foundation, York.

Pike, A., Coombes, A., O'Brien, P. and Tomaney, J. (2018) 'Austerity states, institutional dismantling and the governance of sub-national economic development: the demise of the regional development agencies in England' *Territory, Politics, Governance*, 6: 118–44.

Pitt, T. (2020) *Beyond Levelling Up: The Conservative Case for Tackling Inequalities of Income and Wealth*, Social Market Foundation, London.

Polanyi, K. (1957) *The Great Transformation: The Political Economic Origins of Our Time*, Beacon Press, Boston, MA.

Pugalis, L. and Townsend, A.R. (2012) 'Rebalancing England: Sub-national development (once again) at the crossroads' *Urban Research & Practice*, 5: 157–74.

Raffas, T. (2017) 'Demanding activation' *Journal of Social Policy*, 46: 349–65.

Rafferty, A. and Jelley, R. (2018) 'Ways to promote a responsible business agenda in UK cities: Greater Manchester' Inclusive Growth Analysis Unit Report, University of Manchester, Manchester.

Rallings, C. and Thrasher, M. (2006) '"Just another expensive talking shop": public attitudes and the 2004 regional assembly referendum in the North East of England' *Regional Studies*, 40: 927–36.

Rancière, J. (2007) *On the Shores of Politics*, Verso, London.

Redcliffe-Maud, L. and Wood, B. (1974) *English Local Government Reformed*, Oxford University Press, Oxford.

Rhodes, R. (2007) 'Understanding governance: ten years on' *British Politics*, 4: 1243–64.

Rigby, D.L. and Brown, W.M. (2013) 'Who benefits from agglomeration' *Regional Studies*, 49: 28–43.

Roberts, C. (2017) *The Inbetweeners: The New Role of Internships in the Graduate Labour Market*, IPPR, London.

Royal Society of Arts (RSA) (2014) *Unleashing Metro Growth: Final Recommendations of the City-Growth Commission*, Royal Society of Arts, London.

RSA (2016) *Inclusive Growth Commission: Emerging Findings*, Royal Society of Arts, London.

RSA (2017) *Inclusive Growth Commission: Making the Economy Work for Everyone*, Royal Society of Arts, London.

Rubery, J., Grimshaw, D., Keizer, A. and Johnson, M. (2018) 'Challenges and contradictions in the "normalising" of precarious work' *Work, Employment and Society*, 32: 509–27.

Rutherford, T. (2006) 'Local representations in crisis: governance, citizenship regimes, and UK TECs and Ontario local boards' *Environment and Planning D: Society and Space*, 24: 409–26.

Sandford, M. (2018) 'Devolution to local government in England' Briefing Paper, Number 07029, 4 May, House of Commons Library, London.

Sandford, M. (2019) 'Money talks: the finances of combined authorities' *Local Economy*, 34: 106–22.

Sandford, M (2020) 'Conceptualising "generative power": evidence from the city-regions of England' *Urban Studies*, 57: 2098–114.

Schneider, C. and Cottineau, C. (2019) 'Decentralisation versus territorial inequality: a comparative review of English region policy discourse' *Urban Science*, 3: 1–22.

Scott, A. (ed) (2001) *Global City-Regions: Trends, Theory, Policy*, Oxford University Press, Oxford.

Scott, A. (2019) 'City-regions reconsidered' *Environment and Planning A*, 51: 554–80.

Scott, A. and Storper, M. (2003) 'Regions, globalization, development' *Regional Studies*, 37: 579–93.

Senior, D. (1969) *Royal Commission on Local Government in England 1966–1969. Volume II: Memorandum of Dissent by Mr D Senior*, HM Stationery Office, London.

Shaw, K. and Tewdwr-Jones, M. (2017) "'Disorganised devolution": reshaping metropolitan governance in England in a period of austerity' *Raumforschung und Raumordnung/Spatial Research and Planning*, 75: 211–24.

Sheffield City Council (2011) *Unemployment and Worklessness in Sheffield*, Children and Young People's Services Lifelong Learning and Skills, Sheffield.

Sheffield City Council (2013) *Sheffield Economic Strategy*, Sheffield City Council, Sheffield.

Sheffield City Region Local Enterprise Partnership (2013) *Made in Sheffield: A Deal for Growth*, Sheffield LEP, Sheffield.

Sheffield City Region Local Enterprise Partnership (2014) *A Strategic Economic Plan: A Focused 10 Year Plan for Private Sector Growth 2015–2025*, Sheffield LEP, Sheffield.

Sheffield Fairness Commission (2012) *Making Sheffield Fairer*, Sheffield Fairness Commission, Sheffield.

Sheffield First Partnership (2010) *Sheffield Economic Masterplan*, Sheffield First Partnership, Sheffield.

Sheffield First Partnership (2012) *The Sheffield Employment Strategy*, Sheffield First Partnership, Sheffield.

Sheffield First Partnership (2013) *Sheffield Economic Masterplan*, Sheffield First Partnership, Sheffield.

Sheffield First Partnership (2014) *State of Sheffield 2014*, Sheffield First Partnership, Sheffield.

Sheffield First Partnership (2016a) *State of Sheffield 2016*, Sheffield First Partnership, Sheffield.

Sheffield First Partnership (2016b) 'Devolution: the future for Sheffield. Understanding the challenges and opportunities for our city' Seminar Report, Sheffield First Partnership, Sheffield.

Shildrick, T. (2018) *Poverty Propaganda: Exploring the Myths*, Policy Press, Bristol.

Shucksmith, M. (2008) 'New Labour's countryside in international perspective' in M. Woods (ed) *New Labour's Countryside: Rural Policy Since 1997*, Policy Press, Bristol, 57–76.

Shukaitis, S. (2013) 'Recomposing precarity: notes on the laboured politics of class composition' *Ephemera*, 13: 641–58.

Smith, N. (1990) *Uneven Development: Nature, Capital and the Production of Space*, Blackwell, Oxford.

Smith Institute (2017) *Devo–Work: Trade Unions, Metro Mayors and Combined Authorities*, Smith Institute, London.

SSAC (2018) *Universal Credit: Addressing the Risks of Managed Migration*, Social Security Advisory Committee, London.

Storper, M. (2013) *Keys to the City: How Economics, Institutions, Social Interaction, and Politics Shape Development*, Princeton University Press, Princeton, NJ.

Swansea Bay City Region (2016) *Swansea Bay City Region: A City Deal 2016–2035*, Swansea Bay City Region, Swansea.

Swyngedouw, E. (2009) 'The antinomies of the postpolitical city: in search of a democratic politics of environmental production' *International Journal of Urban and Regional Research*, 33: 601–20.

Swyngedouw, E. (2010) 'Post-democratic cities. For whom and for what?' Paper presented to the Regional Studies Association Annual Conference, 26 May, Pecs, Budapest.

Swyngedouw, E. (2018) *Promises of the Political: Insurgent Cities in a Post-Political Environment*, MIT Press, Cambridge, MA.

Thomas, P., Etherington, D., Jeffery, B., Beresford, R., Beel, D. and Jones, M. (2020) *Tackling Labour Market Injustice and Organising Workers: The View from a Northern Heartland*, Sheffield Hallam University, Sheffield.

Thompson, M. (2020) 'What's so new about New Municipalism?' *Progress in Human Geography* https://doi.org/10.1177/0309132520909480

Thompson, M., Nowak, V., Southern, A., Davies, J. and Furmedge, P. (2020) 'Regrounding the city with Polanyi: from urban entrepreneurialism to entrepreneurial municipalism' *Environment and Planning A*, 52: 1171–94.

Tomaney, J. (2016) 'Limits of devolution: localism, economics and post-democracy' *The Political Quarterly*, 87: 546–52.

Tomaney, J. and Pike, A. (2020) 'Levelling up?' *The Political Quarterly*, 91: 43–8.

Torrance, D. (2020) ' "A process, not an event": devolution in Wales, 1998–2020' Briefing Paper, Number CBP-8318, House of Commons Library, House of Commons, London.

Toynbee, P. and Walker, D. (2017) *Dismembered: How the Attack on the State Harms Us All*, Guardian Books, London.

TUC (2014) *TUC Submission to the City Growth Commission*, TUC, London.

UK Parliament (2016) *Select Committee on the Constitution, The Union and Devolution. 10th Report of Session 2015–16, HL Paper 149*, UK Parliament, London.

UK2070 Commission (2020a) *Make No Little Plans – Acting At Scale For a Fairer and Stronger Future*, UK2070 Commission, Sheffield.

UK2070 Commission (2020b) *Civil Society Perspectives on Inequality: Focus Group Research Findings Report*, UK2070 Commission, Sheffield.

UKCES and Centre for Cities (2015) *City Deals and Skills*, Centre for Cities, London.

Umney, C. (2018) *Class Matters: Inequality and Exploitation in Twenty-First Century Britain*, Pluto, London.

UNISON (2016) 'Public Consultation on the devolved powers in Greater Manchester' UNISON North West response, May, UNISON, Manchester.

Vainikka, J. (2015) 'Identities and regions: exploring spatial narratives, legacies and practices with civic organizations in England and Finland', *Nordia Geographical Publications*, 44: 1–72.

VCSE (2016) 'Greater Manchester Voluntary, Community and Social Enterprise, Devolution Reference Group', GMCVO Information Sheet, Manchester.

Vickers, I., Spear, R., Brennan, G. and Syrett, S. (2017) *Cities, the Social Economy and Inclusive Growth: A Practice Review*, Joseph Rowntree Foundation, York.

Waite, D. (2015) 'City profile: Cardiff and the shift to city-regionalism' *Cities*, 48: 21–30.

Waite, D. and Bristow, G. (2019) 'Spaces of city-regionalism: conceptualising pluralism in policymaking' *Environment and Planning C: Government and Policy*, 37: 689–706.

Waite, D. and Morgan, K. (2019) 'City deals in the polycentric state: the spaces and politics of Metrophilia in the UK' *European Urban and Regional Studies*, 26: 382–99.

Waite, D., MacLennan, D. and O'Sullivan, T. (2013) 'Emerging city policies: devolution, deals and disorder' *Local Economy*, 28: 770–85.

Wales Rural Observatory (2009) *Deep Rural Localities*, Wales Rural Observatory, Aberystwyth.

Ward, K. and Jonas, A.E.G. (2004) 'Competitive city-regionalism as a politics of space: a critical reinterpretation of the new regionalism' *Environment and Planning A*, 36: 2119–39.

Ward, K., Newman, J., John, P., Theodore, N., Macleavy, J. and Cochrane, A. (2015) Whatever happened to local government? A review symposium, *Regional Studies, Regional Science*, 2: 435–57.

Ward, N. (2006) 'Rural development and the economies of rural areas' in J. Midgley (ed) *A New Rural Agenda*, IPPR, London, 46–67.

Ward, S.V. (1988) *The Geography of Interwar Britain*, Routledge, London.

Webber, D., Healy, A. and Bristow, G. (2018) 'Regional growth paths and resilience: a European analysis' *Economic Geography*, 94: 355–75.

Welsh Government (2008) *People, Places, Futures: The Wales Spatial Plan*, Welsh Government, Cardiff.

Welsh Government (2011) *City Regions Task and Finish Group: 'City Regions' Definition and Criteria*, Welsh Government, Cardiff.

Welsh Government (2012) *City Regions: Final Report*, Welsh Government, Cardiff.

Welsh Government (2015a) *Well-Being of Future Generations Act: The Essentials*, Welsh Government, Cardiff.

Welsh Government (2015b) *White Paper, Reforming Local Government: Power to Local People*, Welsh Government, Cardiff.

Welsh Government (2017a) *Reforming Local Government: Resilient and Renewed*, Welsh Government, Cardiff.

Welsh Government (2017b) *Securing Wales' Future: Transition from the European Union to a New Relationship with Europe*, Welsh Government, Cardiff.

Welsh Government (2017c) *Moving North Wales Forward: Our Vision for North Wales and North East Wales Metro*, Welsh Government, Cardiff.

Welsh Government (2018) 'Regional economic and labour market profile, North Wales' *Statistical Bulletin*, SB 44/2018.

Welsh Government (2019) 'City region analysis' *StatsWales*, 27 November, Welsh Government, Cardiff.

Wharton, J. (2016) 'The story so far' in 'Powering on: The Northern Powerhouse, two years on' Supplement to the *New Statesman*, 19–25 February, 8–9.

While, A., Gibbs, D. and Jonas, A.E.G. (2013) 'The competitive state, city-regions, and the territorial politics of growth facilitation' *Environment and Planning A*, 45: 2379–98.

Whitehead, M. (2003) 'In the shadow of hierarchy: metagovernance, policy reform and urban regeneration in the West Midlands' *Area*, 35: 6–14.

Whitehead, M. (2005) 'Between the marvellous and the mundane: everyday life in the socialist city and the politics of the environment' *Environment and Planning D: Society and Space*, 23: 273–94.

Whitham, G. (2018) *The Decline in Crisis Support in England*, Greater Manchester Poverty Action, Manchester.

Wiggan, J. (2012) 'Telling stories of 21st century welfare: the UK coalition government and the neoliberal discourse of worklessness and dependency' *Critical Social Policy*, 32: 383–405.

Williams, J. (2020a) ' "We've seen nothing like this since the 1930s" – how will Greater Manchester's economy bounce back from coronavirus?' *Manchester Evening News*, 29 April, 2.

Williams, J. (2020b) 'Government refuses to promise councils will be paid back for "catastrophic" financial toll of coronavirus' *Manchester Evening News*, 26 April, 3.

Williams, J. (2020c) ' "No way to run a country": why Covid-19 has exposed a key weakness in the British state' *Manchester Evening News*, 24 May, 7.

Wills, J. (2016) *Locating Localism: Statecraft, Citizenship and Democracy*, Policy Press, Bristol.

Winter, M. (2006) 'Rescaling rurality: multilevel governance of the agro-food sector' *Political Geography*, 25: 735–51.

WLGA (2017) 'Consultation on local approaches to poverty reduction: The Well-Being of Future Generations Act and public service boards' Response by the Welsh Local Government Association, Cardiff.

Wood, M. and Flinders, M. (2014) 'Rethinking depoliticisation: beyond the governmental' *Policy and Politics*, 42: 151–70.

Woods, M. and Heley, J. (2017) 'Conceptualisation of rural-urban relations and synergies' *ROBUST Deliverable 1.1.*, Department of Geography and Earth Sciences, Aberystwyth University, Aberystwyth.

World Bank (2009) *World Development Report: Reshaping Economic Geography*. Washington, DC: World Bank.

Yates, E. (2017) 'Reproducing low-wage labour: capital accumulation, labour markets and young workers' *Industrial Relations Journal*, 48: 463–81.

Zuege, A. (1999) 'The chimera of the third way' in L. Panitch and C. Leys (eds) *Necessary and Unnecessary Utopias: Socialist Register 2000*, Merlin Press, London, 87–114.

Index

Note: Page numbers in *italic* type refer to figures; those in **bold** type refer to tables.

A

ABRs (area-based reviews) 68
accelerators 145
accountability, impact of austerity on 65
Adam, R. 3
Adult Skills Budget 46, 60, 68
advice organisations, Greater Manchester 76–7
agency 63, 66
agent 79, 97
  civil society as 36
agglomeration 4, 24, 81, 102, 120, 121, 146
All Change; Why Britain Is So Prone to Policy Reinvention, and What Can Be Done about It, Institute of Government 3
'anchor institutions' 66, 73, 76, 144
Andrews, Leyton 85
Anglesey (Ynys Môn) 100, 111
Apprenticeship Grant for Employers 46
apprenticeships 46–7, 54, 60, 70
area-based reviews (ABRs) 68
austerity 21, 23, 64, 81
  'austerity localism' 150
  austerity resistance/mitigation by civil society actors 63, 64, 66–7, 69–70, 71, 73, **74**, 75–7, 78
  'austerity urbanism' 21, 63–4
    political economy in city regions 64–7
  'downloading' of to regions 65
  GMCR (Greater Manchester City Region) 67–71
  LA (local authority) unions 32–3
  Northern Powerhouse 25
  SBCR (Swansea Bay City Region and City Deal) 132–3
  SCR (Sheffield City Region) 50–1
  Wales 95–7, 106

B

Bakker, K. 56
Barford, A. 72–3
Barnsley 41, 59
Bassetlaw 41, 59
Beardmore, E. 42

Beatty, C. 72
Bebb, Guto 112
Belfast, City Deal 9
Bell, A. 43
Benefit Cap Extension, Greater Manchester 72
benefit cuts 71
Benefit Freeze, Greater Manchester 72
benefit sanctions 71, 76
'better jobs gap' 69
Blanco, I. 63
Bogdanor, V. 2
Bolsover 41
Bolton 64
Braudel, F. 144
Brenner, N. 20
Brexit 113, 118
Bristol 29, 97
Bristow, G. 63
Burnham, Andy 76
Burnham, P. 142
Bury 64

C

Cardiff 105, 122; *see also* CCR (Cardiff Capital Region)
Carmarthen 121
Carmarthenshire 123
CAs (combined authorities) 8, 14, 23, 24, 25, 26, 37, 46, 57, 64, 80, 81, 82, 105
CCR (Cardiff Capital Region) 5, 9, 21, 79–80, 97–8, 99, 105, 140
  austerity geographies 95–7
  CCR Business Council 87–99, *88*
  CCR Business Organisation 87
  CCR Cabinet 87
  CCR Economic Growth Partnership 87
  City Deal 83, 86–9, *87*, **88**, *88*, *90*, 91, 97, 125
  civil society 80, 91–2, 96
  creation of 82–91, *87*, **88**, *88*, **90**
  economic growth model 92–3
  GVA (gross value added) 89
  scale and accountability 93–5
  Transition Board 86, 88, 91
central-local relations, Wales 83–6
Ceridigion 106

charities 29; *see also* civil society
Cheshire 106, 114
Cheshire and Warrington Local
  Enterprise Partnership 111
Chesterfield 41, 59
chimera 41, 43, 62
Cities and Local Government
  Devolution Act 2016 2, 8
City Deals 8, 9, 45–6, 104–5, 109
City Region Taskforce, Wales 84
city regions 5, 6
  competition between 27
  critiques of and missing links 13–17
  futures of 139–42
  growth, neoliberalism and civil society
    contexts 12–13
  limits of 119–21
  solutions 6–9, *10*, *11*, 12
City Strategy Pathfinder (CSP) 45,
  50, 54
city-first approach 15, 25, 99, 105,
  120, 121, 129
city-region building
  Northern Powerhouse 25–8, *26*, *28*
  as a process 19–20, 79
civic repair 140, 144–7, 153–4
civil society 5, 21, 28, 139, 140, 146
  CCR (Cardiff Capital Region) 80,
    91–2, 96
  depoliticisation of 142–4
  GMCR (Greater Manchester City
    Region) 29–30, 32–3, 34–8, **35**,
    39, 73, **74**, 75–7
  Northern Powerhouse 24–5, 27,
    28–38, **35**
  SCR (Sheffield City Region) 29,
    30–1, 33–4, 38–9, 43
civil society actors 16, 18, 21, 141
  austerity resistance/mitigation 63, 64,
    66–7, 69–70, 71, 73, **74**, 75–7, 78
*Civil Society Strategy: Building a Future
  that Works for Everyone*, HM
  Government 1, 2–3
Clegg, Nick 41
Coalition government (Conservative/
  Liberal Democrat), 2010–15 5, 8,
  23, 25, 99, 105
  skills policy 45
combined authorities (CAs) 8, 14, 23,
  24, 25, 26, 37, 46, 57, 64, 80, 81,
  82, 105
Communist Party, Sheffield 44
Communities First 96
Community Care Grants 72
community groups 29
  austerity resistance/mitigation 73
  see also civil society

'competitive city' 145
'Connected North Wales' 110
Conservative governments 1979–90
  (Thatcher Governments) 44–5
Conservative governments 2015–6,
  23–4, 25, 65, 129
Conservative Party 5–6
construal 18, 19, 131
Corbyn, Jeremy 135
Core Cities 8, 105
Coronavirus Act 2020 148
COVID-19, FE (foundational
  economy) in post-COVID-19
  period 147–54
Cox, K. 19, 94
Crisis Loan awards 72
Crouch, C. 5
CSP (City Strategy Pathfinder) 45,
  50, 54
Cumbers, A. 66, 154

D

Darling, J. 14–15
Davidson, M. 63
Davies, Ron 79
DBIS (Department for Business,
  Innovation and Skills) 51
Dean, J. 61
Dear, M. 33
Deas, I. 4, 16, 146, 153
Deeside 111
de-industrialisation 7, 68, 75
  Wales 111
*Democracy: The Missing Link in the
  Devolution Debate* (Lyall) 3
democratic deficit 43, 78, 82
Department for Business, Innovation
  and Skills (DBIS) 51
Department for Work and Pensions
  (DWP) 47, 67
depoliticisation 82, 141
  of civil society 142–4
Derbyshire 59
Derbyshire County Council 59
Derbyshire Dales 41
Derbyshire Employment and Skills
  Board 59
de-unionisation 69
'Devo Manc' *see* GMCR (Greater
  Manchester City Region)
'Devo Sheffield' *see* SCR (Sheffield
  City Region) ('Devo Sheffield')
devolution 1–2, 21
  regional 26
Devolution Agreements 21, 61
Devolution Deals 8, 104–5, 109

disability benefits, GMCR (Greater Manchester City Region) 71
disabled people, SCR (Sheffield City Region) 53, 59
discursive depoliticisation 143; *see also* depoliticisation
'discursive institutions' 144
Doncaster 41, 59
Duncan, S. 79
DWP (Department for Work and Pensions) 47, 67

E

East Midlands 41
economic development
  city region scale 26–7
  FE (foundational economy) school of 22, 141–2, 144–54
economic governance, SCR (Sheffield City Region) 44–8, *48*
elite city deals *see* CCR (Cardiff Capital Region)
embeddedness 145
Emmerich, M. 23, 141
employment crisis, SCR (Sheffield City Region) 51–4, 59
employment regulation 64
Employment Support Allowance, Greater Manchester 71, 72
encounters 5
England
  English Regions 7
  RDAs (Regional Development Agencies) 8
Enterprise Zones, North Wales 111
entrepreneurship, grassroots 145
European Work and Employment Research Centre 70

F

Fall, Kate 23
FE (foundational economy) 22, 141–2, 144–7
  post-COVID-19 147–54
  research agendas on FE city regions 152–4
financial crisis, 2008 25, 65, 150
financialisation 141
  SBCR (Swansea Bay City Region and City Deal) 132–3
Finn, D. 78
Flinders, M. 142
Flintshire 100, 106, 114
Folkman, P. 145–6
food banks, Greater Manchester 71
Fothergill, S. 72

foundational economy *see* FE (foundational economy)
Foundational Economy Collective 152–3
Foundational Economy Challenge Fund, Wales 147
Fraser, A. 94
Fuller, C. 144
'Funding and Structures for Local Economic Growth,' National Audit Office 3
Further Education 51, 60, 68

G

geographies of governance 21
'geographies of representation' 19
globalisation 14
GMCA (Greater Manchester Combined Authority) 34, 35–6, 71, 75
GMCR (Greater Manchester City Region) 81, 140, 141
  austerity and uneven development 67–71
  austerity urbanism 63–4
  civil society 29–30, 32–3, 34–8, **35**, 39
  austerity resistance/mitigation 73, **74**, 75–7
  GVA (gross value added) 69
  health and social care devolution 35, 67, 68
  trade councils 75
  welfare reform and social protection 64, 71–3, 76–7
  see also Northern Powerhouse
Goodwin, M. 79
governance 65, 82
  governance failure 21, 55–6, 58
  governance geography 6
  SCR (Sheffield City Region) 21, 42–3, 55–8, 61–2
governmental depoliticisation 142; *see also* depoliticisation
graduate employment, SCR (Sheffield City Region) 52
Gramsci, A. 17
grassroots innovation/entrepreneurship 145
Gray, M. 72–3
Greater London Authority 1
Greater Manchester 106
  COVID-19 impact 149
  health and social care devolution 37, 67, 68
  'new civic offer' 145–6

see also GMCA (Greater Manchester Combined Authority); GMCR (Greater Manchester City Region)
Greater Manchester Centre for Voluntary Organisation 76–7
Greater Manchester City Region *see* GMCR (Greater Manchester City Region)
Greater Manchester Coalition of Disabled People 77
Greater Manchester Combined Authority (GMCA) 34, 35–6, 71, 75
Greater Manchester Devolution Deal 8–9
Greater Manchester Health and Social Care Plan 75
Greater Manchester Law Centre 76–7
Greater Manchester Strategic Workforce Engagement Board 76
Greater Manchester Voluntary, Community and Social Enterprise (VCSE) Devolution Reference Group 34–7, **35**, 38, 39, 77
gross value added (GVA) *see* GVA (gross value added)
'grounded city' 145
Growth Deals 8, 104–5, 109
growth machines 12–13, 31, 80, 120
Guinan, J. 151
GVA (gross value added) 31, 99, 151
   CCR (Cardiff Capital Region) 89
   GMCR (Greater Manchester City Region) 69
   NWGD (North Wales Growth Deal) 107
   SBCR (Swansea Bay City Region) 125, 128
   SCR (Sheffield City Region) 59
Gwynedd (Meirionnydd) 106

H

Harrison, J. 14, 102–3
Harvey, D. 18
Haughton, G. 13, 83, 121
Haywood, Elizabeth 84
Healey, P. 7
health and social care, devolution of in Greater Manchester 37, 67, 68
Health and Work Programme, GMCR 67
Heinrich, V.F. 5
Heley, J. 83, 84, 102–3
Hindmoor, A. 43
HM Government 89
   Civil Society Strategy: Building a Future That Works for Everyone 1, 2–3

Local Growth: Realising Every Place's Potential Cm 7961 1, 2
HM Treasury 8
housing associations 29; *see also* civil society
housing benefit claimants, Greater Manchester 71
HPM Berwyn 111

I

incapacity benefit claimants, SCR (Sheffield City Region) 53
inclusion 28, 61
'inclusive growth' approach 25
Inclusive Growth Commission, Royal Society of Arts 28, 61, 117
industrial relations 64
Industrial Strategy for the UK 39
innovation, grassroots 145
Institute of Government
   All Change; Why Britain Is So Prone to Policy Reinvention, and What Can Be Done about It 3
Institute for Public Policy Research 68
Internet Coast 126
interstitial places 22, 103, 104–5

J

Jarvis, Dan 59
Jenson, J. 27, 91
Jessop, B. 5, 17–18, 19, 23–4, 25, 55, 57, 58, 59, 91, 142, 143
Job Retention Scheme 148–9
Job Seeker Allowance claimants
   Greater Manchester 71
   SCR (Sheffield City Region) 52–3
Johnson, Boris 147
Johnson, M. 66
Jonas, A.E.G. 16, 113
Jones, G.R. 29
Jones, M. 16, 19
Jones-Evans, Dylan 135, 137
Joseph Rowntree Foundation 72
'Just Work' programme 73

K

Katz, B. 41
Keep, E. 68

L

LA (local authority) unions 21, 32–3, 63
labour conditionality 21
labour market
   Greater Manchester 69–71
   impact of austerity n 64, 65–6

NE Wales 100, 107–8, 114
NW Wales 100, 107–8, 114
Labour Party
  Sheffield 44
  Sheffield Labour Party, Fairness
    Commission 47, 55
  see also New Labour governments,
    1997–2010
LAs (local authorities) 8, 14, 63, 80, 81
  COVID-19 response and support 149
  Derbyshire 59
  impact of UC on 72–3
  Wales 83, 85–6, 87, **88**, *88*, 100, 106
Lee, R. 140
Leeds City Region 81
Lefebvre, H. 144, 145, 149
LEPs (Local Enterprise Partnerships) 8,
  14, 15, 23, 27, 31, 37, 45, 49,
  76, 80
'levelling up' 141
Leyshon, A. 140
Lindblom, C.E. 18, 41
Liverpool 29, 106
Llanelli 121
Llanelli Wellness and Life Science
  Village project 128
local authorities (LAs) *see* LAs
  (local authorities)
Local Enterprise Partnerships (LEPs) 8,
  14, 15, 23, 27, 31, 37, 45, 49,
  76, 80
local government reorganisation 21
  Wales 85–6, 87, **88**, *88*, 100, 106
Local Growth: Realising Every Place's
  Potential Cm 7961, HM
  Government 1, 2
Local Resilience Forums 149
Local Skills Councils 45
localism 2, 21, 49, 58, 61, 140
  'austerity localism' 150
London, centralisation of government
  and finance in 7
lone parents, SCR (Sheffield City
  Region) 53
Lovering, J. 16
Lyall, S. 3

M

MacDonald, John 135
MacLeod, G. 16, 19, 102
Make No Little Plans – Acting at Scale
  for a Fairer and Stronger Justice,
  UK2070 Commission 3–4
Manchester 64;
  see also GMCR (Greater Manchester
    City Region); Greater Manchester
Manchester City Council 72, 73, 76

COVID-19 impact 149
Massey, D. 7
Matthews, Terry 125
Mayoral authorities 8, 14
mayors, directly-elected 2, 41
MDA (Mersey Dee Alliance) 106,
  111, 114
metagovernance 151
  CCR (Cardiff Capital Region) 79
  SCR (Sheffield City Region) 21, 43,
    57–8, 61–2
'Metro' areas, North America 12
Metro-Dynamics 141
metrophilia 101–2, 120–1
  SBCR (Swansea Bay City Region
    and City Deal) 130–2
'Metropolitics' 41
Mid Ulster City Deal 9
Midmore, P. 104
Mid-Wales Growth Deal 9, 117
'more jobs gap' 69
Morgan, K. 101–2, 121

N

National Assembly of Wales 1,
  9, 85; *see also* Welsh Assembly;
  Welsh Parliament
National Audit Office 60
  'Funding and Structures for Local
    Economic Growth' 3
National Institute of Adult Continuing
  Education (NIACE) 54
National Union of Mineworkers 48
NE Wales 114
  labour market 100, 107–8, 114
  see also North Wales; NWGD (North
    Wales Growth Deal)
Neath 121
Neath Port Talbot 123, 125, 137
neoliberalism 13, 61, 62, 64, 143
  Thatcher Governments (Conservative
    governments, 1979–90) 44–5
  US welfare provision 33
new citizenship regimes 25, 27, 37,
  39, 151
'new civic offer' 145–6
New Economics Foundation 3
New Economy Manchester 69
New Labour governments, 1997–2010
  23, 26, 45, 50
  governance policy 7–8
'New Municipalism,' North
  America 12
'new regionalism' 14, 26–7
'new regions' 25
Newman, J. 66

NIACE (National Institute of Adult
Continuing Education) 54
Norris, E. 3
North America, 'Metro' areas and 'New
Municipalism' approaches 12
North East Derbyshire 41
North East Metro 112
North of England 39;
see also NW England
North of UK 9, 26
North Wales 5, 100, 104
LAs (local authorities) 100, 105
as a region 105–8, *107*, *108*
'spatial imaginary' 102, 109, 114
transport infrastructure 110, 111,
113–14, 115
Welsh language speakers 107
see also NE Wales; NW Wales;
NWGD (North Wales
Growth Deal)
North Wales Economic Ambition
Board (NWEAB) 109, 110
North Wales Growth Deal
(NWGD) see NWGD (North
Wales Growth Deal)
North West TUC 75
Northern Ireland 1, 2, 9
Northern Ireland Assembly 1
Northern Powerhouse 9, 14, 19, 20,
21, 23–5, 38–40, 67, 109, 116
building of city regions 25–8,
26, 28
civil society 24–5, 27, 28–38, **35**
'spatial imaginary' 111
see also GMCR (Greater Manchester
City Region); SCR (Sheffield
City Region)
NW England 106, 111
transport infrastructure 114
NW Wales 114
displacement 114–15
labour market 100, 107–8, 114
see also North Wales; NWGD (North
Wales Growth Deal)
NWEAB (North Wales Economic
Ambition Board) 109, 110
NWGD (North Wales Growth
Deal) 5, 9, 22, 100–1, *108*,
109–12, 116–17, 140
agglomeration and spatial
displacement 114–15
critiques of 113–15
evidence base for 112–13
GVA (gross value added) 107
political discourse and geographic
reality 112–14

O

O'Brien, P. 60
obstacle 79, 97
civil society as 36–7
Offe, C. 17, 19
Oldham 64
Oldham Borough Council, Fairness
Commission 76
'onward devolution' 2
Osborne, George 23
Overman, H. 13

P

Paole Plus 47
Parc Adfer, Deeside 111
Peck, J. 24, 63, 83
Pemberton, S. 85, 94
Pembrokeshire 123, 131
People Plus 47, 49, 54
Phillips, S.D. 27, 91
Pike, A. 60, 69
Polanyi, K. 145
'policy transfer' 83
Port Talbot 121; see also Neath
Port Talbot
'post-democratic' frameworks 62
post-political city regions 141, 142–4
'post-political' frameworks 62
Powys 106
PricewaterhouseCoopers 46
private investment, SBCR (Swansea
Bay City Region and City
Deal) 133–4
Public Service Boards 147

R

Raffas, T. 66
Rancière J. 62
RDAs (Regional Development
Agencies) 1, 7–8, 23, 26, 45, 60
Redcliffe-Maud, L. 6
regional devolution 26
regionalisation 25
repoliticisation 143, 153
representation
impact of austerity on 65
'representational regimes' 27–8, 31
'Resilient North Wales' 110
Rhodes, R. 18
Rochdale 64
Rotherham 41
Royal Commission on Local
Government in England 154
Royal Society of Arts, Inclusive Growth
Commission 28, 61, 117
Rubery, J. 78

rural regions 99–101, 102–3, 116, 131;
    see also North Wales; NWGD
    (North Wales Growth Deal);
    SBCR (Swansea Bay City Region
    and City Deal)

S

Salford 64
Salford Borough Council 76
SBCR (Swansea Bay City Region and
    City Deal) 5, 9, 22, 99, 105,
    119–20, 121, *122*, 122–3, *123*,
    124, **125**, 125–6, *127*, 128,
    136, 140
    austerity and financialisation 132–3
    conflicting aspirations in 129–30
    critiques of 128–35
    GVA (gross value added) 125, 128
    metrophilia 130–2
    trickle-out 133–5
scale jumping 32–4, 77, 94
'scalecraft' 80, 94
Scargill, Arthur 48
Scotland 9, 102
    devolution 1, 2, 7
Scott, A. 1, 4–5, 6
Scottish Parliament 1
SCR (Sheffield City Region) ('Devo
    Sheffield') 5, 20–1, 24–5, 27, *28*,
    41–3, 58–62, 81, 140
    austerity, uneven development and
        employment crisis 50–4, 59–61
    civil society 29, 30–1, 33–4, 38–9, 43
    economic governance and skills 44–8,
        48, 59
    governance and metagovernance 21,
        42–3, 55–8, 61–2
    GVA (gross value added) 59
    LEP (Local Enterprise
        Partnership) 45, 46, 47, 49, 51
    political geography *48*
    representation, accountability and
        democratic deficits 49–50
    Skills and Employment
        Partnership 46
    see also Northern Powerhouse
Sector Skills Councils 45
*Select Committee on the Constitution, The
    Union and Devolution. 10th Report
    of Session 2015–2016, HL Paper
    149*, UK Parliament 4
self-employed people, COVID-19
    impact 150
semiosis 18, 19
Senior, D. 154
Serco 47, 49, 54
service industries 44, 53, 68–9

Shared Prosperity Fund 118
Sheffield 41
    Manufacturing Innovation District 48
    see also SCR (Sheffield City Region)
        ('Devo Sheffield')
Sheffield City Council 45
    austerity cuts 51, 59
    political control of 47, 55
Sheffield City Region *see* SCR
    (Sheffield City Region)
    ('Devo Sheffield')
'Sheffield City Region Agreement on
    Devolution,' HM Government 46
'Sheffield City Region Combined
    Authority Devolution Deal,' HM
    Government 46
Sheffield College 51
Sheffield First Partnership 45
Sheffield Labour Party, Fairness
    Commission 47, 55
Siencyn, Dyfrig 14–15
skills, SCR (Sheffield City
    Region) 44–8, *48*, 51–4, 58–9, 60
Skills Funding Agency 46
'Smart North Wales' 110
SMEs (small and medium-sized
    enterprises) 145
    SCR (Sheffield City Region) 52
    skills development 46–7
Snowdonia 111
social enterprises 29, 145;
    see also civil society
Social Reproduction 149–50
societal depoliticisation 143;
    see also depoliticisation
South of UK 26
South West Wales 122–3;
    see also SBCR (Swansea Bay City
        Region and City Deal)
South Yorkshire 41, 47
Southeast of UK 7
'spaces of dependency' 19
'spaces of engagement' 19
'spatial fixes' 18
'spatial imaginaries' 19, 23–4, 25, 29,
    38, 111
    North Wales 102, 109, 112
spatio-temporal fixes 18, 24
Special Interest Group of Municipal
    Authorities 149
stabilisers 145
'state spatial selectivity' 19
state, the 17–19
    centralisation of 26
Stockport 64
Storper, M. 42, 121
Sum, N.L. 18

Sustainability Transformation
	Partnerships, GMCR (Greater
	Manchester City Region) 68
Swansea 106, 120, 122, 123, 125
	metrophilia 130–2
	see also SBCR (Swansea Bay
	City Region)
Swansea Bay City Region and City
	Deal (SBCR) see SBCR (Swansea
	Bay City Region and City Deal)
Swansea Bay Transition Board 125–6
Swyngedouw, E. 142
symptomology 18, 19

T

Tameside 64
Tameside Poverty pledge 76
tax credit claimants, Greater
	Manchester 71, 72
'Team North Wales' 110
Thatcher Governments (Conservative
	governments, 1979–90) 44–5
Theodore, N. 24, 83
third sector 29; see also civil society
Thompson, M. 145
trade councils 75
trade unions 21, 66–7
	austerity resistance/mitigation 63, 73,
		75–6, 78
	CCR (Cardiff Capital Region) 88
	Greater Manchester 69–70, 71
Trafford 64
Training and Enterprise Councils 45
Transition Boards 82
	CCR (Cardiff Capital
		Region) 86, 91
	Swansea Bay Transition Board 125–6
transport infrastructure, North
	Wales 110, 111, 113–14, 115
Travel to Work Areas, Swansea 123,
	123, 124
trickle-down effects 12, 27, 30, 31, 39,
	81, 93, 113, 114, 130–1, 141
trickle-out effects 133–5
Trussell Trust 71
TUC 76–7

U

UC (Universal Credit) 65, 72–3
	and COVID-19 148
	GMCR (Greater Manchester City
		Region) 67, 71, 72, 77
UK Parliament
	Select Committee on the Constitution,
		The Union and Devolution. 10th
		Report of Session 2015–2016, HL
		Paper 149 4

UK2070 Commission 139, 140
	Make No Little Plans – Acting at Scale
		for a Fairer and Stronger Justice 3–4
uneven development 4, 7, 12–13, 14,
	15, 24, 65, 79, 80–2, 137
	CCR (Cardiff Capital Region) 92–3
	GMCR (Greater Manchester City
		Region) 67–71
	Northern Powerhouse 38–9
	NWGD (North Wales Growth
		Deal) 99, 100, 102–3, 104
	SCR (Sheffield City
		Region) 41, 50–4
UNISON trade union 75
Universal Credit (UC) see UC
	(Universal Credit)
University of Manchester, Inclusive
	Growth Analysis Unit 75
US (United States)
	'Metropolitics' 41
	neoliberalism and welfare
		provision 33

V

VCSE (Greater Manchester Voluntary,
	Community and Social Enterprise)
	Devolution Reference Group 34–7,
	35, 38, 39, 77
voluntary groups 29
	austerity resistance/mitigation 73
	see also civil society

W

Waite, D. 101–2, 121
Wales 21
	austerity 95–7, 106
	central-local relations 83–6
	city regions 9
	de-industrialisation 110
	devolution 1, 2, 7, 79–80, 118
	FE (foundational economy) 146–7
	independence 118
	LA (local authority) restructuring
		85–6, 87, **88**, 88, 100, 106
	see also CCR (Cardiff Capital
		Region); North Wales; NWGD
		(North Wales Growth Deal);
		SBCR (Swansea Bay City Region)
Wales Spatial Plan (WSP) 9, 83–4, 106
Ward, K. 15, 16, 63, 113
Ward, N. 103
Warrington 114
welfare conditionality 65
welfare reform 21, 65
	GMCR (Greater Manchester City
		Region) 71–3
welfare-to-work programmes 66, 78

SCR (Sheffield City Region) 45, 47,
    49–50, 60
Wellbeing of Future Generations Act
    2015 (Welsh Government) 95,
    129, 146–7
Welsh Assembly 106
  Economy, Infrastructure and Skills
    Committee 105, 129
  see also National Assembly of Wales
Welsh Government 9, 79, 82, 84–5,
    86, 87, 89, 129, 146–7
  and the NWGD 109, 112
  Wellbeing of Future Generations Act
    2015 95, 129, 146–7
Welsh Index of Multiple
    Deprivation 109
Welsh language speakers 107
Welsh Parliament 9;
  see also National Assembly of Wales;
    Welsh Assembly
'Western Powerhouse' 97
Whitham, G. 72
Wigan 64
Wiggan, J. 65
Williams Commission 106
Wolch, J. 33
women and employment

SCR (Sheffield City Region) 53, 59
Wood, B. 6
Wood, M. 142
Work Choice, GMCR (Greater
    Manchester City Region) 67
Work and Health Programme,
    GMCR 67
Work and Pensions Select
    Committee 76
Work Programme (WP) see WP
    (Work Programme)
Workforce Engagement Protocol 76
Working Tax Credit 73
WP (Work Programme)
  GMCR (Greater Manchester City
    Region) 67
  SCR (Sheffield City Region) 45, 47,
    49–50, 53–4, 60
Wrexham 100, 106, 114
WSP (Wales Spatial Plan) 9, 83–4, 106

Y

Yates, E. 70–1
Yorkshire Devolution Deal 59
young people, labour market in Greater
    Manchester 70–1